Leadership
Theory

Leadership
Theory

︾

A Facilitator's Guide for Cultivating Critical Perspectives

John P. **Dugan**

Natasha T. **Turman**

Amy C. **Barnes** & Associates

JB JOSSEY-BASS™

A Wiley Brand

Published by Jossey-Bass
A Wiley Brand
One Montgomery Street, Suite 1000, San Francisco, CA 94104-4594—www.josseybass.com

Jossey-Bass books and products are available through most bookstores. To contact Jossey-Bass directly call our Customer Care Department within the U.S. at 800-956-7739, outside the U.S. at 317-572-3986, or fax 317-572-4002.

Wiley publishes in a variety of print and electronic formats and by print-on-demand. Some material included with standard print versions of this book may not be included in e-books or in print-on-demand. If this book refers to media such as a CD or DVD that is not included in the version you purchased, you may download this material at **http://booksupport.wiley.com**. For more information about Wiley products, visit **www.wiley.com**.

Library of Congress Cataloging-in-Publication Data is Available

9781118864173 (Print)
9781118864203 (ePDF)
9781118864258 (epub)

Cover design: Wiley
Cover image: © David Marchal/Getty Images, Inc.

Printed in the United States of America
FIRST EDITION

PB Printing 10 9 8 7 6 5 4 3 2 1

CONTENTS

USING THE FACILITATOR'S GUIDE

This guide was created both to support the main text, *Leadership Theory: Cultivating Critical Perspectives* (Dugan, 2017), and as a stand-alone book in its own right. In writing the main text, it became clear that the use of critical perspectives to deconstruct and reconstruct leadership theory might in fact reflect a learning opportunity not just for readers but also for instructors/facilitators. As editors of this volume, we have most certainly been stretched in our thinking about our own approaches to leadership education through the integration of critical pedagogies. This realization made the provision of resources to help instructors/facilitators engage with the material and feel adequately prepared to use it in learning experiences all the more essential.

Thus, the content of the guide may feel a little different than what is typically encountered in an instructor's manual. We have asked outstanding colleagues across disciplinary contexts to share their best practices in how to infuse critical perspectives into teaching leadership theory. What they offer is both a framework for understanding the application of critical perspectives and a set of step-by-step lesson plans. As you read through the guide, keep the following in mind:

- Each chapter aligns with a chapter from the main text, and in many cases there are multiple subchapters in this book designed to support a single chapter from the main text. This was done knowing that the number of concepts and/or theories covered in a single chapter of the main text is large and that instructors/facilitators may want to expose participants to all of these through assigned reading but focus in depth on a singular concept/theory in person. Therefore, chapters in the guide can be combined in a variety of ways to meet the content needs of a particular instructor/facilitator.

- The depth of infusion of critical perspectives in each chapter of the guide is purposefully varied. This is to support its use with participants with varying levels of prior exposure to and developmental readiness for critical perspectives. This variation allows instructors/facilitators the ability to draw on a wider range of content appropriate for their particular audience. Note that each of the chapters can easily be adapted to either deepen or make more accessible the critical perspectives that are employed.

- Similarly, chapters are purposefully varied in approach, with some being decidedly academic and most appropriate for use in a traditional classroom setting, while others are more experiential and ideal for learning experiences outside the traditional classroom. All of the chapters equip instructors/facilitators with resources to adapt content to best serve their own curriculum.

- Each chapter begins with an overview of the theory and an explicit statement of the framework employed for the integration of critical perspectives. Step-by-step directions to implement the curricula follow and typically comprise multiple activities. Note that descriptive instructions for facilitation appear in standard (i.e., nonitalicized) type, while example scripts you can use during the actual facilitation of activities appear in italics.

ACKNOWLEDGMENTS

This facilitator's guide would not have been possible without extraordinary contributions from trusted colleagues and experts in the field of leadership education. We would first like to acknowledge and thank the amazing scholars and educators who contributed as chapter authors and who wrote thoughtful curricula that will undoubtedly help readers gain a greater understanding of critical perspectives and how to apply them to leadership contexts.

We are also grateful to the graduate students and colleagues who served on our respective research teams at Loyola University Chicago and The Ohio State University. These individuals volunteered countless hours conceptualizing, researching, writing, and editing and have made a significant contribution to this creative process. These outstanding educators include Lesley-Ann Brown-Henderson, Stephanie Clemons Thompson, Andrea DeLeon, Kristina Garcia, Willie Gore, James Larcus, Satugarn Limthongviratn, Sarah Mangia, Emiliane du Mérac, Kamaria Porter, Allison Schipma, Suzanne Shoger, and Mark Anthony Torrez.

Finally, we would like to express our appreciation to our friends, family, and colleagues, who provided constant support and encouragement and who inspire us to continue our efforts as critical learners and champions of leadership education. We are especially grateful to a few special people in our lives whose patience and support are endless. In our own words:

From Tasha: I would like thank the Dugan Research Team for their tireless work on this project and my loving husband Matthew for being my support system as I do the work I love.

From Amy: *I would like to thank John, Natasha, and the book teams for being wonderful partners in this journey, my husband Pete for his endless support, and my two amazing kids, Sophia and Luke, who teach me about compassionate, inclusive leadership every day.*

From John: *An enormous thanks goes to the incomparable and brilliant Natasha Turman and Amy Barnes for making this book happen, the "Book Club" for all their hard work, and my family, friends, and especially my husband David "Trey" Morgan for keeping me sane and life fun!*

EDITORS AND CONTRIBUTING AUTHORS

Scott J. Allen
Associate Professor, Management, Marketing, and Logistics,
John Carroll University

M. Sonja Ardoin
Program Director and Clinical Assistant Professor,
Higher Education, Boston University

Amy C. Barnes
Clinical Assistant Professor, Higher Education and Student
Affairs, The Ohio State University

Benjamin Brooks
Associate Professor and Senior Class Advisor, Gallatin School
of Individualized Study, New York University

Lesley-Ann Brown-Henderson
Executive Director of Campus Inclusion and Community,
Division of Student Affairs, Northwestern University

Marilyn J. Bugenhagen
Faculty, Center for Leadership Development, Federal Executive
Institute, U.S. Office of Personnel Management

Stephanie H. Chang
Director, Multicultural Education Department, Guilford College

Natasha Chapman
Coordinator, Leadership Studies Program, University of Maryland

Sharon Chia Claros
Resident Director, Residence Life, University of California
Los Angeles

Kathryn Kay Coquemont
Director, Student Leadership Development and New Student and
    Family Programs, University of Utah

Valeria Cortés
Founder, Tlatoa Consulting

Richard A. Couto
Independent Senior Scholar

Amanda B. Cutchens
Senior Academic Advisor, Honors College, University of South
    Florida

Andrea M. De Leon
Residence Director, Office of Residence Life, St. John's University

John P. Dugan
Associate Professor, Higher Education, Loyola University Chicago

Sara C. Furr
Director, Center for Identity, Inclusion, and Social Change,
    DePaul University

Kristina C. Alcozer Garcia
Program Coordinator and Doctoral Student, Off-Campus Life,
    Loyola University Chicago

Mathew R. Goldberg
English Teacher Grantee, Fulbright Korea

Adam Goodman
Director, Center for Leadership, Northwestern University

Willie Gore
Residence Hall Director, Housing and Residence Life Administra-
    tion, Saint Louis University

Paige Haber-Curran

Assistant Professor, Student Affairs in Higher Education, Texas State University

Kevin M. Hemer

Graduate Research Assistant, Research Institute for Studies in Education, Iowa State University

Daniel M. Jenkins

Director and Assistant Professor, Leadership and Organizational Studies, University of Southern Maine

Renique Kersh

Associate Vice Provost for Engaged Learning, Northern Illinois University

Michelle L. Kusel

Graduate Research Assistant, Leadership Studies Minor, Loyola University Chicago

Satugarn P. Limthongviratn

Coordinator for Social Justice Education, Indiana University-Purdue University Indianapolis

Marc Lynn

Associate Professor, Management, Marketing, and Logistics, John Carroll University

Laura Osteen

Director, Center for Leadership and Social Change, Florida State University

Vijay Pendakur

Dean of Students, Student and Campus Life, Cornell University

OiYan A. Poon

Assistant Professor, Higher Education, Loyola University Chicago

Melissa L. Rocco
Instructor and Doctoral Coordinator, Leadership Studies Program, University of Maryland

David M. Rosch
Assistant Professor, Agricultural Education, University of Illinois at Urbana-Champaign

Ana M. Rossetti
Assistant Dean, Stuart School of Business, Illinois Institute of Technology

Allison M. Schipma
Residential College Director, Office of Residential Life, Washington University in St. Louis

Corey Seemiller
Author, *The Student Leadership Competencies Guidebook*

Matthew Sowcik
Assistant Professor, Leadership Education, University of Florida

Dian D. Squire
Visiting Assistant Professor, Student Affairs, Iowa State University

Clinton M. Stephens
Assistant Professor, Director of Leadership Studies, Emporia State University

Maurice Stevens
Associate Professor, Comparative Studies, The Ohio State University

Mark Anthony Torrez
Doctoral Student, Higher Education, Loyola University Chicago

Natasha T. Turman
Doctoral Research Assistant, Higher Education, Loyola University Chicago

Leadership
Theory

⌄

Introduction and Critical Facilitation

Amy C. Barnes

> *Education either functions as an instrument that is used to facilitate the integration of the younger generation into the logic of the present system and bring about conformity to it, or it becomes "the practice of freedom," the means by which [people] deal critically and creatively with reality and discover how to participate in the transformation of their world.*
>
> SHAULLAS CITED IN FREIRE, 2000, P. 34

This guide was created by a dedicated group of educators committed to teaching, researching, and analyzing leadership theory and organizational dynamics using critical perspectives. As a companion tool for the main book, *Leadership Theory: Cultivating Critical Perspectives* (Dugan, 2017), this guide serves as a resource to help facilitators and educators bring to life a critical pedagogy of leadership studies. This guide is structured to mirror and supplement the main text; however, it can also be used as a stand-alone resource. Using meta-themes from critical theory as the paradigm through which participants learn, the following chapters contain intentional and unique curricula crafted to guide participants toward a greater understanding of how power, privilege, and oppression affect leadership dynamics.

Facilitation design is foundational to rich and insightful group processes. Giving thought to things such as how time is structured, physical environment and space configuration, framing of reflection, whether and when there should be breaks, what materials to use, and whether to provide food and/or drinks (to name a few), can maximize the focus, efficiency, and effectiveness of group learning. Accordingly, each chapter within this guide includes (1) an introduction to the leadership theories or concepts discussed in the corresponding main text chapter; (2) a theoretical or conceptual framing of the specific curriculum; (3) learning outcomes and material lists for each activity; (4) step-by-step facilitation guidelines; and (5) tailored debriefing and facilitator notes to provide you with additional insight and support. Furthermore, if an activity suggests leading small- or large-group discussion, then sample questions are provided; and if supplementary content is needed to facilitate a specific activity, then the requisite instructions, materials, and/or resource links are also provided.

Although the authors have shared a comprehensive plan within each chapter, the curricula are designed to allow for flexibility in timeline and structure so that content can be easily adapted for use in formal classrooms as well as cocurricular or professional training environments. This guide is designed to equip you with ideas, strategies, and tools to effectively facilitate sociocultural dialogue and critical leadership learning. Facilitating curricula from a critical perspective where stereotypes, biases, and privilege are challenged can be difficult. Yet introducing these concepts, discussions, and perspectives is the necessary work of leadership educators. The remainder of this introduction will focus on critical pedagogy and an approach to facilitation that will help to support the teaching of this content.

❯ Experiential, Transformative, and Developmentally Sequenced Learning

The approach to this facilitator guide is activity- and discussion-based and reflects Kolb's (1984) theory of experiential learning. Kolb's theory described learning as "the process whereby knowledge is created through the transformation of experience" (p. 38). The Kolb cycle of learning includes four stages that further learning, understanding, and integration of concrete human experiences through a cyclical process of feeling, watching, thinking, and doing. This approach allows learners to make meaning of current experiences and empowers them to engage in their own learning process.

Mezirow's (1991) theory of transformative learning similarly articulates a cyclical process of experiencing, reflecting, and integrating newly obtained knowledge or insight. However, the scope of this theory extends beyond simple knowledge acquisition and weaves together both experiential and human development approaches to describe a process of learning that results in *cognitive transformation*: encountering and internalizing experiences and ideas that liberate one from "reified forms of thought that are no longer dependable" (Mezirow, 2000, p. 27). Situated at the core of transformative learning is the act of *metacognition*, which refers to critically examining the cognitive process itself (Day, Harrison, & Halpin, 2009; Kegan, 1994; Mezirow, 1991, 2000). That is, the practice of metacognition involves one taking pause to first recognize a present thought or belief, and then interrogating one's own subconscious to unveil the underlying presuppositions framing that thought or belief. Dugan, Kodama, Correia, and Associates (2013) positioned critical self-reflection and metacognition as central mechanisms to effective leadership development, further claiming that leadership educators can increase awareness and attention to the metacognitive processes of learning by leveraging opportunities for critical self-reflection that are appropriately tailored to developmental readiness.

Hannah and Avolio (2010) defined *developmental readiness* as "the ability and motivation to attend to, make meaning of, and appropriate new leader KSAAs (knowledge, skills, abilities, and attributes) into knowledge structures along with concomitant changes in identity to employ those KSAAs" (p. 1182).

Translated to leadership education, *developmental sequencing* is a pedagogical method of intentionally delivering and facilitating curriculum in a manner that appropriately builds in complexity over time to ensure the successful evolution into new ways of knowing, being, and doing (Dugan et al., 2013). Moreover, developmental sequencing acknowledges the interrelationship of lived experience, critical self-reflection, metacognition, developmental readiness, and transformative learning/development by scaffolding learning opportunities that are rooted in the needs of participants, simultaneously validating developmental achievements and encouraging continued growth. The crucial importance of developmental sequencing is well evidenced within leadership literature (e.g., Day et al., 2009; Hannah & Avolio, 2010; Komives, Owen, Longerbeam, Mainella, & Osteen, 2005). In using this guide to inform practice, it is important to consider the unique needs of your participants and adapt the material provided to best align with goals and learning outcomes.

The Art of Critical Facilitation, Teaching, and Learning

Facilitation is an art (and not a science). It involves planning that considers the unique developmental needs of the group, an attitude of openness and willingness to engage participants in shared learning and sociocultural sensitivity. Yet, even with thoughtful design and significant planning, you can never fully anticipate how human identity and emotion will influence a discussion or activity.

The art of critical facilitation includes the ability to anticipate what may occur, but also the capacity to respond to the unknown in a manner that encourages growth and learning while also validating participants' lived experiences and perspectives.

This is especially challenging when one of the outcomes is to help participants develop a *critical* perspective. For some participants, this may be the first time some of their beliefs are challenged and/or their biases uncovered. Therefore, the aim of critical leadership education becomes facilitating the confrontation, deconstruction, and subsequent *re*construction of the biases, presuppositions, and prototypes that inform our conceptualization, development, and enactment of leadership.

It is important to remember that facilitating group conversations and processes is based on the premise that both facilitator and participants share expertise and knowledge as they engage in mutually constructed learning (Griffin & Ouellett, 2007). Furthermore, the priority must be creating a community of learners by empowering participants to learn collaboratively, teach each other, and assume responsibility for learning. You must create opportunities for participants to critically analyze the curriculum as they examine conventional interpretations and introduce alternative narratives (Ladson-Billings, 1995). The remaining sections describe the significant role of sociocultural conversations and the environmental requisite of brave spaces in challenging paradigms, promoting cognitive and metacognitive growth, and evolving facilitators and participants alike in their perspectives and practices of leadership.

Sociocultural Conversations

The importance of teaching individuals how to engage in meaningful dialogue about and across differences cannot be overstated, as the degree to which people interact with peers or colleagues across difference contributes significantly to their leadership development (Dugan, 2011). On the most basic of levels, increasing one's interactions with diverse colleagues leads to individuals being more open-minded (Laird, 2005). Meaningful interaction in diversity-related activities or conversations also promotes individuals' educational growth and cultivates their self-confidence, social agency, and ability to think critically (Chang, Denson, Sáenz, & Misa, 2006; Laird, 2005). In the 2013 report from the Multi-Institutional Study of Leadership (MSL), sociocultural conversations were highlighted as the "single strongest predictor" for building socially responsible leadership capacity (Dugan et al., 2013, p. 9). Findings from the report further concluded that sociocultural conversations create a platform for individuals to clarify personal values and explore others' values, consider their values within larger contexts (social structures, cultural paradigms, or worldviews), and understand how to navigate those differences in an effective manner (Dugan et al., 2013). As such, it is essential that leadership educators and facilitators purposefully create opportunities for participants to engage in these conversations.

Facilitating sociocultural conversations requires emotional intelligence and an acute sensitivity to multiple social identities. These intersecting identities belong to both facilitators and participants, and it is important to first become aware of personal privilege and bias in creating mutual learning environments. As conversations unfold, you should encourage and model inclusivity, use gender-neutral language, and structure activities in ways that share power equally among participants. It is often helpful to allow participants frequent opportunities to share and reflect on their multiple identities and lived experiences; the more opportunities there are for all participants to share in the conversation, the more empowered they will feel and the greater the learning will be for everyone (Adams, Bell, & Griffin, 2007).

The practice of conversations for growth is observed across disciplines, and what follows is a description of a developmentally sequenced, three-part strategy to engage learners in this conversational space. Although Savignon and Sysoyev (2002) offered this cognitive development structure from an applied, cross-cultural linguistic perspective, their framework may be applied to sociocultural conversations addressing general differences:

- In the first phase, *explanation*, Savignon and Sysoyev (2002) suggested time be used to teach or offer rationale for the process that will follow; we further suggest that you establish rules and expectations to create brave spaces (e.g., Arao & Clemens, 2013) where participants are empowered as both learners and teachers.
- The second phase, *exploration*, may take many instructional forms. The core concern of this stage is to engage participants in dialogue by offering the opportunity to work with others, share experiences, and explore difficult questions—all ways to move individuals from curiosity to dialogue with one another (Savignon & Sysoyev, 2002). Asking participants to analyze articles or texts, examine current media, or utilize personal stories are meaningful ways to initiate the dialogue process, which is the primary concern of this stage.
- In the final stage, *expression*, participants must insert their own stories, opinions, or conclusions—ultimately reflecting both on the experiences they share and the overarching process of exchanging perspectives (Savignon & Sysoyev, 2002).

Through the use of this approach, and by providing developmentally appropriate amounts of challenge and support, you can create environments where rich, meaningful sociocultural conversations can occur.

Brave Spaces

Safe space is a phrase often used to describe the environment cultivated by social justice educators when groups create agreed-upon norms or community standards to guide sociocultural or otherwise sensitive discussion. Typically, the goal is that confidentiality can be agreed upon and members of the group can feel their contributions are valued. Although facilitators have the best of intentions in attempting to create an ideal environment for sociocultural conversations, attempting to create safe spaces assumes that the security or safety necessary for every participant is the same. However, the measurement of personal risk associated with sociocultural conversations varies greatly based on social identity, lived experience, power dynamics within the group, developmental readiness, and level of personal experience discussing topics related to social justice. It is, therefore, impossible to remove the risk that someone might assume in these conversations just by agreeing to a few community guidelines. Arao and Clemens (2013) wrote.

> *It became increasingly clear to us that our approach to initiating social justice dialogues should not be to convince participants that we can remove risk from the equation, for this is simply impossible. Rather, we propose revising our language, shifting away from the concept of safety and emphasizing the importance of bravery instead, to help students better understand—and rise to—the challenges of genuine dialogue on diversity and social justice issues. (p. 136)*

In their work as facilitators of sociocultural conversations, Arao and Clemens (2013) found that a commonly used activity that asked participants to take a step forward or back based upon a list of statements about privilege actually left participants with significant feelings of discomfort, and most felt the activity was fundamentally incongruent with the idea of safety. In fact, the authors argued that "authentic learning about social justice often requires the very qualities of risk, difficulty, and controversy that are defined as incompatible with safety" (p. 139). They instead advocated for a new term to better capture the challenges participants experience when they choose to participate in critical dialogue: *brave space*.

To create brave space within a group setting there must be ample time to process what brave space looks and feels like to the participants. It is recommended that you set aside time to either read and discuss the chapter by Arao and Clemens (2013) or introduce the concept and lead a discussion using the following questions: *What does brave space feel like to you? How can we create brave space in this group? What hesitations or fears do you have about our ability to create brave space? How can we help to address each others' hesitations?*

Following the discussion of these questions, the group should articulate ground rules to foster and maintain brave space for the experiences and conversations that will occur. You might also ask a group, *How can we support each other in our bravery to tackle these challenging but important conversations?* By guiding an open, honest conversation where you, as the facilitator, share power, admit the challenge inherit in sociocultural conversations, and commit to the importance and bravery associated with the work, you cultivate a community in which people feel empowered to share their stories, discuss their opinions, and engage openly in dialogue. This approach may take extra time and may need revisions along the way, or the discussion may feel imperfect or unfinished because it is a *process*. But, the authentic conversation that can result from a true commitment to critical pedagogy on the part of the facilitator and critical reflection on the part of the participants can lead to significant growth for everyone.

Glancing into the Mirror

Facilitating dialogue and learning around systems of oppression, power dynamics, and the marginalization of underrepresented identities within leadership settings is vital in today's world. Just as participants are instigated and challenged by the curricula within this guide, you must also engage with this content meaningfully and vulnerably; you must walk, struggle, and advance *together* through this work. It is both appropriate and expected that you will similarly confront, deconstruct, and reconstruct your own biases and presuppositions within the learning community. Understanding your privilege(s), knowing your triggers, and considering how your social identities influence your role as a facilitator, your leadership perspectives, and your participation in the social world are integral aspects of self-awareness.

Critical facilitation is based on the premise that knowledge, expertise, and power are shared, and that teaching and learning are reciprocal, coconstructed processes (Griffin & Ouellett, 2007). Critical leadership development necessitates unlearning deep-seated binaries (e.g., teacher-student, right-wrong, good-bad) and overcoming deep-rooted fears (e.g., making mistakes, acknowledging bias, being flawed). Of course these challenging tasks are wholly dependent on our capacity to look ourselves in the mirror, name what we see, and share ourselves authentically in relationships. However, at the core of this work, being a critical educator and facilitator requires a foundation of bravery and courage. In her book, *Daring Greatly: How the Courage to Be Vulnerable Transforms the Way We Live, Love, Parent, and Lead*, Brené Brown (2012) positioned authenticity and vulnerability as the definitive acts of leadership and self love, claiming that "the willingness to show up changes us. It makes us a little braver each time" (p. 42). Given the nature of critical work, it is important to ensure that the same amount of energy put toward the creation of brave space for participants is also invested in the creation—and safeguarding—of such a space within ourselves.

❯ Conclusion

As a facilitator, you play an important role in shaping the dynamics of learning. When power is shared, you ask open-ended questions, model the behavior you would like to see from participants, encourage collective participation, handle conflicting viewpoints with care, and employ curricula in a developmentally appropriate manner. Using these strategies, you can increase the effectiveness of the climate, learning, and overall experience for everyone. At the same time, the reality is that critical leadership development takes time; it requires revision along the way; and it is certainly an imperfect process. But a commitment to the foundations of critical pedagogy will bolster the possibilities for significant, transformative leadership learning for everyone. Finally, in the spirit of this work, you are invited to critically analyze, deconstruct, and reconstruct this guide itself, as you work with participants to confront conventional interpretations of leadership, explore alternative narratives, and imagine interpretations and narratives of your own.

Chapter 1: The Evolving Nature of Leadership

1 A: Our Evolving Understanding of Leadership

Melissa L. Rocco

Objectives/Goals of Chapter

- Introduce the process of examining leadership through multiple lenses of personal experience, history, social identity, and other elements of context.
- Identify and understand the leadership assumptions and considerations found in participants' personal leadership experiences.
- Develop presentation, knowledge synthesis, and critical thinking skills.

Critical Concepts: *critical self-reflection, oppression, privilege, social perspective-taking*

❯ Chapter Overview

Chapter 1 of the main text prepares participants for reading, internalizing, and critiquing theory, concepts, and approaches in our study of leadership. Leadership theory includes key assumptions about the nature of leadership, uses specific terminology, and presents core considerations. Participants should understand these foundational pieces of leadership theory and use them as a framework for analyzing individual theories, identifying themes across theories, and critiquing theories from multiple perspectives.

First, this chapter introduces and explores four core assumptions for understanding the nature of leadership: (1) leadership is paradigmatically derived; (2) leadership is socially constructed; (3) leadership is inherently values-based; and (4) leadership is interdisciplinary. Second, this chapter introduces key terminology in leadership: leadership theory, leadership development, leadership capacity, leadership enactment, leadership motivation, and leadership efficacy. Third, this chapter introduces core considerations of leadership: born versus made, leader versus leadership, leader versus follower, leadership versus management, authority versus power, and macro versus micro. Participants are encouraged to use the leadership assumptions, terminology, and considerations to critically examine and analyze the theories presented in the rest of the book to form opinions and complex questions about leadership.

› Chapter Framework

To prepare participants to be critical learners of leadership scholarship, Chapter 1 of the main text initiates a conversation about assumptions that continue to dictate how leadership is understood. This curriculum primes participants to consider how these assumptions might reflect majority group narratives and dominate the study and theorizing of leadership. Through social perspective-taking (i.e., the cognitive process of looking through the lens of another to better understand and empathize with alternate perspectives; Gehlbach, 2004; Hoffman, 2000; Underwood & Moore, 1982), participants are encouraged to identify possible counter-narratives to the traditional rhetoric of leadership. Moreover, they are encouraged to examine their assumptions about leaders and leadership through critical self-reflection.

> Curriculum Plan

This curriculum engages participants in activities utilizing creative drawing, personal reflection, and small- and large-group discussion. The activities help prime participants to examine leadership through diverse perspectives, or lenses, through a creative drawing activity titled "Your Leadership Lens." The following curriculum plan should be implemented in one workshop-style session ranging from 2 to 4 hours depending on the number of participants. The plan can also be broken into multiple smaller sessions by activity or by selecting a few activities at a time. For a shorter, single session, elements of this plan can also be assigned as pre- or post-work for participants. Suggestions for variations are indicated throughout each activity.

> Activity 1—Leadership Lens Primer

When studying various approaches to leadership throughout history, it can be helpful for participants to think about each as a set of glasses or lenses through which to examine leaders and leadership. It is first important for participants to identify their own *lens*, or the beliefs and assumptions they have about leadership currently. It is also important for participants to try on different lenses and see leadership through the eyes of the approaches that they may or may not have considered or even been aware existed. This activity helps participants begin to understand how to study leadership from multiple perspectives and consider the context that affects varied leadership approaches.

Learning Outcomes

- Understand leadership as something that should be examined and studied from multiple perspectives.

- Consider how perspectives on leadership differ due to contextual influences and personal experiences.
- Understand and develop comfort with the existence of multiple definitions of and approaches to leadership.

Setting Up the Activity

Group Size: Open to any group size

Time: 35 minutes (10 minutes to draw, 15 minutes to share, 10 minutes for reflection)

Methods: Art, reflection, small and large group discussion

Materials: Colored markers or crayons (a few per person), blank paper (legal size or larger; one per person), craft supplies (optional), computer, projector/screen (optional)

Variations: This activity is adaptable based on session time available, number of participants, and participant needs. It can be turned into a more elaborate creative project using varied art supplies (e.g., stickers, construction paper). It can be done as a take-home assignment prior to the session with participants bringing completed drawings with them to the session. Sharing can be done with partners, in small groups, or with the large group depending on size and time.

Directions

1. Provide the following prompt to the participants, along with a creative or humorous photo or illustration of a pair of glasses (e.g., the funny eyebrow, nose, and mustache glasses commonly seen with costumes). *YOUR LEADERSHIP LENS! Wait, what in the world is a leadership lens? I would like you to take some time to think about how you see/feel/experience/learn leadership. What does the word mean to you? What or who has informed how you personally know or understand leadership? The idea is that we get all of our assumptions and thoughts about leadership out there now, at the beginning of our time together, so*

that we understand the perspectives on leadership that each person brings to the table.

Your leadership lens may not look like this (reference recommended picture), *but someone's could, and that is okay! The point is that everyone's leadership lens is different. This session is about understanding those lenses—whether they are yours, others, or even the lens of a theorist or researcher. So, go ahead: Show us your leadership lens!*

2. Pass out a piece of paper and supplies to each participant.

3. Instruct participants to create their own leadership lens, or a visual representation of what they currently believe about leadership, using the materials provided. This could include definitions or core concepts, characteristics, traits, people they admire as leaders, certain behaviors, personal experiences, or anything else that has informed what the participant believes to be true about leadership. This can be in the form of a life timeline, an abstract drawing, or even a collection of smaller pictures or symbols. Participants should use pictures, but they can also use words to help illustrate their leadership lens. Instruct participants to think deeply and be specific.

4. Provide participants with at least 10 minutes to draw. It can be helpful to walk around and ask the participants questions about their drawings as they work to help push them toward deeper reflection. Time can be extended if more creativity or depth is desired.

5. Participants should share their lenses with others. This can happen in small groups or in the large group depending on participant numbers and time allotted. Each participant should have a chance to describe how the various images and words on their lens drawing have influenced their current understanding or definition of leadership.

6. Engage the large group in a discussion about what they shared with each other. The discussion should help participants see the value in viewing leadership from multiple perspectives and

understand the various elements that influence how individuals define leadership. Questions to consider include these:

- *What similarities did you find between your leadership lenses?*
- *How does your leadership lens differ from how others understand or define leadership?*
- *Why is it helpful to gain insight into how others understand leadership?*
- *Is there a right answer to "What is leadership?" or "What makes a good leader?"*

Facilitator Notes

This activity can stand alone as separate from the other activities in this curriculum plan. If you choose to do this activity separately from other activities, it should still be the first activity done for Chapter 1 reflection. The concept of the leadership lens helps frame the other activities and introduces an important aspect of critical self-reflection. This activity helps participants understand how to begin examining their assumptions as well as consider various perspectives as they discuss the chapter content and engage with each other.

❯ Activity 2—Focusing Our Lenses: Leadership Considerations and Assumptions

This activity builds upon the previous activity by engaging participants in an analysis of their leadership lenses based on the assumptions and core considerations presented in Chapter 1. Each participant's leadership lens is informed by a variety of personal and contextual factors (e.g., background, identity, family, education) that contribute to their informal theory of leadership. This activity helps bring those differences to light and encourages participants to examine the factors and forces that influence their informal view of leadership. Participants will engage in six small group discussions about the leadership considerations presented in Chapter 1 and where they see those binaries showing up in their own leadership lenses, followed by a large group discussion about leadership assumptions.

Learning Outcomes

- Understand the leadership binaries and leadership assumptions discussed in Chapter 1.
- Increase capacity for critically analyzing leadership assumptions and considerations.
- Identify common themes in leadership definitions, approaches, and theories.

Setting Up the Activity

Group Size: Open to any group size, although large groups may make group reflection difficult

Time: 90 minutes (10 minutes to review leadership binaries, 45 minutes for group discussions, 30 minutes for leadership assumptions, 5 minutes for the final large group reflection)

Methods: Small and large group discussion

Materials: Leadership lenses from previous activity, writing utensils

Directions

1. Explain to participants that they will now analyze their leadership lenses based on the assumptions and considerations discussed in Chapter 1. It is important for participants to understand how considerations and assumptions show up in their own leadership experiences before they can engage in a critique of other leadership approaches.

2. Review the six binaries presented as leadership considerations in Chapter 1 with the large group. Ask for a volunteer to

explain each of the six and provide clarification as needed: born versus made, leader versus leadership, leader versus follower, leadership versus management, authority versus power, and macro versus micro.

3. Instruct participants to group back up with the people with whom they shared their leadership lenses earlier in the session. If participants did not share their leadership lenses in small groups, have them create small groups now.

4. Explain that the small groups will be discussing where they see each of the binaries show up in their leadership lenses. For example, if a participant drew a picture of a person standing above another group of people, this image could be related to the leader versus follower binary or to the authority versus power binary. Participants should elaborate on the connections made between their lenses and the binaries. They should also make notes on their leadership lens drawings related to the leadership binaries. Remind participants that a single piece of their leadership lens picture could relate to more than one binary. The small groups will discuss one of the binaries at a time; you can indicate which binary to discuss at which point or allow participants to choose the order.

5. Give small groups approximately 10 minutes to discuss each binary as it relates to their leadership lenses. After each binary discussion, bring the large group back together and ask participants to share highlights from their small group conversations. Point out any themes or interesting points made by the group.

6. Once all six binaries have been discussed, you should review and apply the leadership assumptions with the participants. If multimedia is being used, the following assumptions should be projected onto a screen for easy reference. Ask for volunteers to explain each of the assumptions and clarify as necessary. You should also explain that the elements of our leadership lens, as well as the binaries found in our lenses, are informed by these assumptions. Lead a large group discussion

on what assumptions can be seen in participants' leadership lenses. Possible questions to pose to participants follow:

- Leadership is paradigmatically derived.
    - *Which of the paradigms sounds most like how you see the world? What resonates for you about it?*
    - *How might the way someone defines leadership or identifies a leader change based on each of the paradigms?*
- Leadership is socially constructed.
    - *Who has influenced your definition of leadership?*
    - *What about where you grew up influences how you view leadership?*
    - *What about your culture or heritage influences how you view leadership?*
- Leadership is inherently values-based.
    - *What values are most important to you?*
    - *How do your values influence your definition of leadership or who you consider to be a "good" leader?*
- Leadership is interdisciplinary.
    - *How does your profession or educational path affect how you view leadership?*
    - *How does your field of study or professional field define leadership? Who in your field would be considered a leader? Why?*

7. Conclude the session with any final thoughts from participants or thoughts of your own.

Facilitator Notes

The richness of this activity depends upon participants' familiarity with the material presented in Chapter 1. You may need to adjust the amount of time spent reviewing chapter material before starting the small and large group discussions, depending on participants' needs.

› Conclusion

The session and activities presented here are designed to help participants learn the assumptions, terminology, and considerations found in leadership scholarship as well as reflect critically on their informal theories of leadership. By creating an opportunity for participants to examine their *leadership lens*—the assumptions they hold about leadership—and then by sharing what they learn with others, participants begin to see that leadership is multifaceted and complex. This session should help participants gain a better understanding of the diverse range of leadership approaches and the assumptions that undergird them and how to engage with these differences.

1B: What Is Leadership? Connecting Personal Identity to Social Systems and Power Dynamics

Sara C. Furr & Vijay Pendakur

Objectives/Goals of Chapter

- Explore personal experiences dealing with power.
- Recognize the dynamic interplay between personal experience and social location as an identity-formation process.
- Identify ways to use personal experiences to inform a leadership philosophy.

Critical Concepts: *critical pedagogy, dialectical thinking, power, reflection, social location*

Chapter Overview

This chapter addresses an area of leadership development that is often minimized in dominant literature: the relationship between one's identity, social systems, power dynamics, and one's leadership identity. Let's start by modeling as authors of this curriculum how we situate ourselves in the work of leadership. As student affairs practitioners, we utilize a critical theory lens (e.g., hooks, 1994; Simpson, 2010) to ground our understanding of individuals within a larger matrix of power, privilege, and oppression. As leaders in higher education, we see our leadership identities as extensions of our personal identities; who we are as leaders is critically informed by our life experiences and our social locations.

This chapter offers two new tools to empower learners to engage in reflective and dialogic experiences that can engender deep intellectual and emotional connections between their personal experience, social location, and systems of power. These connections can then form a foundation upon which facilitators can help participants think critically about who they want to be as leaders and how they want to lead. In the following paragraphs, we will briefly review our theoretical framework so that our critical perspective is apparent before we present two curricula that help individuals explore their personal narratives.

Chapter Framework

Central to critical pedagogy is the critique of power. Simpson (2010) affirmed, "Attention to the relationship of knowledge and power represents the most far-reaching and consequential theoretical component of critical pedagogy" (p. 372). Educators might attempt to infuse their classroom or learning environment with a shared ethic of love and cocreation of knowledge as described by hooks (1994), but the bureaucratic frameworks in which educators find themselves often attempt to stop such efforts through the use of systemic discipline. Furthermore, although individual instances of cocreation and noncoercive community development would certainly be positive from a pedagogical perspective, such actions would take place within a broader noncritical pedagogical context.

Cooks (2010) observed that although individuals might attempt to implement critical pedagogy in their classroom or program, participants involved bring a constellation of power relations and behaviors normalized via the broader educational system into the environment every day. This pedagogical situation (i.e., attempting to critically engage learners under a broader system of bureaucratic coercion) is not one that critical educators tackle with any depth or specificity. Freire (1970) did note that usage of some power was necessary when critical educators entered an educational location in which the learners had been previously taught via a harmful pedagogy. All this is to say that educators who attempt to deconstruct power within their program, department, or organization may face resistance because those involved (e.g., students, participants, or other professionals) have been socialized within an existing, dominant understanding of power.

The critique of power just outlined directly connects to individuals' meaning-making and understandings of self. For many, the dominant narrative does not align with lived experience. Therefore, an important starting point, particularly for new learners, is a reflection on one's relationship to power and the development of one's personal narrative. We believe paying special attention to how power shows up in an individual's life provides an integrative understanding of identity moving us beyond the diversity conversation (i.e., a conversation merely acknowledging and accepting differences). Because of this, critical pedagogy, and in particular, power, serves as the starting point for discovering one's personal narrative. Creating dissonance between one's personal narrative and the dominant narrative of social identities can be a powerful start to understanding the experiences of marginalized groups with which we do not identify.

❯ Curriculum Plan

This curriculum plan is broken into two segments titled "Activity 1" and "Activity 2." The first activity is foundational and more appropriate for participants new to the ideas of identity and difference. Activity 1 can help learners examine their formative lived experience alongside their experience of being socially labeled in contemporary American society. This can be followed by Activity 2, which helps participants explore their lived experience with power and how this can be formative, given their privileged and marginalized identities. The second activity can be used independently of the first if you feel participants already possess a strong understanding of their social locations and the constitutive relationship between personal experience and externally applied identity labels. Because this curriculum is experiential and dialogue focused, both activities require a minimum of 60 minutes, with 90 minutes preferred. The two activities can be emotionally intense, so the recommended sequencing (if doing both activities) would be to do Activity 1 and Activity 2 on different days.

❯ Activity 1—Bags: Labels and Stories

In this experiential exercise, participants use a brown paper lunch bag as a tool to reflect on the connections between personal stories and societally applied labels. After being given clear instructions, participants will need 15 minutes of silent work time to use the materials and complete the first part of the exercise. Then, have participants process several key questions in small groups before moving to a large group discussion.

Learning Outcomes

- Ability to articulate new connections between the labels that have been applied to them and how they have come to understand their identities.
- Understand the dialectical relationships between lived experience, social location, and identity.
- Recognition of the need to carefully consider any formation of leadership that discounts the importance of social location or lived experience.

Setting Up the Activity

Group Size: Anywhere between 10 and 30 participants, but no more than 30

Time: 60–90 minutes depending on the length of the large group discussion

Methods: Dialogue, experiential, reflection

Materials: One per person: brown paper lunch sack, 10 sticky labels (mailing labels work well), 5 small pieces of paper (enough space to write 1–2 sentences), writing utensils

Variations: If you have a larger number of participants, have multiple facilitators help process in small and large groups. If you only have 60 minutes, tightly control the processing questions for small group time. If you have less than 60 minutes, this activity *is not* appropriate.

Directions

1. Setting the Tone: *Today we are going to do an activity that might challenge us. It may make you sad. It may make you angry. It may bring up issues that confuse you. After the activity, I hope we can get into a discussion that will be meaningful, understandable, and will leave you with having learned something new.*

2. *Part I—Labeling Your Bags* (How do others perceive you at first sight?): This activity has several preparatory steps that must be clearly explained to the group for the activity to work successfully. Take your time explaining each of these steps as your attention to detail will result in a better learning experience during group processing.

   - *You should have a brown paper bag and five mailing labels in front of you. What I want you to do is quickly write one word or statement for each label that captures your response to these questions:*
     - *How do people perceive you at first glance?*
     - *How do people perceive you if they don't know you?*

- *Don't think too hard; just write down what you believe people see right away if they don't know you. Is it your age? Your body appearance? Your apparel? Where you live? How you speak? Whether you are educated or not?*
- *As you write your labels, stick them on the outside of your bag. Remember to do it quickly; don't over think the exercise.*

3. When the group is done labeling their bags, let them know that you are going to transition to the next set of directions and that they are halfway done with the preparatory steps. Let them know that they will get to share and process soon.

4. *Part II—What Is Really Inside Your Bag?* (Who are you when someone gets to know you?): This set of instructions must be delivered carefully as participants can sometimes be confused by exactly what you want them to put on the inside of their bags. Read through this sample script several times before you facilitate the exercise and think of at least two ways you can articulate instructions so that all of your group members will understand what you want them to do.

    - *Okay, we are going to slow things down a bit. Let's take a moment. Locate your pieces of scrap paper. On each of those pieces of paper, I would like you to take your time and write down one or two sentences that respond to the following:*
        - *What personal, lived experiences have you had that define you?*
        - *What stories do your closest friends and family members know about you?*
    - *Use one piece of scrap paper for each key personal experience or story.*
    - *As you write, please put your pieces of scrap paper in your bag without showing anyone. Again, write down five to six things on separate pieces of scrap paper.*

5. When everyone is done filling out their scraps of paper, remind them to put them inside their bags; let them know that they

are done with the preparatory steps and the sharing portion of the activity is about to begin.

6. *Part III—Small Group Discussion* (Letting it out):
   - *Now it is time to get into small group discussion. I would like for each person to count off by three's and get in respective groups with your bags.*
   - *Now I would like you to share with your group members:*
     - *How have you been labeled? Share up to three labels on the outside of your bag that affect you the most and explain how and/or why.*

7. Check in with groups to gauge discussion. Once everyone has finished sharing labels, ask them to share one story from the inside of their bag and explain how and why it affects them the most.

8. *Part IV—Large Group Discussion:* Shift the dialogue toward a large group discussion by asking the small groups to shift their bodies and their attention to engage the whole room.
   - *Now we are going to get into a large group discussion. I am going to create a list of key labels that emerged as we go along.*

9. Use the remaining time to facilitate large group discussion. See the following debriefing notes for ideas on how to use this time.

Debriefing Notes

In the large group discussion, try to move participants from simply sharing their labels and stories toward thinking about how their identities have been shaped by both the labels and the stories.

- Ask if anyone feels like the labels affected them. If the class does not think that labels matter, ask if anyone has had an experience of rejecting a label and behaving the opposite of a label. Point out that *counter-dependence*, where one's identity is formed in reaction to an external identity, archetype, or stereotype, is still a process of identity formation.

- Ask the participants to think and share their thoughts on whether society pays more attention to the inside of people's bags or to the outside. Try to nuance the conversation by calling attention to the context of public dialogue:
  - *Is the American Dream (e.g., "bootstrap" narratives) rooted in a sense of identity that is informed by the inside of the bag or the outside?*
  - *Are things like judicial systems, school systems, media culture, and so on informed by the inside of the bag or the outside?*
- See if you can introduce a framework of identity that is built on the mutually constitutive tension between the inside of one's bag and the outside. Identity, as a phenomenon, is constantly being formed and re-formed by external and internal forces. How we understand ourselves is intimately tied to our ability to grasp this complexity and make meaning of it time and time again. Furthermore, from a social justice lens, our ability to incorporate an understanding of the systems of power, privilege, and oppression into how we make meaning of our identities is integral to how we understand leadership.

› Activity 2—Discovering Your Story

In this activity participants will be guided through reflection prompts they should complete individually. After a given amount of time, participants will be asked to pair up and share their reflections with one another. Pairs will then find another pair to make groups of four for another opportunity to share. These small groups provide an opportunity to get comfortable with sharing one's story. The final reflection pushes participants to connect their experiences with power to inform their evolving leadership philosophy.

Learning Outcomes

- Reflect on participants' personal experiences with power.
- Understand how power informs participants' views of the world.
- Consider how experiences, particularly with power, inform participants' leadership philosophy.

Setting Up the Activity

Group Size: 10–20 participants

Time: 90 minutes is optimal (60 minutes minimum)

Methods: Facilitation, guided reflection

Materials: Ample writing utensils for participants

Variations: For small groups, consider having the pairs share with the larger group.

Directions

1. Activity Introduction: Begin the activity with some framing language that reconnects participants with learning from Activity 1.
   - *Today we are going to explore issues of power in relationship to our identity and how this informs our informal leadership theories. Developing your narrative requires an introspective reflection on critical moments in your educational experiences. Power is a key tenet of critical pedagogy that may serve to bring forth your narrative. Please write down a specific instance in your life that encompasses the theme of power. Once you have written about power, share with a partner.*
   - Power: *The ability to influence or control, usually connected to the systematic privileging or oppression one experiences based on social location and identities.*
2. Provide 5 to 10 minutes for reflection. The definition of power could be projected onto a screen for reference. It may also be used to put together a handout for participants.

3. Ensure participants are finding pairs as they finish their personal reflection. There should be at least 10 minutes provided for the pair-and-share so that each person has approximately 5 minutes to share as well as time for clarification, questions, and answers.

4. Combine pairs to make groups of four. Participants again have an opportunity to share with their group. This time, ask participants to pay particular attention to any themes that might arise across the stories shared. You should allot 20 to 25 minutes for this section.

5. Bring the discussion back to the large group. You will want to focus the sharing on the themes the participants noticed in their groups of four.
   - *What themes did you notice in your group? Similarities? Differences?*
   - Ideally this will produce some similarities and differences in their experiences. There may have been some individuals who have an affirmative relationship to power while others may not. This is a great place to make connections between social identity and power. What identities were salient in their stories?
   - *Do you see a connection between your experience and any specific social identities?*

6. Depending on time remaining, you may invite folks to share their narrative or story with the large group. This can be more high-risk depending on the group (e.g., size, dynamics). This large group sharing is not necessary to reach the intended learning outcomes but can be added for greater development of trust within the group.

7. Next, participants will return to individual reflection.
   - *Now that we have spent some time specifically reflecting on power, how does this inform your informal theory of leadership? How is your informal theory connected to your identity or narrative? How is power related to your informal theory? What is*

your role in creating a more just society? How will you educate others to understand their role? What will you do to create a culture of social justice in your own life/profession/practice?

8. Debrief: Use the following questions to guide a culminating reflection on how power can manifest in participants' lives and ultimately influence leadership processes.

- *How did it feel to reflect on power in your life?*
- *How did it feel to share your story?*
- *Were you in a position of power or was power being asserted onto you? What feelings arise for you?*
- *Can you identify locations of power in your life? How might you go about deconstructing power?*
- *How can you keep your identity and informal theory of leadership central as you learn more formal leadership theories?*
- *As you learn more about formal theories, how might you consider the role power has played in the development of those theories?*

Debriefing Notes

Much of the debriefing should attend to the process. How are participants feeling? Are there any unresolved feelings or issues? Be sure to make the connection between individual experiences with power identities; depending on the group this might not come out at first. If you are able to spend multiple sessions or more time, this activity works well to be paired with the bags activity described earlier in the curriculum plan.

Facilitator Notes

It is important for you to spend some time going through the reflections within this curriculum yourself to identify your own experiences associated with power. Participants may find it difficult to begin this reflection and it helps if you can share a bit of your own story to provide a starting point for them.

› Conclusion

This curriculum plan provides a holistic reflection of self and system. Activity 1 is great for those new to learning about social justice, critical pedagogy, and power, whereas Activity 2 requires participants to delve deeper into their personal experiences. Both pay particular attention to power, privilege, and social location to develop a clear picture of one's individual story. The context of our experiences matters deeply in the way we understand the world, develop our own narrative, and inform our evolving informal theory of leadership. If you use both Activity 1 and Activity 2 with your group, consider the following reflection questions to help your participants connect their experiences across this curriculum.

- *Activity 1 helped us consider ways in which external labels and internal experiences work in combination to produce what we tend to call identity. How does identity work to inform how you think of yourself as a leader?*
- *Activity 2 challenged us to create a personal narrative that centralized our relationship to power by reflecting on our lived experiences. How do the identities we carry shape the way we think about power and leadership? What aspects of your identity bags from Activity 1 might inform the way you, personally, embody the role of leader?*
- *How can you stay attuned to your story as you grow as a leader? How can you check in with yourself to see if you relate to your stories differently over time as you grow as a leader? The meaning-making process that is at the core of understanding our identities is always in flux, and conscientious leaders must track their shifting relationship to their own identities as they grow and change in the world.*

1C: Social Identities and the Development of Efficacy

Andrea M. De Leon & Allison M. Schipma

Objectives/Goals of Chapter

- Understand efficacy and how it connects to social identities.
- Critically reflect on positive and negative personal experiences with efficacy development and how social identities are connected to these experiences.
- Challenge preconceived notions about power and privilege and their influence on efficacy.

Critical Concepts: *agency, oppression, power, privilege, social identity, social systems*

> Chapter Overview

Although the literature on leadership has become more robust in recent decades, scholars do not agree on a set definition (Dugan, 2017). As expected, the lack of a universal definition can create frustration for learners who are trying to understand the component parts of leadership, like efficacy. However, the lack of a universal leadership definition creates opportunity for learners to think critically, reflect intentionally, and come to their own understandings of what it means to have efficacy as a leader in a formal role or as part of a leadership process.

Bandura (1997) defined *efficacy* as an individual or group's internal belief that they can successfully engage in a particular, domain-specific task. Within the specific context of leadership, there is an important differentiation between leader efficacy and leadership efficacy (Dugan, 2017). Leader efficacy refers to one's internal belief about one's ability to successfully fulfill a positional role, while leadership efficacy reflects belief in one's abilities to engage effectively in the processes associated with leadership. Understanding efficacy on a personal level can advance an individual's leader development and thus positively influence the collective work of a team.

Given efficacy is "a generative capability in which cognitive, social, emotional, and behavioral sub skills must be organized and effectively orchestrated to serve innumerable purposes" (Bandura, 1997, p. 37), it is important to attend to how efficacy can relate to participants' performances. Performance can be broadly defined as the results of participants' actions or behaviors in a setting (Lindsley, Brass, & Thomas, 1995). Self-efficacy and level of performance represent a cyclical relationship that can "result in a downward (decreasing self-efficacy and performance) or upward (increasing self-efficacy and performance) spiral" (Lindsley et al., 1995, p. 646).

› Chapter Framework

The literature is replete with evidence illustrating that efficacy has a positive influence on leader and leadership effectiveness (McCormick, 2001; Leithwood & Jantzi, 2008; Zimmerman, Bandura, & Martinez-Pons, 1992). If the hope is that leaders are effective in their roles, then it is clear that leaders must both understand and work to develop their efficacy. But is it enough to simply define efficacy and talk about ways to develop it? Is it right to assume that efficacy looks and feels the same for all leaders? Understanding leader and leadership efficacy through a critical lens requires understanding how social location influences personal experiences. It is necessary to have conversations about how efficacy might be connected to social identities (e.g., ability status, age, gender identity, race, sexual orientation, socioeconomic status). Furthermore, the concepts of power, privilege, and oppression are closely connected to social identities and can contribute to how an individual experiences efficacy as a leader.

This curriculum introduces the concept of leader efficacy with a focus on the ways in which it is made more complex by considering social identities, lived experiences, and systemic privilege and oppression. When guiding a participant in the creation of a critical framework of self-efficacy and its relationship to leadership, it is essential to link the two concepts through intentional activities and dialogue with one another. This curriculum provides a platform to help participants engage in meaningful learning to support the development of leader efficacy.

> Curriculum Plan

Through traditional lecture, personal reflection, and group dialogue, participants will be challenged to make connections between efficacy and leadership. Participants will begin to make connections between systems of power and oppression and their potential influence on the development of leader efficacy. Participants will also be encouraged to maintain critical hope by discussing tangible ways to continue to think critically while working toward progress and change.

The following curriculum plan should be implemented in one session, lasting approximately 2 hours, with a break between activities. Given the interconnection of the activities, it would be most beneficial for participants to experience the entire curriculum in one session. Though segmented sessions are less optimal, it is certainly possible to break up the activities. If activities are not completed in the same session, it is important to review what was covered in the first session before beginning the second.

Activity 1—Understanding Self-Efficacy

This activity exposes participants to the concept of self-efficacy through lecture and group exercises. First, participants will learn terminology and begin to think about their efficacy. Second, participants will have an opportunity to critically reflect on both positive and negative experiences that have influenced their efficacy and what social identities may connect to those experiences. Participants will have time to process as a group before moving on to Activity 2.

Learning Outcomes

- Understand the concept of self-efficacy and its connection to personal experiences.
- Critically reflect on social identities to foster understanding of their impact on lived experiences.
- Be able to articulate how social identities are connected to self-efficacy.

Setting Up the Activity

Group Size: 10–30 participants

Time: 60–75 minutes

Methods: Lecture, reflection

Materials: Computer, projector/screen, sticky notes (four per person), masking tape, writing utensils, two signs (8.5×11 in size) labeled "Upward Spiral" and "Downward Spiral"

Directions

1. Establish group expectations regarding privacy, confidentiality, and sensitivity and the desire to create a *brave space* (see the Introduction to this book for details on this).

2. Begin by defining the concept of self-efficacy and that it is domain specific. Explicitly discuss the definitions of confidence and capacity and explain the differences between the terms in relationship to leadership efficacy. See Chapter 1 of the main text for support.

3. Explain how self-efficacy can be related to task performance and the cyclical process that connects to the idea of a downward or upward spiral. For further theoretical exploration of this topic, see reading by Gist and Mitchell (1992).

4. Display Upward Spiral and Downward Spiral signs parallel to each other on a blank wall space. Ensure that there are at least two feet of blank space between the signs.

5. Distribute four sticky notes to each participant and ensure that each has a writing utensil.

6. Ask participants to think about experiences in which their leadership efficacy was strengthened as illustrated by the upward spiral. Provide examples (e.g., when you scored the game winning point in a basketball game or received a promotion at work).

7. Ask participants to anonymously write down experiences that come to mind, one per sticky note. Ask them to also think about any social identities that may have been involved in their experience(s) and to also write down the identity/identities on the respective sticky notes.

8. Next, instruct participants to think about experiences in which their leadership efficacy was weakened as illustrated by the downward spiral. Provide examples (e.g., when you received a failing grade on an assignment or when you received a negative performance appraisal at work.)

9. Ask participants to anonymously write down any experiences that come to mind, one per sticky note. Ask them to also think about any social identities that may have been involved in their experience(s) and to also write down the identity/identities on the respective sticky notes.

10. Participants may distribute the sticky notes however they wish. For example, participants can place all four for upward or downward spiral experiences, two for upward spiral and two for downward spiral, or any other combination that makes sense for them. They must, however, use at least two of four sticky notes if they can't use them all.

11. Provide 10 to 15 minutes for participants to complete these tasks, but use more time if needed. Once all participants are finished writing on their sticky notes, instruct them to silently stick their notes under the respective Upward Spiral or Downward Spiral signs.

12. Once all sticky notes are in place, ask participants to silently read and reflect on them.

13. When they are finished, invite participants to share general reactions with the large group. Use open-ended questions such as these: *What are your general reactions to this activity? How are you feeling right now?*

14. Encourage participants to think critically about the things they read on each sticky note. Ask the following questions: *Were there themes around the types of experiences that caused upward spirals in leadership efficacy? What about downward spirals? What social identities, if any, seemed connected to those experiences? What do you believe contributes to these connections?*

15. Inform participants that the next activity will move into further exploration and reflection of leadership efficacy and social identities.

Debriefing Notes

This activity provides a framework for self-efficacy exploration and creates a foundation for group dialogue centering participants' perceptions of their leadership efficacy as it relates to multiple identities and experiences. When debriefing, it is necessary to consider the delicate nature of exploring lived experiences that focus on a participant's social identities. Engage with sensitivity and empathy, pushing participants to disclose only to the degree they feel comfortable.

Facilitator Notes

This activity may be particularly challenging since it asks participants to critically reflect on potentially painful experiences. It also invites participants to think about both privileged and oppressed identities, which can be difficult depending on developmental readiness. To ensure a successful learning experience, remain observant and aware of participants' reactions, and alter the activity as necessary for the group.

Activity 2—Self-Efficacy, the System, and Leadership

This portion of the curriculum builds upon the personal reflection and awareness established during the first activity by inviting participants to dialogue around the topics of social identities and lived experiences.

Learning Outcomes

- Be aware of social identities and how they relate to self-efficacy.
- Understand how societal systems and structures have an impact on self-efficacy.

- Construct ways to positively influence societal systems that affect leader efficacy.

Setting Up the Activity

Group Size: 10–30 participants
Time: 60–75 minutes
Methods: Dialogue, reflection
Materials: Computer, audio, projector/screen

Directions

1. Revisit and amend, if necessary, group expectations regarding privacy, confidentiality, and sensitivity regarding the topics to be explored.
2. Begin by explaining that this activity will build upon the exploration of self-efficacy in relation to social identities and lived experiences covered in the last activity. Explain that this activity further connects these ideas to personal leadership practices.
3. Have participants split into evenly distributed small groups. If possible, participants should arrange their chairs in a way that is conducive to small group dialogue. Display the following questions for participants: *How do we maintain our leadership efficacy when we fail? How do we maintain efficacy when we feel defeated? How do we maintain efficacy when we receive messages that we are not capable? Where do these messages come from?*
4. Allow time for small groups to share with the large group the ideas and concepts they discussed. Then, revisit the question: *Where do these messages come from?* Use this as a prompt to begin a dialogue around these messages stemming from social structures and systems. The concept of *systems* can vary in meaning from family environments to community engagement to media influences to dominant institutions.

5. Have participants consider what specific system(s), if any, influence their ability to sustain leader efficacy. Ask the following: *What system(s), if any, contribute to you experiencing upward spirals in your efficacy as a leader? What about downward spirals in your efficacy as a leader?* Provide examples of systems to support understanding.

6. Guide the discussion to a consideration of how the system is related to self-efficacy and leadership by posing questions such as these: *How does the system influence our efficacy? What messages does the system send? How do you as an individual reject and/or disrupt any systems that negatively influence your efficacy? How do you as an individual maintain any systems that positively influence your efficacy?*

7. Move the conversation toward a discussion of leadership and the connection to leader efficacy. Pose questions like these: *How does this connect back to your own understanding of leadership? What does leader efficacy mean to you? What are ways in which you can further build your leader efficacy? How can you use your leader efficacy to build agency for others?*

8. To wrap up the conversation, encourage participants to share with the large group one take-away from the discussion. This can be in regard to any part of the activity or dialogue, but work to focus the attention on the positive ways in which participants can apply what they have learned.

Debriefing Notes

The conclusion of this activity is constructed to provide a space for participants to think critically about the ways in which societal structures are connected to social identities and the development of self-efficacy. When engaging participants in the dialogue, it is necessary to consider the sensitivity of exploring lived experiences that center on a participant's connection to their social identities, both privileged and oppressed. The topics discussed may lead to feelings of frustration or hopelessness. It is important to be aware of this and to guide the discussion to a hopeful place as necessary.

Facilitator Notes

Discussing self-efficacy can bring about a range of emotions that may or may not be predictable. It is important to allow participants to feel what they feel and to encourage introspection and reflection, but to also be aware of the overall tone and feel of the group. Furthermore, topics regarding power, privilege, and oppression may come up in conversation about systemic influences. It is necessary to recognize how participants are reacting and engaging and guide the conversation to a constructive, yet understanding place. Remember that not every participant will experience this dialogue in the same way, but that engaging them in the critical thinking process is a significant step in the right direction.

› Conclusion

This curriculum was intentionally developed in a way that would allow participants to understand the concept of self-efficacy, apply that understanding to reflections on personal experiences, and develop an ability to think critically about social identities and systems of power that influence leaders' development of self-efficacy. Through lecture, reflection, and dialogue, participants are able to make connections between lived experiences, the experiences of others, and the ways in which social systems and structures inform and shape an individual's development of efficacy. Moving individuals from a place of personal reflection to social perspective-taking, and then to broader thinking about larger societal systems, allows participants to understand systemic issues personally—ideally making the learning more powerful and salient. As scholars continue to research ways in which leadership self-efficacy is connected to leader effectiveness, it is important for all to understand that leaders' experiences are unique. Self-efficacy is developed in different ways for different people, and much of that development is predicated on one's social identities. Leaders who implement a critical approach to understanding self-efficacy prepare themselves to lead better.

1 D: Exploring Cultural Sensitivity, Acceptance, and Understanding in Leadership

Mathew R. Goldberg & Michelle L. Kusel

Objectives/Goals of Chapter

- Understand the importance of culture in global leadership using Hofstede's dimensions.
- Expand views of leadership beyond the Western canon of leadership theory.
- Be able to analyze global situations and develop solutions while using a variety of cultural lenses.

Critical Concepts: *critical self-reflection, power, social perspective-taking*

❯ Chapter Overview

This curriculum offers an examination of the influences and impact of globalization. "When in Rome, do as the Romans do" is a common aphorism to remind individuals that to truly connect with a culture and a place you need to act as the people act. The underlying implication of this saying is that all cultures have a set of behaviors and values that we may fail to appreciate unless we truly try to understand them. As the world becomes more global, it is critical to understand how to integrate into a culture that may be different from our own. The challenge becomes this: How does one connect with a culture other than their own without being offensive or insensitive? How does one understand a culture without using their own culture as a lens of right and wrong and inflicting one's culture on another? In leadership, what are the potential influences of defaulting to the Western canon of theory? How does one identify themes and values of cultures without creating labels and boxes that seem prescriptive?

Chapter Framework

To understand globalization, one must first understand culture. Culture can be defined as "the collective programming of the mind distinguishing the members of one group or category of people from others" (Hofstede, 1980, p. 43). Culture is expressed in many ways but can be categorized by symbols, heroes, rituals, and values (Hofstede, Hofstede, & Minkov, 2010). At the simplest level, symbols are things, heroes are people, rituals are actions, and values are feelings that are inherent to a culture. These elements that comprise culture influence how individuals perceive and process information. Because culture is the foundation for how people interact with the world, it is critical for leaders to recognize cultural diversity and the need to readjust behavior to connect with peoples' values and expectations. Without cultural sensitivity, U.S. leaders likely operate under the assumption of a Western canon of leadership and fail to acknowledge context. The Western canon is problematic in a global age because it perpetuates an ethnocentric view of what it means to be a leader and a rigid definition of effective leadership. When leaders expand their worldview they are able to acknowledge the cultural similarities and differences and respect and integrate into a culture while working to engage, change, and grow the organization.

The connection between culture and leadership is evident in Hofstede's work (e.g., Hofstede, 1980; Hofstede, Pedersen, & Hofstede, 2002). Hofstede's original research was a comprehensive study that examined 40 countries and questioned if they possessed common cultural dimensions (Hofstede, 1980). The results identified four key dimensions:

- *Power Distance* (Hierarchy): What is the level of separation between those in power and those who do not hold power?
- *Individualism versus Collectivism* (Identity): Does a member of a culture express themselves as "I" or "we?"
- *Masculinity versus Femininity* (Gender): Is there a preference for competition or cooperation?
- *Uncertainty Avoidance* (Truth): How is ambiguity handled? Is it embraced or feared?

An additional dimension was later added (Hofstede et al., 2002; Hofstede et al., 2010):

- *Long-Term Orientation versus Short-Term Orientation* (Virtue): What level of importance is placed on long-term benefits versus saving face?

Hofstede's dimensions acknowledge that cultures have common themes that are expressed differently. Understanding Hofstede's theory is necessary for global leaders to meet the needs and values of a team. Hypothetically, if you are a leader working in China, where the power distance score is ranked high (80 out of 100) and individualism is marked low (20 out of 100), how one engages in leadership would need to reflect these cultural norms. However, this leadership style would change drastically if you were leading a team in Finland, where the power distance score is low (33 out of 100) and the individualism is high (63 out of 100; Hofstede et al., 2010). This example signifies how leadership is a constant set of changing choices that necessitate cultural awareness, knowledge, and competence. Although these dimensions are extremely helpful to provide an understanding of a culture and how leaders may enhance effectiveness, it is important to remain vigilant and resist comparing cultures, particularly benchmarking one's culture to another. Rather, culture needs to be examined without a bias of one's own cultural influences.

Ultimately, Hofstede's research falls short in celebrating the plethora of cultural diversity. It solely examines national cultural values likely reflecting the dominant norms of a particular society. It is undeniable that individuals and places will possess rich nuances and multifaceted cultural elements. Additionally, it is naïve to believe that global leadership theories are only applicable in international settings. The access to technology and the growing globalization of the world enables diverse attitudes and perspectives to exist in many countries. Exercising vigilance demonstrates your willingness to accept that truth is relative and that effective leadership requires an understanding of culture, people, and context but that no single framework can provide the full complexity of cultural influences.

> Curriculum Plan

The purpose of this curriculum is to engage participants in critical self-reflection and social perspective-taking with regard to global leadership. Through the use of performing arts and discussion, participants will begin to formulate and understand the challenges that exist with global leadership by turning theory into action. This curriculum is designed for participants to imagine culturally uncomfortable situations and learn how to analyze situations and respond applying Hofstede's theory. The curriculum should be implemented over at least 1 hour of time, but this is flexible depending on the length and depth of the discussion.

Activity 1—Scene Around the World

Participants will interpret and examine different cultural scenarios with a critical lens to navigate their responses, emotions, biases, and analyses of Hofstede's dimensions and its applicability to global leadership. This curriculum assumes that the participants have a working knowledge of Hofstede's dimensions. If this is not the case, a brief overview should be provided. Please see the reference section for some suggestions of literature. The curriculum will challenge participants to adopt a cultural lens that feels unnatural to them and attempt to view a problem through that lens. One goal of the activity is to create discomfort in a controlled setting so that participants will be better prepared to adapt when faced with real-world global experiences.

Learning Outcomes

- Understand how global leadership theories translate into real situations.
- Identify triggers, challenges, and perceptions when learning in a different culture.
- Demonstrate cultural sensitivity and adaptability of cultural values.

Setting Up the Activity

Group Size: Optimal group size is 12 participants.

Time: 60 minutes

Methods: Dialogue, lecture, reflection, role-play

Materials: Blank paper, writing utensils, handouts detailing each scenario (three copies of each scenario, one per participant); hat or other receptacle from which participants can anonymously choose a slip; slips of paper listing "cultures," whiteboard/chalkboard, markers/chalk (optional)

Directions

1. Divide participants into four groups of three people (adjust to accommodate your group size).

2. Explain the activity: *Each group will be provided with a scenario for which they will be asked to determine a resolution and then act it out for the collective group. After I have passed out the scenarios, I will ask you to take a slip of paper out of this hat. On the paper is your culture as defined using Hofstede's dimensions. You should assume that although your culture is not extreme in each dimension, it shows strong preferences toward the dimensions listed. Working together, your group is responsible for scripting this scenario and devising the solution using the norms of your culture. Each performance should be about 3–5 minutes. You will have 15 minutes to prepare.*

3. Before the first group presents, instruct participants to take active notes on the presentation, including which dimensions they witness and where the culture falls in the dimension. After the last group presents, debrief using the questions proposed in the next section, your observations, and following the lead of participants.

Debriefing Notes

Below are some questions that can guide the conversation:

- *Did any group find it hard to apply their assigned culture to the situation? Why? Why not? To what degree might this be a function of your own cultural value orientation?*

- *How did the culture you were assigned align with your typical disposition? What would this mean if you were visiting or living in a culture different from your typical disposition? If you could change your culture, would you? Why? Why not?*

- *Did you identify any cultures incorrectly? Explain. How might the ways in which we act as well as interpret cultural dimensions different than ours be a function of our cultural lenses? For example, how might collectivism be described by someone operating from an individualistic versus collectivistic lens? To what extent is our ability to interpret a cultural value a function of our dominant cultural lenses?*

- *Is global leadership only important to think about when abroad? How is it important in your daily life? How can you incorporate this critical thinking in your own community? What are the implications of this for how leadership is practiced?*

> Conclusion

Global leadership and Hofstede's dimensions are not challenging in concept but become incredibly complex when brought to life. While writing this curriculum plan, we were reminded of the movie *Dead Poets Society*. A student is asked to read the introductory chapter about understanding poetry. The instructor in the film begins to plot a graph on the proper way to rate a poem according to the author's instructions. After he plots the graph, he tells the students that this rating isn't enough. He wants them to experience poetry and think for themselves. Similarly, although Hofstede's dimensions provide an excellent baseline from which to understand global leadership, it is critical for participants to not only identify global leadership and cultures, but to experience what it means to be a global leader. This is where the magic happens.

Therefore, since this curriculum cannot provide actual experiences in another culture, this simulation was based on real examples and authentic discussion in hopes of providing participants with a perspective on both the importance of global leadership and also the execution of leadership theories involving this concept. This chapter is meant to lure participants into a messy and challenging situation that will feel unnatural. When this takes place, participants can name the uneasiness in a controlled setting. Then, when the participants are exposed to global leadership in the real world, they will be better equipped to understand, grow, and adapt to a situation. Ultimately, the goal is to help learners recognize how leadership is socially constructed and that this construction is a function of cultural values.

Handout 1.1: Scenarios

Scenario 1 You are a new employee working overseas and you are having trouble accomplishing your tasks. Simple jobs seem difficult because the computer is in a foreign language and you don't know what resources are available. You are debating whether to ask for help or if you should try to resolve the issues on your own. You are struggling with the decision because you still feel uncomfortable with everyone and are trying to prove you are valuable to the company. Ultimately, if you want to ask for help, you are not sure who you should even ask! At the company, there are several other new employees from the United States, a coworker from the host country who is responsible for helping with your transition, other coworkers from the host country with whom you are still trying to build relationships, and the office supervisor who is also from the host country. What should you do?

Scenario 2 You have been living abroad for three months and a friend from the host country invites you to dinner. At dinner, you are served a traditional dish typical of the area. In your opinion the food looks unpalatable and you are worried it will make you sick. Your friend is really excited to share this meal with you and teach you about his culture. What should you do?

Scenario 3 You currently work for a large U.S. corporation. This month at work you have a new colleague from an overseas office. She is really friendly and a hard worker. She is always bringing in small gifts for the office and asking if you need any help on your projects. One day you head back to the office late at night because you forgot something and find her still working. She is surprised to see you but smiles and exchanges small talk before returning to her work. You are confused about why she asks to help with your work when she has so much of her own that requires her to stay late. You become worried that she is overworking herself, but you are not sure what to do. How do you proceed?

Scenario 4 You are living abroad and working on a group project with a diverse team of international and local students. Your group is charged with planning a community event at the university to help foster relationships between international and local students. You have several ideas already but haven't presented them to the team yet. You are worried about the conversation because you have noticed there is already a great deal of conflict and that cliques are forming. How do you proceed?

Cultures

	Culture 1	Culture 2	Culture 3	Culture 4
Identity	Individual	Individual	Collective	Collective
Hierarchy	Low-Power Distance	High-Power Distance	High-Power Distance	Low-Power Distance
Gender	Feminine	Feminine	Masculine	Masculine
Truth	Uncertainty Tolerance	Uncertainty Avoidance	Uncertainty Avoidance	Uncertainty Tolerance
Virtue	Short-term orientation	Short-term orientation	Long-term orientation	Long-term orientation

Note: The cultures and scenarios do not need to align. For example, Culture 1 does not need to be assigned Scenario 1.

Chapter 2: Critical Perspectives as Interpretative Frameworks

2A: Understanding Core Critical Concepts: Experiential Explorations into the Contextualization of Knowledge Production

Maurice Stevens

Objectives/Goals of Chapter

- Understand ideals of reciprocity in the coconstruction of knowledge and reflexivity-based learning.
- Identify and understand the effects of introducing critical perspectives to leadership practice and knowledge production.
- Analyze and describe shifts in participants' notions of leadership domains.

Critical Concepts: *contextualized knowledge, critical self-reflection, ideology*

> ## Chapter Overview

Critical social theory (CST) points to several things at once. First, it indicates a commitment to using the production of knowledge or theorizing to engage in social action intended to improve conditions for oppressed members of society (Dant, 2004). Critical social theory is, therefore, about application of knowledge in a political and social sense. CST also assumes that everyone can benefit from this process because we are all under the influence of ideology as members of society who do the work of the "State" by submitting to our own domination in multiple ways. From this perspective, we can understand CST as a tool of personal liberation through courageous self-reflection. CST also points to particular objects of analysis in that it is interested in analyzing material social relations and the ideas that inform them (Dant, 2004).

Chapter Framework

Some theorists trace CST to the radical, Marxist theorists of the 1930s through the 1960s and their desire to emphasize the degree to which all knowledge production is emergent from particular social contexts, or radically contextualized, and therefore both reflective and reproductive of dominant ideologies (Nealon & Giroux, 2012). The critical social theorist was, therefore, called upon to turn an analytic lens on society, knowledge production practices, and to engage in leadership by applying what was learned to enhance socially just relations.

This curriculum draws on critical pedagogical theory, participatory leadership techniques like open space technology, science and technology studies, critical trauma theory, Althusser's (1971) theory of ideology, and intersectionality theory (Cho, Crenshaw, & McCall, 2013). Some of the primary assumptions that emerge from the interdisciplinary intersection of these theoretical and methodological frameworks include these:

- Our sense of self or *subjectivity* is the result of intersecting and interacting narratives of self, presented to us through multiple social institutions.

- Objects of knowledge emerge out of social and material relations; they are not discovered.
- Identity is a practice of identification and not an object one possesses.
- Difference, rather than a chasm to be bridged, is a point of contact, friction, and information sharing.

This curriculum also assumes that none of these frameworks are static. They fluctuate and come to crisis in relation to one another, shifting as needed to respond to the contexts of their application.

> Curriculum Plan

The following curriculum plan stresses the importance of understanding knowledge formation as a practice of making and not simply an activity of encountering free-floating forms of knowledge waiting to be discovered "out there." This curriculum plan understands CST to be built first and foremost on the practice of reflexivity and reflection on concepts and modes of material engagement that have come to be accepted as common sense or simple truths. Not only do participants begin to reflect upon who they are and what they know (and how these have come to be), but they begin to reconsider normative frames for leadership and adjust these if they find doing so useful (Dant, 2004). The curriculum plan is best implemented across three sessions of 1 hour and 20 minutes each. These sessions can take place across multiple meetings or be developed across the course of a single day or discreet workshop period. Although this is a suggested format, you can easily adapt it to meet the needs of your particular learning context.

❯ Activity 1—Knowledge Has a Context: Understanding the Coconstruction of Knowledge

This section of the curriculum introduces the notion that knowledge and practices of knowledge production are situated; they emerge from very particular and complex contexts. It suggests that because of the highly contextual nature of knowledge practices and the knowledge objects that emerge from them, a critical perspective is necessary to effectively evaluate the knowledge we encounter from day to day.

Learning Outcomes

- Develop the capacity to trace the history of an important concept or idea and thereby enhance the capacity for critical information literacy.
- Understand basic aspects of ideology and increase the sense of the coconstitutive nature of knowledge and interpretations of that knowledge.

Setting Up the Activity

Group Size: Open to any size group

Time: 80 minutes

Methods: Large group reflection, lecture, small group interaction

Materials: Whiteboard/chalkboard and markers/chalk (optional)

Multimedia: Computers with Internet access for each small group

Directions

1. Remind participants that a core component of CST involves understanding that knowledge is situated and that it develops in relation to sociocultural and historical forces. Review Chapter 2 of the primary text (Dugan, 2017) for support associated with these ideas.

2. Explain that our social identities are critical aspects of who we are and how we experience life and leadership.

3. Discuss how social institutions like the family, school, and media deliver narratives about who we are. Allow time for participants to ask questions.

4. Explain that every field of study has certain ideas that are central to understanding the function of that field. These threshold concepts are critical to developing a sense of understanding in a field. Allow participants to ask questions about these concepts.

5. Ask participants to divide into pairs and talk about one concept or idea they have encountered that completely shifted how they thought of or understood themselves. Harvest these concepts and ask participants to name them. Write them on the board.

6. After the concepts have been written on the board, ask participants to reflect and see whether any of these terms can be condensed or if there are repetitions. Then ask participants to form four-person working clusters with one computer per group.

7. Ask each group to agree upon one threshold concept they want to explore further.

8. Have each group search for and find at least five sources of information about the threshold concept of their choice. These sources should all be different formats (e.g., scholarly articles, websites, podcasts, newspaper articles, magazines, videos).

9. Have participants construct three lists ranking their source material in relation to level of authority, volume of information, and degree of user contact (i.e., How often is this utilized as a source of information? To what degree is it perceived as legitimate?).

10. In large group discussion, ask participants what they notice about the differences between their three lists and what they

notice about different opinions group members may have had about the truth and/or value of the information they found.

Debriefing Notes

At the end of this portion of this curriculum, participants are becoming aware of the ways knowledge is constructed in relation to social institutions and dominant ideas. Moreover, they are beginning to become sensitive to the fact that the authority or legitimacy of particular knowledge objects derives from the particular forms used to represent them. Moreover, they are coming to understand that certain ideas or concepts have more impact on particular areas of knowledge than do others. Awareness of the metacognitive aspect of this activity can be encouraged by asking participants to notice what they are learning throughout the process.

Facilitator Notes

It is important to be mindful of how participants may become uncomfortable as they realize the constructed and contextualized nature of knowledge. It is common for someone to say something like, "Hey, wait a minute! If this is true, then what does that say about what I believe and know? Are you saying that my beliefs are just programmed into me?" It is possible for the group conversation to move toward a sense of helplessness and hopelessness. It is important to allow for this expression and to identify it as part of the context as well; we need to be aware that this is a discursive option presented to us. You could share with the group something I myself often consider, which is—*I'm impressed by the fact that people keep getting up every day even when they are aware of this*—and wonder with the group—*what keeps people going in the face of such daunting social realities?*

❯ Activity 2—Knowledge Is a Conversation: The Effects of Bringing Critical Perspectives into Dialogue

This section introduces the notion that knowledge is produced in dialogic fashion, and the best questions are those that show us what we do not know while troubling us when we ask them. The production of "wicked" questions and dialogic engagement in this activity is designed to demonstrate to participants how questioning and dialogue are themselves knowledge practices by allowing participants to see knowledge production unfold before them.

Learning Outcomes

- Develop the capacity to create probing and open-ended questions otherwise known as *wicked* questions.
- Enhance capacity for dialogue.
- Increase the view of dialogue as a coproductive learning process.

Setting Up the Activity

Group Size: Open to any size group

Time: 80 minutes

Methods: Lecture, small group interaction, large group reflection

Materials: Whiteboard/chalkboard and markers/chalk (optional), 3×5 cards for each participant

Directions

1. Begin the activity by explaining that a core component of CST involves learning how to formulate questions that move beyond commonsense understandings of ourselves and

our actions in the world and that uncover assumptions
and unquestioned beliefs. Share the need to develop these
questions through dialogue.

2. Give each participant a 3×5 card and ask them to write down
   a question that is important to them that has emerged out of
   their participation in the first activity.

3. Explain how participants can create powerful questions by
   enhancing question architecture (e.g., using "why" questions
   instead of the "yes/no" question structure); increasing the
   scope or scale of a question (e.g., Does the question pertain to
   an individual or a larger group/ population?); and by increasing
   the depth of the meaning of a question (e.g., Does it trouble
   me to ask it?).

4. Have participants break into dyads and work together to
   make their questions more wicked. Allow 5 to 7 minutes for
   this. Ask each dyad to pick one question as being the most
   compelling or important to them.

5. Have two dyads come together into a quad and repeat the
   process in Step 4. Have two quads come together in a group
   of eight and compare their questions, work on increasing how
   wicked they are, and then choose one question to post on the
   board. A group of 40 participants should yield five or fewer
   great questions.

6. Divide the large group into subgroups, one for each tough
   question. Have one person respond to the question and
   another participant reply to that response, first by paraphrasing their understanding of the first person's response, and
   then by making an argument for why they agree or disagree
   with the first person's response. Another participant will then
   reply to the second person's response, first by paraphrasing,
   and then by responding with an argument for why they agree
   or disagree, and so on. This process continues until the conversation appears to be ending. At this point, if time allows,
   one of the group participants will ask another question, the

group will go through another round to enhance their wicked question, and then the revised question will be posed to the group and anyone will be allowed to respond. The process continues as before, starting with Step 5.

7. Bring the group back to the full circle and reflect on what happened, what insights and surprises people encountered, and what they learned from the process.

Debriefing Notes

Activity 2 takes participants through a process that asks them to experiment with not knowing and to understand this condition as the place from which the development of new knowledge or frameworks for analysis can emerge. Moreover, this activity centers on the notion of the power of inquiry and the useful-ness of questions that do more than simply corroborate given understandings. Additionally, because they work together to produce, assess, develop, and finally choose questions they find most challenging through dialogue with peers, participants also come to appreciate the value of dialogue as a practice that supports knowledge production.

Facilitator Notes

Although this activity may not be as potentially unsettling for participants as the first activity can be, it is important to pay attention and give guidance to groups as they work to decide how to enhance questions, and then decide which question to put forward to the next group. Encourage participants to slow down and notice how they are making decisions and how they are feeling while these processes take place. *What is it about the question that makes this process unsettling? Is there something about the linguistic architecture (e.g., the use of open-ended structures instead of yes or no questions) or the scope of the question that makes it feel particularly relevant to participants? Does the question unsettle taken-for-granted assumptions or stocks of knowledge?* Asking participants about how the form of questions can influence their impact can raise metacognitive awareness and reflexivity.

❯ Activity 3—Knowledge in Coformation: Distinguishing Different Knowledge Forms

This section of the curriculum introduces the notion that knowledge and practices of knowledge production are situated not only in social contexts but also in the very methods through which they are created. In this activity, participants think through the practice of writing, first individually, then in response to one another. These reflections will relate to responses to a short talk about participatory leadership and social justice engagement.

Learning Outcomes

- Develop capacity to articulate, evaluate, and respond to ideas that are in written form as well as through writing.
- Develop ability to articulate an understanding of participatory leadership and its relationship to social justice engagement.

Setting Up the Activity

Group Size: Open to any size group

Time: 80 minutes

Methods: Dyad interaction, individual work, lecture, large group reflection

Materials: Individual journals for participants, whiteboard/chalk board with markers/chalk

Multimedia: Computers with Internet access. You are encouraged to use "Insights and Revelations from The Art of Participatory Leadership and Social Change" (https://vimeo.com/31028710). An alternative is Lex Schroeder's blog "There's a Conversation

Brewing About Power That Needs #MoreVoices" (http://lexschroeder.com/theres-a-conversation-brewing-about-power-that-needs-morevoices/).

Directions

1. Begin the activity by explaining that the purpose is to develop our capacities to use writing as a process of/for thinking.

2. Explain to participants that this dialogic writing activity will begin with a shared text. This particular text offers one perspective on participatory leadership and its relationship with social justice engagement.

3. View the video with participants, and afterward give participants time to free write for 5 minutes in loose response to the video.

4. When the free-write is complete, write the following questions on the whiteboard or chalkboard and ask participants to spend 30 minutes writing in response to them:

   - *Who is the speaker?*
   - *Who seems to be the speaker's audience?*
   - *What is the primary argument or points the speaker is making?*
   - *What contribution is this speaker making to our understanding of participatory leadership?*
   - *In what ways do you (or your leadership practices) align with this position?*
   - *In what ways do you (or your leadership practices) depart from this position?*
   - *So what? How are you surprised, moved, inspired, rocked, or otherwise affected by this speaker's presentation or something it sparked within you?*

5. Ask participants to get into pairs and share their journal entries with one another. Allow readers to spend 10 minutes reading their partners' journal entries. Ask pairs to share with

one another any questions they may have for clarification purposes.

6. Ask participants to then spend 10 minutes developing wicked questions in response to the journal entries their partners have produced.

7. Have partners share their wicked questions and then have the other partners spend 5 minutes responding to them.

8. Have participants return to the large group to discuss what they have observed about thinking through the writing process, and what insights they gained in relation to their understanding of participatory leadership and social justice engagement.

Debriefing Notes

Activity 3 builds on what the participants have been learning and experiencing in the first two activities. However, instead of encouraging participants to disrupt their sense of knowing, this activity begins supporting them in the process of drawing things together into both a coherent understanding of what they have learned (orderly, due to feedback, and captured in a written document that also bears traces of its own shifts in the form of notes between reader and writer), and a clear sense of new directions for inquiry and research.

Facilitator Notes

It can be useful, and powerfully instructive, to have participants consider their written material as being a kind of record of their thinking processes. It can be a rich experience to have them revisit these documents after a few weeks have passed and describe what they "see" in their documents. It is best to have them write what they see down on the documents themselves so that their responses become a kind of trace as well.

> Conclusion

The curriculum presented in this chapter is designed to develop an experiential context through which participants can encounter and understand concepts and principles important to CST. These contexts for experiential learning have focused on participants achieving a level of vulnerability and self-reflexivity through collaborative and dialogic activities. These activities demonstrate that knowledge is coconstructed and contextualized, that it emerges from spaces of not knowing and the release of habitual understandings, and that it comes in many forms that are themselves significant conveyors of knowledge and the power that determines legitimacy and authority. Participants come to understand themselves as knowledge makers, and not merely consumers of information.

2B: Fundamental Skills for Applying Critical Perspectives to Leadership: Practicing the Art of Deconstruction and Reconstruction

OiYan A. Poon & Dian D. Squire

Objectives/Goals of Chapter

- Encourage questioning of normalized notions of social inequalities.
- Critically examine generally accepted notions of social inequalities.
- Cultivate agency to rethink social conditions and generate innovative solutions.

Critical Concepts: *critical consciousness, power, praxis, social justice, willful blindness*

Chapter Overview

This chapter starts with the premise that bold leadership for social justice requires a spirit of revolutionary thinking or a willingness to go beyond commonly accepted notions of how the world works. It draws from the philosophies of Freire (2000), who outlined the importance of critical consciousness as "learning to perceive social, political, and economic contradictions, and to take action against oppressive elements of reality" (p. 17). It ultimately affirms the idea that another world is possible and rejects the idea that little can be done to ameliorate deep injustices present in our society.

This chapter asserts that critical reflections and investigations into why and how inequalities are produced can lead to collective actions that transform social conditions for justice. Freire (2000) called this combination of dialogical reflection and informed action *praxis*. Engagement in praxis may seem logical and simple in its call for reflective action; however, there is often a deep-seated fear of criticizing and rejecting societal norms, even if they serve to produce inequalities and injustices—especially when normative standards are inherently tied to power dynamics and hierarchies (Freire, 2000).

The 1999 film *The Matrix* can help explain the complexities of engaging in a praxis of deconstructing and reconstructing social realities. The film explores the relationship between two different, but related, worlds. The first is a dream world, where people's perceived realities are actually projections and illusions. The people in this dream world are unaware that their perceived realities are actually produced by an inhumane system of oppression. The second is the real world; in this world, the state of wanton oppression is revealed, and a group of liberated human rebels, who have rejected illusory human existence, fight the inhumane power hierarchy.

A pivotal scene from the movie palpably illustrates the fear and anticipation inherent in choosing to critically understand the complexities of social systems. In it, Laurence Fishburne's character Morpheus, a rebel leader, presents Keanu Reeves's character, Thomas Anderson, with a choice to take a blue pill, which represents ignorance, or a red pill, which allows Mr. Anderson to gain emotionally hard-to-accept knowledge about the realities of the world and develop an entirely new identity to become Neo. There is an inherent anxiety in rejecting, or even questioning, the long-presumed ways our world operates to maintain systems of oppression and choosing to embrace what is unknown. It can lead to new, often challenging understandings of self-identity, the world, and leadership possibilities for revolutionary, social change.

The purpose of this curriculum plan is to guide participants through an exercise in deconstructing and reconstructing normative conceptualizations of how the world works. The curriculum encourages participants to engage in a deep questioning of the world in which they live, to work to identify underlying and often ugly social dynamics and power hierarchies that produce injustices, and to courageously imagine more just ways of leading, living, and working together. This act of deconstructing and reconstructing one's worldview, or the development of critical consciousness, is not a simple task because it can represent the choice to fundamentally destabilize one's normative notions of the world and self-identity. At the heart of the humanizing process of critical consciousness development is the choice to begin understanding and reclaiming one's subjectivity to reflect and take responsibility and action toward social justice.

Because the choice to engage in deconstructing and reconstructing one's worldview can be so challenging, Freire (2000) argued that it must not be forced upon individuals. However, offering the opportunity to recognize, understand, and remove the blinders obscuring a clearer understanding of how systemic inequalities and oppression are produced is to begin the process of building a critical consciousness. It is the choice Morpheus presented to Keanu Reeves's character in *The Matrix*. By choosing the red pill of knowledge, Reeves's character chose to awaken from the dream world to see the harsh oppressive system that maintained what he had perceived as reality. With new knowledge, Mr. Anderson assumed a new identity as Neo and became a leader in the resistance against dehumanizing forces.

By being offered an opportunity to begin developing a critical consciousness, participants will have a similar choice to begin seeing their place in the world more clearly, to open their minds to alternative understandings of systems around them, and ideally to consider strategic opportunities to effectively act for social justice. Building a critical consciousness and learning how to deconstruct and reconstruct the world is a lifelong journey where "knowledge emerges only through invention and re-invention through the restless, impatient, continuing, hopeful inquiry human beings pursue in the world, with the world, and with each other" (Freire, 2000, p. 72). This chapter is a starting point for that journey.

> Chapter Framework

This chapter applies the thinking of Freire (2000) and his text *Pedagogy of the Oppressed* to leadership for social justice. Widely recognized as a foundational text on critical pedagogy, *Pedagogy of the Oppressed* explores the concept of *conscientização*, or critical consciousness. In the context of leadership development, becoming a critically conscious leader allows one to lead with justice at the forefront of one's actions. Critical consciousness helps one better understand the world by unveiling previously accepted power dynamics and circumstances, by revealing oppressive systems and structures, and by reframing how individuals view their roles as leaders in relation to those with whom they work. It leads to a courageous spirit of creativity and energy for innovation in producing novel solutions to perplexing problems. Leaders with a critical consciousness engage their communities and themselves in dialogues to identify, counter, and transform contexts and relationships that perpetuate forms of oppression.

The development of critical consciousness begins with critical pedagogy, which engages learning communities in a "struggle to understand how culture and social structure have shaped their lives. The ultimate goal is for learners to develop a critical consciousness, engage in social and cultural transformation, and help create a more just and equitable society" (Rhoads & Black, 1995, p. 413). Freirean critical pedagogy engages people in a collective process of learning and investigation "about complex power relationships, histories of struggle, and the consequences of oppression," allowing participants to recognize that "conditions of injustice are produced, not natural; are designed to privilege and oppress, but are ultimately challengeable and thus changeable" (Cammarota & Fine, 2008, p. 2). At its heart, critical pedagogy, and its related processes of deconstructing and reconstructing understandings of social systems, is inherently and critically hopeful (Duncan-Andrade, 2009). Preskill and Brookfield (2009) noted that critical hope, unlike naïve hope, "comprehends at a profound level how complex and multifaceted is the fight for social justice … the fight for justice can never be anything but a never-ending struggle … Critical hope is hard, practical, and angry … [Critical hope can be a] positive catalyst for change" (p. 171).

Freire's (2000) model of critical pedagogy emerged from his critiques of the dominant mode of education, the banking system, as anti-dialogical and dehumanizing. In this system, teachers, or leaders and supervisors, are positioned to deposit knowledge into their students, peers, colleagues, followers, or supervisees, much as one deposits money into a bank account. Individuals are perceived as empty vessels and presumed to lack existing, relevant knowledge. This type of education is devoid of subjectivity, critical thinking, personal experience, creativity, engagement with world events, and the community in which one lives. It ultimately dismisses human experiences and agency, positioning individuals as objects, incapable of intelligent thoughts or acts. This may be likened to a more managerial and bureaucratic understanding of leadership. One in which a hierarchy of top leaders provide orders to those working beneath them without contemplation of their existing experiences and knowledge of the processes that they encounter on a daily basis.

In place of banking education, Freire argued for a model of problem-posing education to humanize both students and teachers in the process of teaching and learning. Students and teachers are not seen as depositories or owners of knowledge, but rather people who are "becoming—as unfinished, uncompleted beings in and with a likewise unfinished reality" (Freire, 2000, p. 84). In this model of critical pedagogy, education is a dialogical activity between student, teacher, society, literature, community, and others. It also inherently disrupts traditional conceptualizations of the relationship between leader and follower, asserting that all members of a group possess valuable knowledge and expertise. In organizations where positional leaders exist, those leaders are transparent, communicative, engaging, and reflective on the experiences of the group, and the group's experiences, knowledge, and skills. Leaders in these organizations recognize that they do not know all of the answers, but rather help guide the group in collective decision-making and learning in times of the unknown. Critical pedagogy is intended to be a project of radical liberation that unlocks human potential to work toward a more socially just world.

Freire's (2000) model of critical pedagogy is manifest through praxis, which is a process comprised of both dialogical reflection and action to transform unjust social circumstances. Praxis requires both reflection and action. It is not enough to theorize about and reflect on the existence of oppressions in society without taking action to engage in social change. It is also insufficient to act for social change without appropriate reflection to understand how social realities have been developed and maintained.

In this relationship between reflection and practice, a "radical interaction [occurs where if] one is sacrificed—even in part—the other immediately suffers" (Freire, 2000, p. 87). In the end, successful leadership for social justice requires deep reflection, and transformative change can only result from the balanced interaction between reflective dialogue and actions for change. The interplay between the two elements of praxis humanizes people, combats domination, rebuilds equitable systems, and constructs a foundation for dialogue—doing so in ways that embrace love, humility, faith, mutual respect, trust, and hope. Ultimately, Freire's (2000) notion of praxis and critical pedagogy sustains the concept of critical hope, which "rejects the despair of hopelessness … [and] demands a committed and active struggle" against unjust circumstances that appear overwhelming and difficult to overcome (Duncan-Andrade, 2009, p. 185).

By engaging with problem-posing education, leaders and "followers" recognize and respect each other's humanity. They view each other as equals whose collective body of experiential wisdom is invaluable to the generation of collective knowledge for solving jointly identified problems and promoting social justice. Doing so is a continuous process that requires that all those within organizations engage in deep self-reflection and critical thought that may at times be uncomfortable but can ultimately strengthen collective resolve and the ability to meet organizational missions and positively affect social change. This is particularly important as critical leadership studies continue to explore how "leader/follower, power/resistance, and consent/dissent are shaped by gender, class, race, age, etc. [which] demonstrate that leadership dynamics are inescapably situated within, and reproduced through multiple, intersecting, and simultaneous differences and inequalities" (Collinson, 2011, p. 190).

The process of deconstruction and reconstruction is, at its core, humanizing and liberating, and a critical skill for social justice leadership. The curriculum guides participants through the practice of deconstructing normative social systems that produce injustices and assists participants in reconstructing their conceptualizations of potential structural changes they can affect as social justice leaders. Indeed, it is not enough to simply acknowledge and understand how social systems create injustices. We must also remember to trust that people possess strengths and agency to engage in the reconstruction of "the conditions under which they live, work, and learn" (Giroux, 1983, p. 274).

❯ Curriculum Plan

The following curriculum engages participants in a process of deconstructing the social systems around them to identify ways dominant and normative social systems produce and reproduce inequalities. The activity leads participants through a process of reconstruction to identify ways to transform social contexts to be more just. Though there are many widespread, oversimplified concepts defining public understandings of issues related to social inequality, this activity guides participants through a process of questioning three particular concepts: poverty, welfare, and diversity in higher education. Through the use of multimedia, critical self-reflection, and group dialogue, the activity seeks to encourage participants to question prevailing notions of these concepts. Although these topics might not be directly relevant to your organization, learning to deconstruct and reconstruct such notions provides an opportunity for skills development, which is transferable to a wide range of leadership challenges. This curriculum should be implemented during a single 2-hour session. You may adapt structure and format to best complement the specific learning environment.

› Activity 1—Practicing the Praxis of Deconstruction and Reconstruction

This activity introduces participants to the Freirean concept of critical consciousness and the praxis of reflective deconstruction and collective reconstruction as part of a humanistic process to advance systemic social justice transformation. The activity challenges participants to reflect on how they have come to understand injustices, to reconsider generally accepted notions of how class and racial inequalities are reproduced, and to collectively identify and assess strategic actions to reconstruct social conditions and arrangements that maintain inequalities.

Learning Outcomes

- Understand critical consciousness and praxis as tools for creating social justice change.
- Develop skills in reflectively deconstructing and collectively reconstructing.
- Reflect on one's social positioning, responsibility, and agency for critical leadership.

Setting Up the Activity

Group Size: Open to any size group. The optimal size is 20–30 participants.

Time: 120 minutes

Methods: Dialogue, lecture, reflection, video screenings

Materials: Whiteboard/chalkboard, marker/chalk, paper, writing utensils, laptop/computer, projector/screen, Internet access, and audio capability

Multimedia: Consider using video clips such as *Who Is Dependent on Welfare* with Ananya Roy (https://www.youtube.com/watch?v=-rtySUhuokM) and *See the Stripes* by A. D. Carson (https://www.youtube.com/watch?v=tl1cSgbnZTo).

Directions

1. Begin by explaining that how we develop initiatives for social change depends significantly on how we construct or understand contributing factors toward identified problems. Therefore, it is important to critically evaluate commonly accepted assumptions.

2. Give an overview of the key concepts: critical consciousness, praxis, deconstruction, and reconstruction.

3. Explain that for this session, the group will engage in an activity that demonstrates and allows them to develop and practice critical consciousness and the praxis of deconstruction and reconstruction. They will do this through the exploration of their assumptions about the concepts of poverty, welfare, and diversity in higher education.

4. Have the group brainstorm definitions of and contributing factors toward poverty, welfare, and diversity in higher education. Ask these questions:
   - *What does* poverty *mean? What creates conditions of poverty? What are some solutions to ending poverty based on these definitions?*
   - *What is* welfare?
   - *What is* diversity in higher education? *How should colleges and universities value diversity?*

5. Facilitate viewings of video clips that explore the concepts of poverty, welfare, and diversity in higher education. It is particularly important to select video clips that examine the concepts from critical perspectives. Consider using the examples *Who Is Dependent on Welfare* with Ananya Roy and *See the Stripes* by A. D. Carson; however, by reading the following prompts and the rest of this curriculum, you can identify other video clips that will similarly stimulate participant learning around these concepts.

6. Facilitate a self-reflection activity. Have participants engage in a written reflection in response to the two videos. Provide the following prompts:

   - *How did these videos' definitions of poverty, welfare, and diversity in higher education compare or contrast with your initial definitions and understandings of these concepts?*

   - *Within the social structures and systems described in the videos, where do you personally fit? In other words, are you positioned in a place of privilege within these structures? Why or why not? In acknowledging a privileged identity, what implications might there be for your engagement in social justice?*

   - *How did watching these videos make you feel? Why?*

7. Facilitate a collective large group (or small groups) dialogue with the following prompts:

   - *How did these videos' presentation of poverty, welfare, and diversity in higher education compare and contrast to our group's initial definitions?*

   - *How did the videos deconstruct common assumptions about the three concepts?*

   - *What motivations might lie behind videos like these? Is everything we watch inherently biased?*

   - *In what ways can we attend to power dynamics and systematic motivations as we strive to lead and promote change for the common good?*

   - *With these reframed views on the three concepts, how might we reconstruct, or reconceptualize solutions or initiatives to address these issues?*

8. Optional: If the dialogue was facilitated through small groups, ask groups to report back to the large group key points from their discussions.

9. Facilitate a free-write individual reflection. Provide the following prompts:
   - *What were the skills you employed when reflecting on these major societal topics (e.g., social perspective-taking, empathy, naming of power, racism, sexism)?*
   - *How might you continue to recognize when you must utilize these skills and help others to do the same?*

10. Conclude the session with a "next steps dialogue" by having the group discuss the following prompt: *Now that the group has practiced examples of conceptual deconstruction and reconstruction, how might the skills of this praxis help you address a specific problem facing you as an individual or your organization? How will you gather the types of information you need to make decisions that better address issues of inequality? How will you judge those sources of knowledge?*

11. To continue processing this content after the session concludes, and for assessment of concepts learned, have participants engage in an additional written reflection (one to two pages in length) in response to the following prompts:
    - *Reflect on what it feels like to critically question commonly accepted concepts.*
    - *How might these challenges to dominant understandings lead to new ways of thinking about their individual and organizational actions and efforts to initiate social justice change?*
    - *How has the development of critical consciousness, through this activity, informed your understanding of your own leadership identity and the enactment of leadership for the common good?*

Debriefing Notes

Questioning commonly held assumptions about how the world works can lead to anger or resistance. Participants might assert that the videos present biased views, perhaps claiming the need for more "neutrality." As Freire (2000) warned, the oppressed can fear "freedom," or general critiques of dominantly held notions of how the world currently works. It is important to acknowledge that resistance is not necessarily disrespect, but rather, it potentially reveals anxiety over questioning long-held beliefs and accepted assumptions about one's position in society. It may also bring up discomfort over personal, undeserved privileges within social structures of inequality. If charges of bias and lack of neutrality arise, take time to discuss how and who gets to judge ideas as neutral, and ask questions to find out from where the resistance and emotional responses arise.

＞ Conclusion

The purpose of this chapter is to guide participants through a curriculum that highlights the critical tools of deconstruction and reconstruction in leading for social justice change. Participants are introduced to Freirean notions of critical consciousness development and praxis. Through personal reflection and group dialogues, participants are introduced to the possibilities of critical consciousness, which are necessary for engaging in conceptual deconstruction and reconstruction. By engaging participants in critical self-reflection and collective dialogue about commonly accepted assumptions about how the world operates, you can provide opportunities for participants to safely engage in questioning and reframing their understandings of why injustices and oppression exist. When individuals and groups are unbound from singular perspectives about problems, it opens up possibilities for creativity and more socially just efforts for problem-solving and systemic transformation. They are guided to better understand their personal and collective responsibility, agency, and possibilities to work toward a better world.

2C: Ideology and Leadership

Sharon Chia Claros

Objectives/Goals of Chapter

- Understand ideology and its relation to leadership and culture.
- Identify and accurately characterize both dominant and counter-dominant ideologies.
- Analyze how different ideologies influence leadership and interactions within a group.

Critical Concepts: *counter-narrative, critical self-reflection, ideology, normativity*

> Chapter Overview

Ideology has been defined in various ways by scholars (see Chapter 2 of the main text), but at its core, it is a concept that causes individuals and groups to have beliefs that they accept as true (Dugan, 2017). Dominant narratives as well as counter-narratives influence people's ideologies. In turn, ideology reflects how members of a society construct and structure thought processes to validate and operationalize an existing social order; it shapes how people think the world works (Bartolomé, 2010). Different forms of ideology fall on a continuum. On one end of the continuum, there is dominant ideology such as whiteness, colorblindness, and heteronormativity and on the other end there are counter-narratives that push against the dominant ideology, such as multiculturalism and social justice. In acknowledging the continuum of ideologies it is important, however, to avoid defaulting to false binaries.

Exploring ideology is relevant to leadership because it will enable people to understand what they bring to both leader positions and leadership processes in terms of how they construct their worldview. Individual exploration on where one falls on the continuum of ideology will enable leaders to critically reflect on and understand their thoughts and actions. Leaders who understand their thoughts and actions will have the capacity to be more inclusive and considerate of various cultures and perspectives. Furthermore, leaders will also gain the agency to challenge dominant ideologies.

Leaders in any organization and role must be able to engage in reflection and inner work. According to Palmer (2000), "If people skimp on their inner work, their outer will suffer as well" (p. 91). Leaders must understand that to engage in meaningful self-reflection, the community and the collective within the organization must be engaged in the process as well.

› Chapter Framework

As leaders work and live in diverse communities, it is important to understand how ideology shapes and influences their environment. Leaders are expected to create an inclusive environment and to do so, it is crucial for them to understand their ideology. Bartolomé (2010) asserted that cultural practices and norms as well as symbols in a society personify dominant ideologies. These ideologies form people's thoughts on a subconscious level and, in turn, members of society implicitly allow current practices and approaches to occur with the belief that it is a "natural" and "normal" course of action. These natural and normal courses of action privilege individuals with dominant identities while marginalizing individuals with targeted identities. In a counter narrative form of ideology, Syed (2013) offered a definition of multicultural ideology as recognizing and celebrating group differences, which are associated with positive life outcomes and experiences for society at large. Additionally, social justice as a counter-narrative ideology includes "a vision of society in which the distribution of resources is equitable and all members are physically and psychologically safe and secure" (Adams, Bell, & Griffin, 2007, p. 2).

The breadth of literature on ideology can be overwhelming. For the purpose of this curriculum plan, ideology will be narrowed to a few interrelated concepts including the following: dominant ideology (e.g., colorblindness and heteronormative ideology) and counter-dominant ideology (e.g., multicultural ideology and social justice ideology). Although there are many concepts of dominant and counter-dominant ideologies, this chapter will focus on the aforementioned constructs as they relate to further understanding a leader's ability to be more inclusive and create space for various cultures as well as become agents of change who support marginalized individuals in their respective organizations. Given that leaders will have multiple perspectives and diverse social identities, it is to be expected that they will express some degree of internalization of both dominant and counter-dominant ideological perspectives. The following activities are framed using a U.S. reference point. Those working in other cultural contexts are encouraged to consider modes of social stratification that parallel what is presented here and adapt accordingly.

Dominant ideology. One aspect of dominant ideology in the Unites States is the sense that being White, male, cisgender, and heterosexual are ideals; invisible constructs make people think they are in control of their lives when in reality they have been socialized and constructed to follow and live within the status quo, maintaining systems of oppression (Dugan, 2017). Brookfield (2005) contends that "ideology becomes hegemony when the dominant ideas are learned and lived in everyday decisions and judgments and when these ideas (reinforced by mass media images and messages) pervade the whole existence" (p. 94). The central schema of hegemony is the distribution of an ideology that serves the interest of the privileged few while failing to represent and serve the marginalized majority.

Counter-narrative ideologies: Pushing against the dominant. Historically underrepresented groups (e.g., women, People of Color, lesbian/gay/bisexual/transgender/queer [LGBTQ] people, and persons who are differently abled) experience marginality in various societal locations (e.g., schools, work, family, and communities of worship). *Marginality* is a sense of not fitting in that can lead to self-consciousness, irritability, and depression (Evans, Forney, Guido, Patton, & Renn, 2009). Those who are marginalized may doubt their value and their mattering to their community, and ultimately, they might sense a disconnection and alienation from broader social structures (Evans et al., 2009). Lack of support, pride for themselves and their achievements, and confidence in their abilities to succeed are all sentiments that marginalized people must contend with and navigate (Evans et al., 2009). This issue of marginality has great implications for people's self-esteem, self-efficacy, and well-being (Evans et al., 2009). People who are marginalized do not fit within the dominant narrative and are challenged by dominant ideologies. Alternative forms of ideology that counter dominant ideologies are important to explore because they give people another paradigm through which to see and perceive the world. Alternative ideologies open up possibilities to interrupt the status quo, challenge oppression, and see the world through a social justice lens.

› Curriculum Plan

This curriculum integrates ideology and leadership to provide participants with a critical perspective to process their leader roles and leadership processes. Leader roles and leadership processes can then be directed toward creating an environment that is more inclusive and has space to challenge the dominant status quo. Alternative forms of ideology that provide a counter-narrative to the dominant ideology will be explored—specifically, multicultural ideology and social justice ideology. Through the use of articles, multimedia, critical reflection, and intentional group discussions and activities, participants will be challenged to question and unlearn the potentially compromising nature of their dominant ideologies surrounding leadership. Additionally, participants will also explore ways to integrate counter-dominant ideologies that create individual and collective agency within leadership. The curriculum plan can be implemented in one session, ranging from 2 to 2.5 hours. However, segmenting the activity components is encouraged to provide participants with time to process.

⟩ Activity 1—Exploring Dominant and Counter-Dominant Ideologies

This activity introduces both dominant and counter-dominant ideologies as frameworks for understanding why leaders think and act the way they do in various group and/or organizational environments. The activity will gradually challenge participants to critically reflect on how their ideologies form, where they fall along an ideological continuum, ways they can unlearn dominant ideologies that serve a privileged few, and ways to embrace counter-dominant ideologies that give agency to challenging the status quo.

Learning Outcomes

- Understand both dominant and counter-dominant ideologies.
- Identify the problematic nature of dominant ideologies.
- Recognize the usefulness of exploring ideologies in leadership.

Setting Up the Activity

Group Size: Optimal group size is 25 participants to ensure intentional dialogue.

Time: 2–2.5 hours

Methods: Individual reflection, lecture, small group dialogue

Materials: Poster paper; markers; smart phone, tablet, or laptops with Internet access to take the Implicit Association Test; blank paper; writing utensil; Handout "A Six Step Framework to Cultivate a Social Justice Ideology"

Variations: The gallery activity can be converted to a small group activity. Larger participant groups can be accommodated by increasing the number of facilitators.

Directions

1. Begin the activity by engaging participants in a discussion about ideology. Ask participants to form groups of three to four and have them discuss what comes to mind when they hear the word *ideology*. Give participants about 5 minutes for the discussion and ask two to three groups to report back to the large group.

2. Tell participants that they will now engage in a gallery activity that focuses on their early learnings. There should be at least three large sheets of poster paper with topics that have ideological underpinnings (e.g., racism, sexism, homophobia, genderism, xenophobia). Include other topics and increase the number of sheets of poster paper depending on the number of participants and relevance of particular topics to the audience with which you are working. Have participants divide into groups based on the number of topics selected. Ask participants to think back to their early learnings and what they remember being taught about a particular topic/issue. Have someone from the group write

down people's ideas on the poster paper. After 5 to 7 minutes, have the groups rotate until all groups have commented on all topics. Ask someone from each group to summarize what was written. Allow time for participants to ask questions or provide clarifications once everything has been read.

3. Thank participants for engaging in the activity. Emphasize that one's ideology is a set of conscious and unconscious ideas that form one's belief system and world view. Although most people do not recognize it, people who grew up in the United States have been, and continue to be, socialized to form dominant ideologies. It may be helpful here to share how stocks of knowledge often contribute to and are informed by dominant ideologies.

4. Use examples from the gallery activity to introduce dominant ideologies. Talk about whiteness, colorblindness, patriarchy, ableism, and heteronormativity as forms of dominant ideologies. Ask participants the following: *How do you feel about these ideologies and how have you seen these ideologies actualized? Think about how these forms of dominant ideologies inform someone's leadership style and actions.*

5. Transition the conversation to explore other forms of ideology such as multiculturalism and social justice. Talk about what multicultural and social justice ideologies entail. For example, you could focus on critical perspectives as described in Chapter 2 of the main text (Dugan, 2017) as elements of an ideology stemming from critical social theory. Ask participants these questions: *How have you seen examples of multicultural/social justice ideologies actualized in group settings? How did members of the group respond to leaders who actualized this type of ideology?*

6. Transition to discuss the importance of being cognizant of the ideologies we hold as leaders in various capacities. *In order to know ourselves and where we fall in the continuum of*

ideology, we have to be explicit about individual self-reflection. One way of knowing is by taking the Implicit Association Test (IAT; facilitators should take a few IAT tests online prior to this activity so they can role-model and talk about their results).

7. Have participants take out their smart phones, tablets, or laptops and tell them to go to the Project Implicit site (https://implicit.harvard.edu/implicit/). Choose a topic/test for everyone to take. This will take about 10 minutes to complete.

8. Share your results with the participants to role-model the group dialogue they are about to engage in with each other. Have participants break into small groups and talk about their results. Write the following on the board for the groups to discuss:

   1) *Share your results with your group and talk about your initial thoughts and feelings.*

   2) *How do you think this IAT represents your ideology?*

   3) *What do you think influenced your results?*

   4) *How will you use this to inform your exploration of your personal ideologies?*

   5) *How might you utilize your IAT results to inform or modify how you engage in leadership?*

9. Introduce the Six-Step Framework to develop a social justice ideology (see handout). Give participants a few minutes to read the framework and ask them to underline things that are challenging for them to do, star things that they feel they have the capacity to do, and put question marks next to things they are uncertain about (feel free to role-model and share personal insights). Have participants break off into small groups to discuss their thoughts and why they underlined, starred, and/or questioned certain

aspects. Have a few share in the large group after the small group discussion.

10. Engage in a large group discussion to connect personal biases and counter-dominant ideologies back to leadership. Some questions to consider include the following:

   - *In what ways, if at all, have your personal biases influenced how you understand leadership?*
   - *When you think of leader what characteristics/types of individuals come to mind? How might this reflect ideological beliefs?*
   - *How might the application of counter-dominant ideologies like multicultural and social justice change how leadership is understood, experienced, and enacted?*

11. Close the session by validating participants and thanking them for going out of their comfort zones to engage in what can be a challenging topic. Remind participants that everyone in the United States carries both dominant and counter-dominant ideologies because of how people were and continue to be socialized. However, emphasize the point that the dominant ideology that they have learned can be unlearned. Embracing this notion can be both powerful and life changing, as it is the action of unlearning that begins the cultivation of a social justice ideology. The cultivation of an ideology rooted in social justice and multiculturalism is essential to engaging and leading in an ever-changing and diverse society. It is important to note, too, that the goal is to prevent ideologies from being rigidly enforced, hegemonic, or understood as a singular truth. Even social justice and multicultural ideologies can fall into this trap if we fail to continuously challenge the perspectives we adopt. Leadership for the common good is predicated on the notions that difference is embraced, those who are marginalized are centered, and alternative ideologies that welcome unique perspectives inform our thoughts.

Debriefing Notes

This curriculum is designed to intentionally practice critical self-reflection to raise one's consciousness about their ideologies and how their ideologies influence their abilities to enact leadership. Please note that debriefing activities that involve sensitive topics, such as one's ideology and worldview, should always be structured based on the readiness of the group.

Facilitator Notes

This activity may be challenging to participants who have never questioned their ideology and how their ideology shapes how they view the world. It may be easier for some to begin with the concept of stocks of knowledge and then move into a discussion of ideology. Additionally, some participants might not be ready to discuss facets of how they support dominant ideology either consciously or unconsciously. As facilitators, feel out the capacity of individuals to share their ideologies on various issues/topic. Some participants may experience guilt, shock, resistance, or frustration.

❯ Conclusion

Who we are and how we've come to make meaning of the world around us shapes our ideologies and these in turn shape how we lead and understand the phenomenon of leadership. This curriculum challenges dominant ideologies that often perpetuate marginalization. Through critical self-reflection and dialogue, participants were encouraged to confront personal biases and examine ways in which learned dominant ideologies shape their understanding of leadership. By advocating for counter-dominant ideologies, participants explore how liberatory frameworks such as these are paramount to thinking differently and ultimately leading more justly.

Handout 2.1: A Six-Step Framework to Cultivate a Social Justice Ideology

1. Begin by understanding oppression and how it is a part of social structures that make it self-sustaining and challenging to eradicate.
2. Recognize and understand the interactions among different oppressions as society's ability to socially construct the separation of groups tends to place oppressions in hierarchy.
3. Recognize and understand the pain that comes with increased understanding of one's role in the cycle of oppression so that healing can occur to break the cycle; people must work on their own liberation.
4. Recognize different ways that oppression touches different social groups/identities based on social location and take individual and collective action toward change.
5. Examine previous roles as oppressors and learn new skills on how to be allies by focusing on listening to and supporting others rather than co-opting an oppressed group's movement; an important aspect of this step is the ability of allies to educate dominant group peers about the reality of oppressive systems and individual behaviors.
6. Recognize that having a social justice ideology is strenuous and demanding because it goes against the dominant status quo so it is crucial to sustain and keep hope and idealism alive while working for positive change.

To sustain a social justice ideology, one must embrace the "sincere belief that what is learned (racism, sexism, homophobia, etc.) can be unlearned" (Davis & Harrison, 2012, p. 20).

Davis, T. L. & Harrison, L. M. (2012). *Advancing social justice: Tools, pedagogies, and strategies to transform your campus.* San Francisco: Jossey-Bass.

Reason, R. D., & Davis, T. L. (2005). Antecedents, precursors, and concurrent concepts in the development of social justice attitudes and actions. *New Directions for Student Services, 110,* 5–15.

Chapter 3: Interpreting Leadership Theory Using Critical Perspectives

3A: Interpreting Leadership Theory Using Critical Perspectives

Melissa L. Rocco

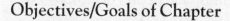

Objectives/Goals of Chapter

- Understand the multiple, varied approaches to leadership throughout history.
- Develop ability to critically analyze leadership scholarship and action.
- Develop presentation, knowledge synthesis, and critical thinking skills.

Critical Concepts: *context, deconstruction, dominant narratives*

❯ Chapter Overview

Formal and informal leadership theories offer varying insights and understandings of leadership, often determining who can claim the identity of leader as well as what it means to engage in the process of leadership. Leadership theories can be organized into a variety of thematic clusters (see Chapter 3 of the main text for examples of this) that represent varying approaches.

These approaches describe what leadership looks like, and at times how individuals understand it or how it is developed.

Scholarship on the history of leadership theory first notes the heredity-based approaches from the 19th century and earlier (Dugan, 2017). Skill and behavior-based leadership approaches appear next in the literature, followed by contemporary approaches featuring relational and process-oriented leadership (Dugan, 2017). To understand contemporary leadership, the history of the concept and its evolution must first be explored and critiqued. This chapter highlights formal leadership theories, models, and approaches found in the dominant narratives of leadership studies, providing a platform for their critique, deconstruction, and reconstruction.

The evolution of formal leadership theories reveals a variety of context-based assumptions and biases that emerge from (1) the disciplines and fields in which theories originated, (2) social and political events dominating the time, and (3) larger systems of privilege and oppression. Many individuals and organizations still utilize antiquated approaches to leadership that continue to limit leadership access to a select few (e.g., affluent, cisgender, White males, those with particular personality traits, or those with formal education; Day & Harrison, 2007; Dugan, 2017; Lord & Hall, 2005). Uncovering the contextual factors and limitations of formal leadership theories can help learners better understand how to recognize, address, and change individual, organizational, and community perceptions and practices of leadership to be more diverse and inclusive.

Chapter Framework

This curriculum invites participants to hone their critical analysis skills and examine their own thoughts and experiences to deconstruct and reconstruct the "story most often told" or dominant narratives in the history of leadership theory. In Chapter 2 of the main text, participants are presented with several tools that can be used to deconstruct leadership theory: ideological critique, commodification, flow of power, and willful blindness (Dugan, 2017). Chapter 3 then demonstrates this process by highlighting the ways dominant groups have co-opted the leadership styles and processes of traditionally marginalized groups and authored a false history, commonly known as the "evolution of leadership theory" (Dugan, 2017). Chapter 3 of the main text then suggests an example of reconstructing the dominant narrative of leadership into theoretical clusters rather than the chronological pattern often presented in the literature. This curriculum similarly invites participants to engage in the process of deconstructing and reconstructing dominant leadership narratives. Participants are encouraged to further critique the deconstruction and reconstruction presented in the main text to create a more critical and socially conscious narrative of leadership theory.

> Curriculum Plan

The activities presented here use peer education and presentations to serve as catalysts for participants to understand and critically analyze the dominant narrative of leadership theories throughout history. Although it is important for participants to have general knowledge about each theory, it is even more imperative that they begin to ask critical questions about the leadership theories presented in the main text and approaches they have personally experienced. The curriculum also helps participants synthesize chapter content and begin to see patterns, themes, and contextual influences on leadership theory and practice through a peer-to-peer teaching activity. Participants then engage in a large group critique of the leadership approaches presented in the chapter. What is missing from these approaches? Who gets to lead, and who is left out? What was happening in the world at the time the theory was created that affected its formulation and use? Finally, participants will apply their knowledge by blogging about how they see people in their own lives exhibiting a particular leadership approach and the positive and negative aspects of that approach from their perspective. This curriculum is designed as one in-person session with a follow-up reflection experience; however, the two activities can be integrated into a single session as appropriate.

> Activity 1—Peer-to-Peer Teaching: A Review of the Evolution of Leadership Theory

This activity serves as an engaging way to review the various leadership theories and approaches presented in Chapter 3 of the main text. Participants will work together in small groups to review a particular leadership theory and design a presentation for their peers about the approach highlighting important concepts, definitions, assumptions, and historical context. Following each small group presentation, the large group engages in a critique of the approach and discussion of the evolution of leadership theory.

Learning Outcomes

- Understand how and why approaches to leadership have changed over time.
- Recognize the history and context that affect how individuals and organizations engage in leadership.
- Develop information synthesis, presentation, and critical thinking skills.

Setting Up the Activity

Group Size: Optimal group size is 10–40 participants. Small groups should include no more than 5 participants each. A large group discussion is an important component of the activity and can be difficult to manage with a group larger than 40.

Time: Dependent on number of participants (small group preparation for 30 minutes, 5 minutes for each group presentation, 5 minutes for large group discussion following each presentation)

Methods: Presentations, small and large group discussion

Materials: Poster or flip chart paper for each small group (two sheets per small group if the activity will be done without technology), markers (a few colors per group), computer, projector/screen (if small groups use technology)

Multimedia: It will be helpful for participants to have access to smart phones, tablets, or computers with Internet connections to search for information about each leadership approach as well as to integrate multimedia into their presentations.

Variations: Small groups may be assigned more than one approach. Similarly, for larger participant numbers, a single approach can be divided across small groups or multiple groups could be assigned the same theory.

Directions

1. Prior to the session, determine how many total participants will be involved in this activity. Participants should be divided into small groups of three to five and assigned at least one leadership approach found in Chapter 3. Note that you should use the approaches as identified in the "story most often told."

2. Explain to participants that the purpose of this activity is to help them review and better understand the dominant narratives in leadership literature and to deconstruct those narratives. Explain that rather than hearing a lecture or taking a test, they will work with their peers to design and implement creative presentations to share with each other on each of

the approaches to leadership (i.e., clusters and themes used to group formal theories).

3. Divide the participants into small groups, pass out materials, and assign each group a leadership approach.

4. Provide the following instructions to the participants:

- *Your small group has been assigned a leadership approach from Chapter 3 to review and then "teach" to the rest of the participants in this session.*

- *Step 1: Review the portion of the chapter related to your assigned approach. You may also need to search the Internet for additional information.*

- *Step 2: Discuss the following as a small group: What does this approach presume about leadership? When was this approach developed and/or most widely used and what may have been happening in the world at that time that contributed to the approach's development or applicability? Identify and discuss any sub-theories, key concepts, definitions, or other ideas associated with your approach.*

- *Step 3: Design a multimedia slide/poster (depends upon participant access to technology) to present to the large group that provides an overview of your conversation from Step 2.*

- *Step 4: Draw a picture on a piece of poster paper that illustrates what leadership would "look like" according to this approach. This could include anything from physical traits to abstract images. Creativity is encouraged! For example, for more collaborative approaches, participants might draw people all together in a circle with network lines connecting each person, rather than drawing just one single person.*

- *Step 5: Present your approach to the large group. This should include a summary of your discussion using your multimedia slide/poster and an explanation of your drawing illustrating what leadership looks like according to this approach.*

5. Once small groups have completed their presentation preparations, bring everyone back to the large group and explain that presentations will be done in the order that the leadership

approaches are presented in the chapter. Explain that they should pay close attention to the presentations because they will be asked to critique each leadership approach (not the presentation itself) using tools of deconstruction after it is presented.

6. Following each small group presentation, engage the large group in discussion of the following questions:
   - *How does this approach improve upon or further develop earlier approaches to leadership?*
   - *What does this approach assume about leadership and/or who can and cannot lead?*
   - *How does this approach address power in leadership? Who has or can have power according to this approach? How is power used and for what purpose?*
   - *Who or what is missing from this approach?*
   - *What is this approach lacking or not considering that it should?*
   - *Think back to the leadership assumptions and considerations discussed in Chapter 1 of the main text. How do the assumptions and considerations show up in this leadership approach?*

7. End by posing the following reflection questions to the large group and solicit a few responses:
   - *What did this activity teach you about the evolution of leadership theory over time?*
   - *What did you learn from our critique of each approach?*
   - *Where and how do we still see these theories and approaches to leadership used today? Why do you think this is the case?*
   - *What is problematic about using these approaches?*
   - *Why is it important to understand the big-picture landscape of leadership theory?*

Facilitator Notes

The purpose of this activity is twofold: (1) to help ensure that participants understand the various theories, models, and approaches presented in Chapter 3 of the main text, and (2) to help participants begin to develop a critical lens in preparation for their engagement with concepts and ideas in subsequent chapters. You should demonstrate genuine curiosity as participants answer the reflection questions in Steps 6 and 7 regarding critical perspectives outlined in this activity. Your role is to move participants beyond summarizing content and toward critical reflection. It is okay for the conversation to also generate new questions that may or may not be answered in the activity. Lingering questions serve as helpful tools for further discussion.

❯ Activity 2—Personal Reflection Blogs: Applying Approaches to Leadership

This activity should be assigned as homework following the in-person workshop. By blogging about a personal leadership experience that illustrates one of the leadership theories/approaches from Chapter 3, participants will engage in further reflection and application. Participants will also read the blog entries of their small group members and provide each member with a feedback comment or question for further consideration.

Learning Outcomes

- Apply knowledge of leadership theories to personal experiences.
- Consider ways in which current and historical approaches to leadership are conceptualized and implemented today.
- Critically reflect on the benefits and drawbacks of particular theories in today's increasingly diverse and complex world.

Setting Up the Activity

Group Size: Open to any size group. Small groups should be three to five participants each.

Time: This activity should be done for homework. The time each
   participant spends will vary but should be approximately 1 hour.
Methods: Blog writing, peer feedback, reflection
Materials: Computer, laptop, tablet, or other device with Internet
   access
Multimedia: Participants may wish to integrate video clips, music,
   images, or other multimedia into their blog post.
Variations: This activity can also be done without technology in
   the form of a reflection paper.

Directions

1. Prior to facilitation, determine how participants should
   blog or otherwise engage in reflection for this assignment.
   For example, participants could be asked to create a personal
   blog using a free blogging website. Participants could also
   complete this activity using course management programs
   operated by an institution or organization. Be sure participants
   have a way to access one another's blog entries. If you choose
   to conduct this activity without technology, then blogs should
   take the form of reflection papers in which you determine the
   style, format, and logistics.

2. At the end of the in-person session(s), introduce the blogging
   assignment and instruct participants on how to set up blogs.
   Share that participants should work with their small groups
   to agree upon a day and time before the next session to post
   their blog entries with enough time for each group member
   to read and comment on one another's contributions. Comments should be in the form of feedback, further conversation
   prompts, or questions posed to the blog author. Comments
   should also indicate that the reader both read and reflected
   upon the author's blog.

3. Provide participants with the following blog prompt:
   *Think about the various theories/approaches to leadership we
   discussed. Which of these do you see people using in your everyday*

life? Pick one approach to highlight. First, share in 140 characters or less a summary statement of your chosen approach. Creativity is encouraged! For example: "Royalty is the way to be! Without the bloodline, I can't lead. If only I were a 'Great Man.'" Then, share a personal story of when you or someone you know utilized that theory/approach. It can be a story of success or failure, and it can be from any part of your life (e.g., friends, family, school, work). Provide us with the background information, the story of what happened, and specific examples of thoughts and actions in the story that align with the approach you discuss. You should use concepts from the text to critically analyze the approach and how it was used in the example you have chosen. Finally, consider any assumptions that may have been at play related to the leadership approach. Use the themes of stocks of knowledge, ideology/hegemony, and social location, along with the tools of deconstruction, to examine the example and theory used in it.

Debriefing Notes

It is not necessary to engage participants in a large group reflection once the blog assignments have been completed, but you could discuss this activity further at a later session if desired.

Facilitator Notes

Consider the value of having participants set up a blog during this session and then utilizing it for other leadership reflections in future sessions. Blogging is a great way to keep conversations going outside of dedicated learning time. Since blogs can be easily shared with other participants, blogging also allows those who may not be as likely to speak up in a session to have a voice and engage in dialogue with peers and the facilitator. Blogging also challenges participants to communicate their thoughts in new ways using language that is often more casual and conversational than formal papers. Blogging also encourages participants to enhance their message and apply their learning by finding and posting related media such as videos, images, music, and news articles.

› Conclusion

The activities presented here engage participants in the process of critically analyzing specific leadership theories/approaches often found in the dominant leadership literature. Having participants teach each other about leadership theories/approaches requires that they synthesize and internalize content from the main text by putting concepts into their own words. Critiquing each approach using the analysis tips and deconstruction tools helps participants become critical learners of scholarship and develop efficacy in the study of leadership. Finally, the personal reflection blog helps participants recognize examples of everyday leadership happening around them and the diversity of approaches with which they and the people they know engage in leadership.

3B: Applying Critical Perspectives to the Evolution of Leadership Theories

Stephanie H. Chang & Natasha Chapman

Objectives/Goals of Chapter

- Recognize systemic/institutional and personal experiences of power.
- Evaluate one's personal connections to critical perspectives.
- Understand the benefits of applying critical perspectives to leadership theories.

Critical Concepts: *critical race theory, homophobia, oppression, power, privilege*

> Chapter Overview

The purpose of this chapter is to introduce general principles of critical theory and apply these perspectives to the evolution of leadership theories. This chapter highlights the importance of understanding power relations in social systems/institutions and personal social identities as a means to encourage the adoption of a critical lens when doing leadership work. As is evident in depictions of the evolution of formal leadership theory, theories increasingly espouse more relational and integrative perspectives but have yet to fully infuse critical perspectives.

The adoption of a critical perspective requires not only an exploration of leadership theories, but also a deeper look at key principles of critical social theories (see Chapter 2 of the main text for more on this). To be critical means believing and knowing power dynamics exist and function at all levels of society (Carr & Kemmis, 1986). This requires an exploration of personal social identities and the ways power flows in society to create and perpetuate positions and experiences of privilege and oppression (Johnson, 2006). How do social identities influence decisions about which leadership theories to use? What are systemic and institutional benefits and barriers that exist for groups based on social identity group membership, or in other words, privileged and oppressed identities? What biases present themselves in leadership approaches and literature that reflect dominant values and perpetuate one-dimensional ways of understanding leadership? Whose contributions and perspectives to the field have been ignored, dismissed, or co-opted because of biases? Adopting and internalizing a critical lens when interpreting and enacting leadership theories is an ongoing and iterative process of persistently defining and redefining what is "critical" and who is influenced by theory.

> Chapter Framework

Key principles of critical perspectives involve recognition of power and an ability to see and believe identities are socially constructed. Critical perspectives submit that personal experiences of privilege and oppression are real and meaningful, and there is a need to highlight the experiences of traditionally oppressed and marginalized identities to liberate and emancipate individual and group experiences (Delgado & Stefancic, 2001; Johnson, 2006; Solórzano, Ceja, & Yosso, 2000). These principles are evident in descriptions of critical race theory (CRT; Delgado & Stefancic, 2001). Although CRT has disciplinary roots in legal studies, it has become highly interdisciplinary and serves as a useful tool in analyzing individual and group experiences around race and racism. CRT concentrates on how race and racism unfold in society and the implications of power and oppression associated with race (Delgado & Stefancic, 2001; Ladson-Billings, 1998). Through a CRT lens, it is clear that power dynamics around race place People of Color as the oppressed group and Whites as the privileged group in society. In other words, in a U.S. context, People of Color struggle and experience racial discrimination and marginalization whereas Whites tend to receive the privileges associated with being the dominant group in society (Delgado &Stefancic, 2001; Johnson, 2006; Solórzano et al., 2000). Keeping this critical perspective in mind when educating about leadership theories results in a greater likelihood that social stratification and discrimination based on racial group membership can be redressed.

Another way to look at critical perspectives is to see critical social theory as an epistemology. As a lens, a critical theory paradigm or epistemology centers on the experience of oppression and marginalization with the intent to promote and seek a sense of emancipation or liberation for oppressed and marginalized populations (Guba & Lincoln, 1994; Kincheloe & McLaren, 2005). By claiming and adopting a critical theory paradigm, individuals will see themselves as subjective parts of the emancipation process. They might wonder, "What are my social identities and how do they relate to oppressed and privileged identities? Where do I have systemic, institutional, and social power? Historically, how have people who look like me experienced privilege and oppression in society?" These are the types of questions elicited by a critical perspective.

Developing as a leader, in part, means locating the meaning of social identity group membership and exploring the influence one's oppressed and privileged identities have with respect to one's relationship with others. While working with groups and organizations, a critical perspective is a useful way to reflect on group composition and to consider the influence or impact an organization can have on others based on their social identities and group memberships. Critical perspectives incite a largely reflective process of relating and seeing power as it presents itself in both systemic/institutional and individual experiences of oppression and privilege. This process provides a unique avenue for bringing attention to salient factors, such as social identity, that may be ignored or deemphasized when describing the leadership process, leadership approaches, or the evolution of these approaches over time.

Curriculum Plan

The activities for this chapter provide participants with two different ways of seeing how and why a critical approach to interpreting leadership theories is necessary. Both activities relate to individual and societal perspectives on privilege and oppression. These activities are introductory ways to explore critical perspectives of leadership. The following curriculum can be done in one consecutive or two stand-alone sessions. Activity 1, as a stand-alone activity, will minimally take 1 hour to 75 minutes. Activity 2, as a stand-alone activity, will minimally take 45 minutes to 1 hour. These times include debriefing and reflection.

Activity 1—Critical Perspectives as a Theoretical Tool: Scanning and Surveying Images

This activity uses the general principles of critical social theories to evaluate how social identities and systemic/institutional power, privilege, and oppression influence the evolution of leadership theories. Participants will also develop and interpret a narrative of selected images and photographs to experience an application of a critical perspective.

Learning Outcomes

- Understand the utility of critical perspectives in leadership.
- Evaluate how social identities and systemic/institutional power, privilege, and oppression influence the evolution of leadership theories.
- Recognize the paradigm shift represented in leadership literature as a dominant perspective.

Setting Up the Activity

Group Size: Open to any size group. Consider engaging participants in large and small groups (three to five participants) to diversify reflection.

Time: 60–75 minutes depending on approach to debrief and discussion questions

Methods: Dialogue, discussion, lecture, reflection

Materials: Five to eight printed images, whiteboard/chalkboard, markers/chalk, projector/screen (optional)

Variations: This activity requires a selection of images or photographs. You can use either preselected, printed images or ones that can be displayed using a projector. You may want to use preselected, printed images and display the same images as participants deconstruct and reflect on them. An alternative is to instruct participants to find their own images in advance or during the session. This activity can be accomplished with or without access to the Internet, a computer, or a projector. Without technology, have enough copies of preselected and printed images for small groups to review.

Directions

1. Walk through the evolution of leadership theories described in Chapter 3 of the main text. Review leadership theories as transitioning from trait-based to process and relational approaches. It will help to have a visual timeline of the evolution of these approaches. Note that this exercise is most effective if used with the "story most often told" about how leadership theories have evolved.

2. Ask participants to name people (e.g., commonly known celebrities, politicians, or historic figures) who embody the different approaches and theories of leadership. Use the chalkboard, dry-erase board, or easel paper to display the names of these individuals.

3. Review general tenets of critical perspectives (see Chapter 2 of the main text):

   - Importance of recognizing social location and its role in social stratification
   - Systemic power dynamics reinforced through experiences of institutional and personal privilege and oppression
   - Mechanisms for reinforcing power dynamics in historic events, culture, politics, media, and laws through ideology and hegemony
   - An emphasis on liberation and emancipation

4. Refer participants to the list of names previously identified in Step 2 of this activity when reviewing different leadership approaches and theories. Ask participants to name common themes or share any observations they have about the collective list of people. Prompt the participants to think about the social identities of these individuals and name the identities as belonging to privileged and/or marginalized groups. Anticipate participants mostly identifying privileged identities such as White, male, cisgender, upper socioeconomic class,

and able-bodied persons. Ask participants which identities or groups of people are largely missing from the list of names. Anticipate participants mostly identifying oppressed or marginalized identities such as People of Color, females, transgender people, middle or lower socioeconomic classes, and persons with disabilities.

Note: Often times, in an exercise like this, the names of people like Martin Luther King, Jr., Barack Obama, César Chávez, Hillary Clinton, and Margaret Thatcher may come up. When this occurs, it becomes important to name the extent to which these individuals are tokenized representations. It is important to explore the challenges of identifying numerous examples of leaders/leadership outside of dominant groups and to bring attention to the role of tokenization as it contributes to myths about equity and access. For instance, ask participants to wrestle with the significance of Hillary Clinton as not just a prominent leader, but also a prominent female leader. What is the significance of President Barack Obama's service as the first African American and Black President of the United States? You may also consider incorporating the following prompts to elaborate on this idea:

- *How does the reference to these individual's social identities change the perception of who they are as leaders?*
- *Are the social identities of prominent leaders always relevant?*
- *If we can identify a few commonly known people of marginalized identity groups, how does this tokenize these individuals and their marginalized identity?*
- *Are there themes in the way these (tokenized) individuals embody the leadership approaches we've discussed? Do these themes align with the rest of the individuals on this list? What are the similarities? What are the differences?*

Additionally, you will want to call attention to visible versus invisible social identities during this exercise along with what it means to make presumptions about a person's social identities. For example, are invisible identities such as sexual orientation, socioeconomic status, or faith tradition among others even less likely to be acknowledged in the dominant narrative? What happens when we make presumptions about a person's perceived social identity status?

5. Next, ask participants to name historical movements they are aware of, such as the women's movement and labor movements or those found in Communities of Color and lesbian, gay, bisexual, transgender, or queer (LGBTQ) communities. Add them to the list of "commonly known people." Ask participants to take a moment to consider the timeline for the evolution of leadership approaches as it intersects with the dates of the specific social movements identified. If your space allows, it may help to write dates next to the movements or add the movements chronologically on the evolution of leadership approaches timeline.

6. Discussion should center on how the traditional paradigm of the evolution of leadership was influenced by the dominant perspective and how it neglects to consider social movements and marginalized community perspectives. Dominant leadership theory has omitted important narratives and experiences. Chapter 3 of the main text provides useful figures you may want to use for visual reference points. Continue with the following:

   - *Describe what leadership looked like in these social movements.*
   - *Which leadership theories or approaches do these social movements embody?*
   - *What do you notice about the timeline as it intersects with the social movements?*
   - *Why do you think these social movements and their contributions on the evolution of leadership are overlooked? What are the implications of this?*

7. Now that participants have had an opportunity to understand the utility of critical perspectives in examining how we understand, value, and study leadership, they will move into an activity that will give them an opportunity to apply a critical lens to leadership images. Prior to the lesson, identify and print at least five images that include people from multiple social identities. The images should capture a crowd of people posing for a camera and working together in some capacity. The various images should reflect people with presumed similar and presumed different social identities. For example, using the Internet, search for images that capture a group of five to six people in which one or two members of the group may be female or People of Color. Some of the images should contain people of all similar and visible social identities and some of the images should have a group with visibly different social identities. Additionally, consider images that may produce diverse assumptions about what is occurring, who has power and influence and who may not, and how leadership is happening. Determine how many images to use based on the size of the group.

8. Share the images with the group. You can display, discuss, and cycle through the images as a large group or you can divide the participants into small groups.

9. Ask participants to review the images and come to conclusions about what is happening in the images. Questions to explore may include these:

   - *What do you see in this image?*
   - *What is happening in this image? How do you know what the group is doing?*
   - *Who do you see in this image? Who is managing and leading this group? Based on whom you see, what are they doing?*
   - *What observations do you make about the social identities of this group?*
   - *With which leadership approach would you associate this image?*

10. Cycle through a number of images asking the same or similar questions. Ideally, participants will begin to see how their inherent perspectives on social identities, based on systemic/institutional and personal experiences with power, privilege, and oppression, reinforce and influence their perspectives on leadership. The following large group discussion prompts can be used to facilitate this process:

    - *How did you determine what was happening in the image? What factors contributed to your conclusions? How was leadership reflected?*

    - *How did you decide who was managing or leading the group? Where did your assumptions about this/these person(s) as the leader(s) or manager(s) come from? What role did social identities play in your decisions? Were you conscious of multiple identities? If yes, in what ways? If no, why not? Were invisible identities discussed at all? Did everyone in the group agree with what was occurring? Did everyone in the group agree with who was managing or leading? Share some significant aspects of your conversation.*

    - *How did your conversations reflect the earlier activity on prominent figures and social movements? Do you think our earlier conversations prompted you to see the image differently? In what way(s)?*

11. Close out the lesson by asking participants the following prompts:

    - *Share your perspectives on how social, systemic, and institutional experiences shape and relate to the evolution of leadership theories.*

    - *How might you apply this information outside of this space?*

12. Return to the general principles of critical perspectives to emphasize how the dominant perspective influences the evolution of leadership and why the use of critical perspectives as a tool to critique our study and understanding of leadership is so important.

Debriefing Notes

At the conclusion of the activity, ask participants to think about their own social identity group membership and how it does or does not affect their roles as leaders. Encourage participants to use a critical perspective as a way to evaluate the inclusiveness of approaches to leadership. Remind participants that applying critical perspectives to the evolution of leadership is a process and takes a great deal of reflection on and awareness of systems of power, privilege, and oppression and individual social identities.

Facilitator Notes

To facilitate this activity, you will need to reflect on your own social identities and knowledge of systems of power, privilege, and oppression. The social identities and epistemology of the facilitator(s) can influence the way a critical perspective is communicated, presented, and promoted. Thus, it is recommended that you and other facilitators be keenly aware of your own experiences with power, privilege, and oppression prior to facilitation.

› Activity 2—Critical Perspectives as an Epistemology: Exploring Internalized Homophobia and Systematic Heterosexism

Using homophobia and heterosexism as an example, this activity highlights the relationship between social and personal experiences of systemic/institutional power, privilege, and oppression. As a result of this activity, participants may have an increased awareness of issues related to homophobia and heterosexism, but the main purpose is to demonstrate how a critical approach to leadership may be applied and implemented.

Learning Outcomes

- Be able to apply critical perspectives through exploration of personal levels of internalized homophobia and heterosexism.
- Understand the utility of critical perspectives as an approach to leadership.
- Be able to use critical perspectives in alternative scenarios.

Setting Up the Activity

Group Size: Open to any size group. You want to consider engaging participants in large and small groups (three to five participants) to diversify reflection on discussion questions.

Time: 45–60 minutes depending on approach to debrief and discussion questions

Methods: Dialogue, discussion, lecture, reflection

Variations: Activity can be done with another nonvisible social identity (e.g., ask participants to imagine themselves with a cognitive disability or being of a lower socioeconomic status).

Directions

1. Walk through the evolution of leadership theories as described in Chapter 3 of the main text. Review leadership theories as transitioning from trait-based approaches to process-based and transformative approaches. Ask participants to focus on transformative, social change, and social justice leadership perspectives. Invite participants to consider the relevance of their social identities when doing change-oriented leadership work.

2. Ask participants to name people (e.g., commonly known celebrities, politicians, or historic figures) and social movements that may embody the different phases and theories of leadership. You could refer to the list created in Activity 1 if the sessions are done consecutively. Ask participants how much is actually known about the people and these

communities in relation to their social identities and interests. For example, how many of the identified people (or those involved in different social movements) are known to be part of a LGBTQ community? Similar to the previous activity, review the tenets and skills of critical perspectives detailed in Chapters 2 of the main text.

3. Without prompting the group to think about homophobia and heterosexism as an example of applying a critical perspective to leadership, prepare the participants for the activity. Tell participants they will only need themselves to participate. Ask participants to put away any personal belongings and materials. Let participants know the activity requires participants to go outside or to travel to another nearby location. Act as if participants will actually travel to this location. Ask participants to identify a partner who they assume holds their same gender. Once participants have identified their partners, ask participants to sit next to their partners.

4. Let participants know that they will be traveling to a pre-selected location. Share that they are required to spend between 10 to 15 minutes together in a highly populated location. Then, reveal that they will not only spend time with their partners in this highly public location, but they will also spend their 10 to 15 minutes holding hands.

5. As a facilitator, pause and observe participants' reactions to the direction about holding hands. Anticipate that some participants will shift or move their bodies physically away from their partners and others may decide to verbally reject the activity and decide to no longer participate. However, also anticipate a smaller group of participants may be completely comfortable with the directions and the assignment. The moment of revealing that partners will hold hands in public and move through a highly public area together can exemplify participants' internalized homophobia. Again, the point is not to hone in on the topic of homophobia, but to exaggerate the

connections between social systems and personal identities and experiences. If participants experience or show some level of discomfort with the activity, then this illustrates (on a basic level) a degree of unsettled internalized homophobia and the privileging of heterosexuality (or heterosexism).

6. Ask participants to reflect on their reaction to all the directions. Direct participants to respond to the following questions:

   - *How do you feel? What are you thinking?*
   - *If you are feeling discomfort, what is the root of your discomfort? If you are not feeling discomfort, what makes you comfortable with all the directions?*
   - *How does this exercise relate to what was discussed about adopting a critical perspective?*
   - *What are you discovering about your internalized beliefs and how your beliefs are or are not communicated to others?*

7. At this point, let the participants know there are no intentions of actually asking participants to carry out all the previous directions. Relate back to change-oriented leadership theories and critical perspectives. Let the participants know the purpose of the activity is to illuminate the connection between a system and social issue with personal values and beliefs. Consider the following prompts:

   - *Discussing what you are feeling at this moment in the activity is the actual purpose of the exercise. We will not be venturing to another site where you will be in physical contact with another person. The purpose is to put you in a scenario that is outside of dominant norms. A perceived man and a perceived woman holding hands, in a U.S. context, reflects that dominant norm.*
   - *Learning that we will not be carrying out the assigned instructions, what are your thoughts? How have your thoughts, opinions, and perspectives changed throughout the entirety of this activity? How do your beliefs and values translate into your perceptions of leaders and leadership?*

- *Where we have comfort and discomfort around systems of privilege and oppression can teach us a great deal about others and ourselves. What has this activity taught you about yourself and others?*

Debriefing Notes

At the conclusion of the activity, ask participants to think about their own social identity group membership and how that does or does not affect their roles as leaders. Encourage participants to use a critical perspective as a way to evaluate the inclusiveness of approaches to leadership. Remind participants that applying critical perspectives to understanding leadership is a process and takes a great deal of reflection and awareness on systems of power, privilege, and oppression and individual social identities.

Facilitator Notes

To facilitate this activity, you will need to reflect on your own social identities and knowledge of systems of power, privilege, and oppression. The social identities and epistemology of the facilitator(s) can influence the way a critical theory lens is communicated, presented, and promoted. Thus, it is recommended that you be keenly aware of your own experiences with power, privilege, and oppression before facilitating this activity.

It would be a good idea to explicitly state that this activity is highly contingent on the U.S. cultural context as well as regional/institutional cultural norms. Because of cultural contingency, it is important to recognize that the same internalized heteronormativity and potential homophobia could put a spotlight on participants whose gender performances and/or sexual identities do not conform to dominant assumptions. These participants may be fine with this or they may be uncomfortable with it. You should consider these dynamics in advance as well as issues of safety that might be specific to institution or region.

Furthermore, you should be prepared to support participants who identify as members of the LGBTQ community throughout the activity ensuring that any negative reactions from other participants about holding hands is not allowed to move from general discomfort to overt hostility. Processing should also attend to LGBTQ participants' needs, avoiding using them as a response mechanism in the activity or neglecting their personal reactions to it. Finally, facilitators should be ready to clearly distinguish between gender identity and sexual identity since this may be participants' first exposure to the concepts.

A central part of the learning from this activity stems from the assumption that participants will be momentarily placed in an unexpected position and will realize this was done intentionally as part of the process. You should be prepared to handle the potential ego threat that comes with this realization and consider options for coaching participants through it to avoid the risk of shaming and/or having them reject the activity as an opportunity to learn.

> Conclusion

The application of critical approaches to formal leadership theories is a process of reflecting on systemic/institutional and individual power related to privilege and oppression. By adopting and using a critical perspective, participants must be prepared and committed to seeing the emancipation of marginalized populations as possible and needed in society to change existing experiences of racism, sexism, genderism, heterosexism, classism, and other forms of social inequality. Looking at images and formulating stories about people depicted in an image is an indirect way to reflect on the diversity of groups and organizations. Physically engaging in an act, albeit not actually doing the directed task, is a more direct way of experiencing power and the need for emancipation from heterosexism. The activities proposed in this curriculum plan are ways to introduce participants to power dynamics by varying the personal connection to privilege and oppression; they also make visible the ways in which systemic oppression instigates our own biased attitudes and inhibits the advancement of truly relational, transformative, and liberatory practices of leadership. Additionally, the activities highlight the evolution of leadership theories and bring to light the ways in which these are influenced by a dominant perspective while the role of marginalized identity groups has been minimized, tokenized, and neglected.

3C: Implicit Leadership Through a Critical Lens: How Implicit Biases Support the Dominant Narrative

Amy C. Barnes

Objectives/Goals of Chapter

- Be aware of personal biases toward leaders and followers.
- Understand how implicit assumptions about leadership are influenced by social identities/stereotypes.
- Recognize the impact of preconceived ideas of social identity on leadership contexts through analysis of microaggressions.

Critical Concepts: *biases, critical self-reflection, flow of power, microaggressions, stereotypes*

› Chapter Overview

Leaders must learn to navigate and negotiate a wide variety of situations, relationships, and organizational politics to create a shared vision, meet goals, and motivate teams. In complex systems, leaders are often judged by their ability to successfully achieve goals regardless of obstacles placed in their way. Implicit leadership theory is based on the premise that everyone has assumptions that frame how they understand what leadership is and is not. Connected to personal experiences, leadership is defined implicitly through an individual's cultural, racial, gendered, and other mental models. Navigating implicit assumptions represents a challenge for leaders, especially those who are not part of a dominant identity group (Dugan, 2017).

Often people from minoritized identities are forced to navigate less obvious or hidden biases. Preconceived assumptions that both leaders and followers have of "good" or "effective" leadership play a significant role in the evaluation of leader behavior. How a leader is perceived is not just through a single lens but through the collective sum of leadership perceptions held by every individual they encounter and every relationship they navigate. In addition, the intersection of perceptions held by both leaders and followers can affect how power is distributed, how decisions are made, who is invited to participate, and the relative inclusivity of a leadership context. Barriers to success for leaders from underrepresented populations are reinforced through implicit leadership assumptions that fail to include diverse perspectives (Dugan, 2017).

> Chapter Framework

This chapter promotes an analysis of implicit leadership theory through critical perspectives using activities, guided reflections, and small group discussions so participants can increase their awareness of personal biases and how assumptions influence leadership contexts. This includes the impact that stereotypes, privilege, and covert/hidden oppression (microaggressions) have on the distribution of power and perceptions of leadership in various settings (Sue et al., 2007). A critical approach to implicit theory challenges leaders to bring the unconscious assumptions or biases they might have about others to consciousness and realize the implications of those assumptions within leadership contexts.

Consciousness-raising techniques utilize a small-group format and allow group members to share personal experiences to better understand the lived experiences of people who have different backgrounds or experiences from their own. Consideration of the individual's marginalized or privileged identities along with the impact of oppression are important. Typically, the goal is to "facilitate students' self-awareness and social awareness of oppressive systems" (Leonard, 1996, p. 91). Similarly, the goal of applying a critical perspective to implicit leadership is to help participants uncover potential biases that occur within leadership contexts. Critical self-reflection allows leaders to explore the complex personal narratives that individuals bring to leadership contexts while honoring the ways in which their identities and past experiences matter.

Curriculum Plan

The following curriculum helps participants increase their awareness of personal implicit biases that lead to assumptions about their roles as leaders as well as how this influences others. The following curriculum encourages participants to consider how the flow of power in leadership contexts might be influenced by implicit leadership assumptions held by both leaders and followers, especially as it is mitigated by social identity and privilege. This curriculum should be implemented in one session lasting 3 to 4 hours or two sessions each lasting 2 hours.

Activity 1—Implicit Leadership Storytelling

During this activity, participants have the opportunity to consider their experiences with and assumptions about leadership and how those negatively and positively affect both leaders and followers.

Participants will reflect on their implicit leadership biases through an artistic project, a written assignment, and group discussion.

Learning Outcomes

- Understand how personal views of leadership are developed/influenced by past experiences.
- Identify implicit leadership biases that result from past experiences and assumptions.

Setting Up the Activity

Group Size: Open to any size group

Time: 45 minutes to 1 hour, plus a homework assignment

Methods: Self-reflection, group processing, small group discussion

Materials: If drawings are done in the learning session, then paper and art supplies (markers, writing utensils)

Directions

1. (Homework provided before the session) Ask participants to draw what they believe a leader to look like on paper. Allow 20 to 30 minutes for this activity. Then direct participants to write a reflection on the following prompts:

   - *Looking at your artistic representation of a leader, consider where your assumptions about leadership come from. What life experiences have contributed to those assumptions?*
   - *What do you expect from a leader and why? What about your background leads to those expectations?*
   - *When you are the leader, what do you expect of followers? Do your own assumptions about leadership affect your expectations of followers?*
   - *Do any of your assumptions about leadership not involve the traditional leader/follower dyad?*
   - *Thinking about your own life, what or who informed your understanding of leadership/leader?*

2. (During the In-Person Session) Begin the discussion with a quick overview of implicit leadership. Additional information can be found in Chapter 3 of the main text (Dugan, 2017). Here are a couple of prompts you could consider:

   - *A person's ideas about what leaders are and the characteristics or behaviors they should demonstrate make up their implicit theories of leadership.*
   - *Leadership is in the eye of the beholder.*

3. Ask participants to reflect silently on experiences they have had where implicit leadership has been at play (they can refer to the homework for a reminder).

4. Ask participants to find a partner. Instruct each pair to discuss the following prompts. Participants will share their responses one at a time.

   - *Tell your partner about a time when you were a leader or a follower and the situation was not positive. Were assumptions made from one or both sides? What were those assumptions? To what extent were assumptions a function of leader prototypes? How did they influence the experience for both leaders and followers?*
   - *As you consider your particular role in this experience, what may have been gaps in your knowledge that led to those assumptions?*
   - *How might this situation have been handled differently to produce a more positive outcome?*

5. After approximately 20 minutes of paired discussion, bring the group back together. Ask for volunteers to summarize their stories and share what they learned about implicit leadership. Use the following questions to steer group discussion:

   - *What common themes emerged in your discussions about implicit leadership? What new information do you possess that may change your views of implicit leadership in the future?*
   - *How did your homework reflection influence your in-person discussions? How does your implicit leadership lens affect your relationships in leadership settings?*

> - *To what extent did social identities come up in your conversation? How did you address social identity? How does social identity affect your implicit lens?*
> - *How do you think your newfound knowledge on implicit leadership theory will inform how you lead in the future?*

> Activity 2—Identifying, Defining, and Dispelling Microaggressions

Participants will spend time exploring different types of microaggressions and reflect on their impact on an individual's development as a leader. This further illuminates the subtle ways that oppression can affect leadership contexts and the distribution of power. This activity also considers how perfectly logical explanations (PLEs) are often used to defend distributions of power that favor dominant narratives in leadership contexts (routenberg & Sclafani, 2011).

Learning Outcomes

- Identify three types of microaggressions and discuss potential impacts on leaders.
- Understand how to respond to and create strategies for confronting microaggressions when experienced directly or indirectly.

Setting Up the Activity

Group Size: Open to any size group

Time: 90 minutes total (45 minutes for Part 1, 45 minutes for Part 2)

Methods: Self-reflection, small group discussion, and group processing

<u>Materials</u>: Computer, Internet access, projector/screen (laptops or tablets are be ideal)

<u>Multimedia</u>: *The Microaggressions Project* (http://www.microaggressions.com)

Directions

1. *Part I—Go Over Definitions of Microaggressions and PLEs:*
   - The concept of *microaggressions* first emerged from critical race theory to call attention to the use of "brief and commonplace daily verbal, behavioral, or environmental indignities, whether intentional or unintentional, that communicate hostile, derogatory, or negative racial slights and insults toward people of color" (Sue et al., 2007, p. 271). Microaggressions are pervasive in nature; they can target a person or a group; and they can be initiated either intentionally or unintentionally (Solórzano, Ceja, & Yosso, 2000). Over time, the fundamental concept of a microaggression (i.e., the subtle communication of bias and prejudice) has been extended to also recognize negative slights made on the basis of other social identities, such as gender and sexual orientation (Solórzano, 1998; Sue, 2010).
   - A *microinsult* is characterized by nonverbal or verbal comments that convey rudeness to demean a person's identity. These comments clearly convey a hidden insult diminishing the contributions of that person (e.g., a female physician in an emergency room being mistaken by a male patient as a nurse; Sue et al., 2007).
   - *Microinvalidations* are verbal comments or behaviors that exclude or negate the thoughts, feelings, or reality of a person's identity. This includes comments such as, "There is only one race—the human race," or "You speak English very well," said to people who have English as their first language (Sue et al., 2007).

- A *PLE* is when an individual attempts to defend, rationalize, or otherwise justify dominant ideologies (i.e., perspectives that ignore systems of power and privilege) to discredit or invalidate concerns raised regarding the use of microaggressions, microinsults, and/or microinvalidations (routenberg & Sclafani, 2011).

2. Visit The Microaggressions Project website (http://www .microaggressions.com). Have participants access this site from a computer in the room or pass out a handout with a screen shot of the website.

3. Provide participants with a homework assignment to explore the website and identify three microaggressions that satisfy one of these conditions:

   1) *You have experienced that microaggression yourself in some way.*

   2) *You feel empathy for someone in your life who has experienced the microaggression.*

   3) *You are upset by this microaggression and want to learn more about how to help address this sort of discrimination.*

   All three can be from one category or participants can identify one in each category. Once they have selected three microaggressions from the website, they should write a two-page, typed, double-spaced reflective paper answering the following questions:

   - *Describe a time you witnessed or personally experienced a microaggression. What was the underlying message? How did you feel? What did you do?*

   - *Consider the microaggressions you chose from the website. Recognizing that responding to microaggressions can be challenging, personally exhausting (especially when it is directed at you), and situationally unique, the following questions are designed to elicit ways that implicit bias can be appropriately interrupted:*

     ○ *How might different power dynamics influence how you would respond?*

      ◦ *Recalling personal experiences with microaggressions or putting yourself in the shoes of others, what type of approach could you use to interrupt bias (e.g., humorous, calm, inquisitive, rejecting)?*

      ◦ *What are potential PLEs that you may encounter?*

4. Conclude by asking if there are any questions about the homework assignment and remind participants that their reflections are due for the next session.

5. *Part II—Continuation of Activity 2 from Previous Day:* Split participants into small groups. The recommended size is three to five people per group. Give each group a large piece of paper or newsprint and markers.

6. Ask participants to share their reflections generally on the microaggressions they wrote about and then answer the following question as a group: *What are some of the strategies that you came up with in your reflections for addressing microaggressions?*

7. Ask each group to share the strategies they discussed and lead a large group discussion using the following discussion prompts:

   • *What are your reactions to the strategies identified by the groups? Do you feel they can be effective? What are other strategies that can be used to combat microaggressions before they occur?*

   • *How do microaggressions potentially affect implicit leadership assumptions? How can microaggressions have an impact on the distribution of power in leadership?*

   • *Some critics feel that acknowledging the existence of microaggressions creates problems where none exist (i.e., it furthers discrimination by portraying minorities as victims). These critics feel the best way to deal with these exchanges is to ignore them. How would you respond to these critics?*

Facilitator Notes

Most individuals consider themselves to be good, moral people who strongly believe in equity and fairness. When a microaggression is exposed, it may be difficult to accept ownership of a biased attitude. A common reaction is to reject this notion with a nonbiased rationale, or a PLE (routenberg & Sclafani, 2011). To avoid being judged negatively, individuals enacting dominant narratives may simultaneously provide context to justify their perspectives, cite limited exposure, or suggest they have witnessed marginalized groups participating as well. These responses can make it difficult to challenge in dialogue settings. It is important that you invite participants to dissect nuances of dominant narratives to recognize their limitations and encourage the contributions of counter-narratives. This is achieved when you ask questions that participants have never had to think about before and this introspection is critical to understanding the complexities of social identity. It is also important, however, that targets of particular microaggressions are not forced to defend the validity of these issues themselves or speak on behalf of their respective communities. Similarly, facilitators should be aware that asking participants to engage around microaggressions they have personally encountered can be triggering. Appropriate attention should be directed toward supporting participants and acknowledging that the process of sharing is by choice and not compulsory.

❯ Activity 3—Implicit Leadership in Cross-Cultural Contexts

Through this activity, participants examine the cultural lenses that inform leadership across culture and countries. This lesson incorporates a brief introduction to the six dimensions of culture (Hofstede, 1983) and uses the Hofstede Centre's research and website to guide discussion on the cultural differences of varying countries. This analysis informs how each individual's implicit understandings of leadership through cultural lenses can allow or disallow for effective and inclusive forms of leadership.

Learning Outcomes

- Identify the six dimensions of culture established by Hofstede.
- Understand implicit biases toward leadership through a cultural lens utilizing Hofstede's six dimensions as a tool for analysis.
- Recognize strategies for adapting implicit leadership lenses for cross-cultural interactions.

Setting Up the Activity

Group Size: Open to any size group

Time: 45 minutes

Methods: Online investigation, self-reflection, small group processing

Materials: Electronic device with access to the Internet

Multimedia: *The Hofstede Centre* (http://geert-hofstede.com/national-culture.html)

Directions

1. Begin this activity with an introduction to Hofstede's six dimensions of culture. Hofstede first published on his landmark cultural exploration and comparative studies in 1983, examining the differences in cultural responses across four primary categories:
   - *Power Distance*: The distance in relationships between a superior and subordinates
   - *Uncertainty Avoidance*: The degree of comfort with perceived rules and ambiguity
   - *Individualism vs. Collectivism*: The relative interdependence or independence sought by group members
   - *Masculinity vs. Femininity*: The degree to which heroism, success, and competition are valued as these are seen as traditionally masculine traits

Over time, two additional themes were added to more fully address roots of cultural and organizational differences:

- *Long-Term Orientation vs. Short-Term Orientation*: The overall willingness to maintain past traditions or prepare for the future
- *Indulgence vs. Restraint*: A culture's balance between suppressing gratification and having fun

Hofstede's study on cultural dimensions is significant as it provides a framework to more effectively recognize implicit biases when relating across cultures.

2. To help participants contextualize this mini-lesson, break them up into six small groups. Designate each group to one dimension as found on The Hofstede Centre (http://geert-hofstede.com/national-culture.html). Provide groups with about 10 minutes to learn, discuss, and author an example of their dimension. Then, ask small groups to share their definition and example with the large group. Group sharing should take about 5 minutes.

3. Transition the group by asking participants to select an individual country from the list provided in your earlier Internet search of Hofstede's cultural dimensions.

4. Provide each person with 10 minutes to analyze their country of choice with respect to another country of their choice (it is suggested that participants choose the United States if they do not have another cultural lens). Ask participants to individually respond to the following:

- *Describe the similarities and differences between your countries of choice using the dimensions of culture as a framework.*
- *Discuss how leadership could be portrayed or enacted from each cultural lens you selected.*
- *Understanding your implicit leadership lens, consider how you might respond to be an effective leader across your cultures of analysis.*

5. Ask participants to divide into pairs for about 5 minutes of discussion of their responses.

6. If time permits, consider hosting a large group discussion on the revelations of the activity. The following are suggestions for large group discussion questions:

   - *How was this process? How were you challenged to think differently about your leadership assumptions and the degree to which these implicit understandings translate across cultures?*

   - *How does this inform how you approach leadership moving forward?*

Facilitator Notes

For additional content related to Hofstede's cultural dimensions, see The Hofstede Centre website (http://geert-hofstede.com/national-culture.html) and/or Hofstede's original article included in the reference section at the end of this guide.

› Conclusion

This chapter was designed to help participants begin to critique the assumptions that occur with implicit leadership by providing opportunities for personal reflection, dialogue around bias and stereotyping, and an introduction to microaggressions. Implicit leadership theory essentially calls out how people naturally categorize others based upon a prototype that they hold in their minds. However, there is no single prototype of leadership that applies to all contexts (Lord, Brown, Harvey, & Hall, 2001), and perceptions of leaders, followers, the situation, and the environment all intersect to influence these implicit ways in which leadership is understood. When considering the impact of social identities on perceptions of leadership, it follows that biases related to race, gender, and socioeconomic status (just to name a few) will affect an individual's evaluation of leader or follower behavior. When those biases are covert—hidden by the dominant paradigm due to systemic oppression, or explained away using PLEs, as is often the case with microaggressions—then implicit understandings of leadership become a threat to social justice. Identifying implicit bias, confronting and overcoming stereotypes, and understanding ways in which microaggressions can be addressed is essential to addressing systemic barriers to leadership.

3D: Critical Considerations in Gender and Leadership

Renique Kersh

Objectives/Goals of Chapter

- Understand gender schema theory and foster a deeper awareness of gender, gender identity, and gender roles.
- Recognize the social construction of gender and the complexity that is missed when gender is dichotomized.
- Examine dominant gender narratives and explore how these influence perceptions of effective leaders.

Critical Concepts: *gender schema, dominant narratives, power, privilege, stocks of knowledge*

Chapter Overview

"The single story creates stereotypes, and the problem with stereotypes is not that they are untrue, but that they are incomplete. They make one story become the only story" (Adichie, 2009). The social construction of gender governs the ways in which we act, think, and behave. Social construction, at its core, means that the way we have learned to understand gender is based on the norms and meanings established within our society (Berger & Luckmann, 1966).

Much of the literature on leadership takes a particular stance on what are traditionally considered to be roles that men and women embody within organizations (Eagly & Johannesen-Schmidt, 2001; Eagly, Johannesen-Schmidt, & Van Engen, 2003). It is thought that women have a higher degree of emotional intelligence, are more relational, are more adept at being resourceful, and are aware of the needs of followers (Eagly & Johannesen-Schmidt, 2001; Eagly et al., 2003). Men, on the other hand, are often cited as being more authoritarian and task-oriented as well as more adept at negotiating and advocating for their needs (Eagly & Johannesen-Schmidt, 2001; Eagly et al., 2003). The dichotomization, or separation of gender, based on sex and roles, suggests that those who lie outside of these socially constructed boundaries will be less effective or unevenly matched. The research on gender roles in leadership leaves us with more questions than answers particularly related to how individuals come to understand gender and, therefore, construct differences in expected roles and abilities.

Gilligan (1982) brought attention to the extensively damaging ways that the gender dichotomy has influenced generations. She highlighted the ways that theory promulgates the tendency to judge behaviors from a gendered lens and encourages the assignment of value based on whether such behaviors align with internalized notions of proper gender roles. Using Kohlberg's (1976) theory of moral development as a backdrop, she explored the ways in which researchers evaluated the moral development of girls and boys. In response to a simple anecdote about whether a man should steal a drug that he cannot afford to save his wife's life, she found that the girl and the boy responded from drastically different perspectives. Although both were responding to the same circumstance, judgment was informed by prior knowledge and experiences that were deeply connected to how both had been socialized. Gilligan argued that there is an assignment of value to certain behaviors, which serves to determine what is considered the right or acceptable response and the wrong or unacceptable response. In the case of the Kohlberg experiment, the value of the girl's behavior suggested that she was less intelligent and thoughtful, was indecisive and passive, and lacked logical decision-making skills—while suggesting that the boy was more logical, analytical, and strategic.

When considering the characteristics assigned to gender according to leadership research, similar categorizations of gender-based leader behavior and characteristics can be found. For example, researchers suggest that men tend to employ more task-oriented behaviors, are more autocratic, direct, and transactional, whereas women have been classified as more relationship-oriented, democratic, and transformational (Eagly et al., 2003; Shapiro, Ingols, & Blake-Beard, 2011). The assignment of certain characteristics to gender supports the expectation that both women and men should behave a certain way when in leadership, thus creating ideal leader prototypes. It also highlights characteristics that have been socially constructed and deeply embedded in our understanding of what leadership means and who is capable of being successful in the role of leader. Furthermore, this dichotomization does not honor the complexity of gender identity and causes problems for leaders when they display characteristics or behaviors that have been historically connected to particular gender roles other than their own (Eagly et al., 2003).

This chapter explores gender schema and further defines the ways that gender and the expression of gender can lead to challenges in leadership. The discussion includes an overview of the impact of dominant gender narratives, power, and privilege on access to and success in leadership and highlights how these issues challenge our ability to actualize gender equality.

› Chapter Framework

The American Psychological Association (APA; 2012) defined gender as the "attitudes, feelings, and behaviors that a given culture associates with a person's biological sex" (p. 11). This suggests an inherent connection to cultural norms and socialization patterns that define what these feelings and behaviors may be. The APA also indicated that an individual is gender-normative when attitudes, feelings, and behaviors are congruent with cultural expectations. However, when they are not, individuals are considered gender nonconformist. Complicating the matter is the expression of gender, which does not have to be associated with an individual's biological sex, but instead is an expression that may or may not be aligned with gender identity. Evans, Forney, Guido, Patton, and Renn (2009) noted that congruency between gender identity and biological sex is typically referred to as *cisgender identity* whereas gender identity that does not necessarily match up with sex is referred to as *transgender identity*. Additionally, it is critical to recognize that gender identity should not be conflated with sexual orientation (Evans et al., 2009). This understanding increases the complexity of gender identity, how it is constructed, and what impact it may have on leadership.

Bem (1981) explored the complexities of gender identity through gender schema theory, which states that it is a natural tendency to associate particular behaviors and characteristics with sex (i.e., male and female) through the process of sex-typing. Sex-typing results in roles, characteristics, and behaviors that are considered masculine and feminine, which in turn link back to sex categories. In effect, gender schema theory "proposes … that the phenomenon of sex-typing derives, in part, from gender-based schematic processing, from a generalized readiness to process information on the basis of the sex-linked associations that constitute the gender schema" (Bem, 1981, p. 355). Gender schemas enable individuals to cognitively organize information into associated gender-based categories. In essence, schemas represent a stock of knowledge, which creates meaning for information and allows individuals to form an understanding—consciously and subconsciously. Left unchallenged, schemas can result in unconscious bias and discrimination. The constructed meanings also influence an individual's self-concept and can lead to incongruence if behaviors do not conform to socially constructed norms. It is important to note that gender schema theory suggests that gender is, in fact, the dominant lens from which the individual processes experiences and it may not always be the dominant lens from which judgments are made. Bem (1981) also asserted that the relative importance of this schema may have to do with its role during developmental years, which is when socialized constructs are learned.

Gender schema can lead to power dynamics that deeply influence the way individuals experience and practice leadership. Schema categorize information in ways that promote a dominant gender narrative or script based on the normative behaviors associated with gender categories. These scripts can create visible and sometimes not-so-visible barriers within organizations that lead to gender-stratification and a systemic understanding of "good" leadership based on gender norms. In leadership, there tends to be an underlying conflation of power with masculinity, which suggests that individuals who have power exhibit characteristics more traditionally assigned to men. Shapiro et al. (2011) explained that implicit definitions and assignments of power often lead to a gendered way of understanding who has the authority to be in a position of influence. Leadership cannot be discussed without the inclusion of power as a base given that leadership involves influence.

The result of internalized dominant gender narratives can also lead to *double binds*. Jamieson (1995) defined the double bind when describing the experiences of women in leadership. She asserted that the outcome of the double bind is guilt that results from stepping outside of gendered norms as well as guilt for embodying those norms. It sets up a double standard that demonizes the individual who is not accurately affirming the dominant gender narrative. It reduces an individual to being defined by this narrative and not by ability and effectiveness. Bem (1981) asserted that the gender schema is a direct result of "society's ubiquitous insistence on the functional importance of the gender dichotomy" (p. 362), which paves the way for systemic gender inequality and affects the accessibility of leadership. Understanding both gender schema and power dynamics that can result from them are essential components of leadership education that provide an opportunity to unpack dominant gender narratives, or the ways that sex and gender shape the beliefs about what constitutes effective or ineffective leadership.

Curriculum Plan

This curriculum will challenge participants to reflect on their gender schema and the dominant gender narrative that influences how they view gender relative to leadership. This chapter is in the service of understanding implicit assumptions to leadership from a gendered perspective. Participants will unpack societal and personal narratives associated with gender and explore their unintentional outcomes. Given that power dynamics play an important role in the perpetuation of gender dichotomization, participants will also discuss how power dynamics propagate gender inequities in leadership.

Activity 1—Mapping Your Gender Schema

For this activity, encourage participants to create mind-maps (i.e., diagrams that help to organization information) that will be used to associate particular characteristics and behaviors with sex categories. Participants will then explore their individual gender schemas and begin to discuss the sources that have contributed to dominant gender narratives that they have along with those that they believe are related to societal expectations. Participants will also be asked to reflect on how leaders might be viewed based on the sex category for which they are associated and why. This activity will encourage participants to consider how gender has been constructed and how power has influenced this construction. The activity will also challenge participants to consider how the dominant gender lens, both individually and societally, may unfairly increase the acceptance of one set of behaviors/characteristics over another.

Learning Outcomes

- Understand the complexity of gender identity.
- Distinguish between the terms gender identity, sex, and gender expression.
- Develop a greater understanding of personal gender schema and the dominant gender narratives that influence perceptions of leadership.

Setting Up the Activity

Group Size: Optimal group size is no larger than 30 participants with small groups no large than 7 people each given the sensitive nature of the topic and the need for reflection.

Time: 90 minutes

Methods: Personal reflection, small and large group discussion

Materials: Paper, writing utensils, distributed copies of the APA's (2011) "Definition of Terms: Sex, Gender, Gender Identity, Sexual Orientation." (This document can be found online by searching with the complete title and year.)

Directions

1. Explain to participants that a mind-map is a visual display that organizes information. Explain that mind-maps work in ways that are similar to how we cognitively organize information in our brains and solidify associations.

2. Have each participant take out a piece of blank paper and draw a circle in the middle. In that circle, have each participant write either male or female. Participants can choose freely; their selection does not have to coincide with how they personally label their sex.

3. For the next 5 minutes, ask participants to identify characteristics that come to mind that they associate with male or female. Participants should draw connecting circles with these characteristics in the circles.

4. Once they have completed this task, have participants get into groups based on the sex they wrote about and ask that they create one group mind-map for that sex. Take note of any comments you hear during this process, as they can be useful for discussion.

5. Engage participants using the following prompts:
   - *What made it easy to think of and assign associated behaviors and traits with a particular sex?*
   - *What made it difficult to think of and assign associated behaviors and traits with a particular sex?*

6. Next, discuss gender schema theory and explain that it is not unusual to quickly come up with behaviors and traits associated with sex based on our gender schema. Discuss how our schema is highly dependent upon how we were socialized and what dominant gender narratives we grew to understand as our social framework. Note that these dominant gender narratives are both a result of our internalized discussion of gender and the discussions that we learn from our interactions within society (e.g., through discussions in the media). Further discuss the complexity of sex and gender identity given they may not align nor will they necessarily reflect the same forms of gender expression or fit neatly into masculine or feminine categories. This may be a natural place to engage in a detailed discussion on gender schemas by problematizing the stocks of knowledge from which they are drawn and the accuracy of the "recipes"

that inform them. This will lead nicely into the discussion about how gender identities and expressions influence the acceptance and trajectory of leaders.

7. Engage participants in a discussion by asking this: *How do our gender schema influence our expectations and acceptance of leaders? How might they affect the experiences of leaders or those aspiring to become leaders?* Consider discussing the court case, *Hopkins vs. Price Waterhouse*, specifically looking at the comments made by the partners when deciding whether Ann Hopkins should be appointed as a partner. This case highlights the ways that gender schemas affect women in leadership. Lastly, consider asking: *How might factoring in other socially constructed categories like race complicate the expectations and acceptance of leaders?*

8. It may be useful to include factual information from the Bureau of Labor Statistics that show the gender gaps in pay and the comparative percentages of women versus men in leader positions and ask participants the following: *How might dominant societal gender narratives be attributing to these disparities? What other factors might be important to consider?*

Debriefing Notes

The debriefing of this topic may be uncomfortable for some participants particularly if they are not used to thinking deeply about how their narratives may contribute to the perpetuation of inequity. It is not uncommon to encounter participants who do not share their opinions on this issue because they are processing whether their opinions are valid or whether it is okay to share. Conversely, be prepared to engage with participants who push back and/or reject even the exploration of gender schemas because they threaten stocks of knowledge too deeply. Find ways to engage these participants attempting to keep them in the conversation without allowing them to override the learning experience of others.

It is important to engage participants in a discussion about how they have taken the first step that involves self-awareness and perspective-taking, which will inevitably influence the lens that they will view leaders from in the future as well as how they view themselves and their role in helping others become more self-aware. It is also important to note that the goal is not to solve the issues, but to become aware of them in an effort to increase leader sensitivity to double standards, inequities, and narratives that may contribute to marginalizing and oppressive behaviors. Further, it is important to engage participants in a reflection on how these narratives may affect their leadership journey (e.g., the impact on self-esteem, self-efficacy, and sense of belonging) and what that means.

Facilitator Notes

It is possible that some participants may be more connected to their racial identity or another identity category, which may make it difficult for them to engage fully in the discussion. It is not unusual for intersectionality to come up in a discussion and this can allow for a more detailed exchange about how dominant narratives can tell only one story, which can influence an individual's self-concept and sense of competence as a leader.

> Activity 2—Deconstructing Dominant Gender Narratives

For this activity, show the video clip, *There's Gotta Be a Downside to Having a Woman President*. Participants will then engage in an in-depth discussion that captures reactions and asks them to consider ways that the statements in the clip support or disprove the idea that dominant gender narratives influence the acceptance and trajectory of leaders. Participants will reflect on what it might mean to have this discussion being led by a male reporter and will analyze whether this is more or less likely to influence the acceptance of this idea by viewers. Participants will also consider personal gender narratives and societal gender narratives that support the statements made in the video and their overall impact on gender equity in leadership.

Learning Outcomes

- Understand the impact of dominant gender narratives as perpetuating factors for gender inequity in leadership.
- Articulate the negative impacts that gendered messages have on individuals and society.
- Articulate what understanding both the damages of dominant gender narratives and the challenges presented by inequitable assumptions means as they pursue leadership roles.

Setting Up the Activity

Group Size: Optimal group size is no larger than 30 participants with small groups no large than 7 people each given the sensitive nature of the topic and need for reflection.

Time: 90 minutes

Methods: Multimedia, personal reflection, small group discussion

Materials: Computer, projector/screen, Internet access, paper, writing utensils

Multimedia: *There's Gotta Be a Downside to Having a Woman President* (https://www.youtube.com/watch?v=085FHc5uA64)

Directions

1. This video is best shown without providing too much context. One of the reasons for this is to ensure that as a facilitator, you can capture the raw emotion and response of the participants. Prior to showing the video, you might ask the question:

Do you believe there is a downside to having a woman president? Have participants privately write down their answer. Ask that they take notes on the video paying particular attention to comments that support the prior activity on dominant gender narratives. Show the video (5 minutes).

2. Ask participants to share their initial thoughts. It is highly likely that the clip will invoke strong responses. Provide 10 to 12 minutes for personal reflection on what they saw and heard using the following questions:

   - *What messages did you hear that are most disturbing to you?*
   - *What messages did you find to be true and worth further exploring?*
   - *How might what Bill O'Reilly is suggesting affect you?*

3. Have the participants get into small groups to discuss each question. After about 10 minutes of small group discussion, ask participants to share key thoughts with the larger group. It is likely that there will be room for a discussion about power and privilege and the ways that we often do not see how our own power and privilege positions us to be taken seriously in leadership in ways that others with less power and privilege are not afforded.

4. Ask the large group to think back to the earlier discussion about dominant gender narratives using the following prompt: *Knowing what you now know about dominant gender narratives, how does this knowledge inform your thoughts on this clip?*

5. Discuss the role that dominant gender narratives play in perpetuating gender inequality in leadership. It will be useful to ask participants to think about the two correspondents and consider their comments, particularly those made by Kirsten Powers when she is asking what the downsides are for a man being president. This can also connect to the aforementioned discussion about power dynamics that privilege one group over another and can allow for questions to be asked about

the competence of one group that may not also be asked about the competence of another group.

6. Ask participants to briefly share whether they believe what O'Reilly stated is true or false. Ask that sharing be concise and simply share whether they find truth in the statements.

7. Then, have participants break into two groups based on their responses. You can have participants break into groups according to similar responses (i.e., all those who believe the statements to be true are grouped together) or, if you want to challenge the group even more, you could instruct them to take the stance *opposite* of their actual belief. The second option can engage participants in powerful social perspective-taking.

8. Give participants about 10 minutes to develop supporting rationale for their stance, and then have them report out. Encourage participants to be open-minded and respectful to one another throughout the process. Once each side shares, ask the questions:

   - *For those of you who did not agree with the position of your group, but followed the assigned rules, how did this experience challenge you? What did you learn or take away from the experience?*
   - *Were you able to identify how particular stocks of knowledge might be influencing thinking?*
   - *How did this discussion help you to understand the issues related to gender and leadership?*

9. Further engage participants in a discussion as a large group considering the following questions:

   - *Why is understanding dominant gender narratives important in terms of leadership? How does it impact leaders? How does it impact leadership?*
   - *What are the challenges to leadership that you anticipate as a result of developing an awareness of dominant gender*

narratives? What are the benefits to leadership that you anticipate as a result of developing an awareness of dominant gender narratives?

- *How might knowledge of gender schema provide a path forward for disrupting them and creating greater equity in leadership?*

10. Have participants write a final reflection identifying what they learned about themselves through this discussion. Push participants to honestly reflect from a vulnerable place. Suggest that they note when gender schemas and dominant gender narratives may have influenced their acceptance of leaders and how this new knowledge will impact how they will view leadership and gender in the future.

Debriefing Notes

Participants may be frustrated and angry about the comments in the video and it is important to allow space for the expression of these emotions. The expression gives way to further discussion about how harmful dominant gender narratives can be both from the individual and societal perspective. It also allows for a discussion about how important it is, particularly for those who have power and privilege, to advocate for changing the narrative to move society toward honoring the differences that individuals bring to leadership. Lastly, it allows the participants to reflect personally on how they respond to others' leadership potential and how others may respond to theirs.

❯ Conclusion

The intent of this curriculum plan is to engage participants in a critical exploration of gender and an examination of dominant gender narratives influencing leadership. This curriculum guides participants through complex learning about gender schema, sex, gender identity, gender expression, and gendered bias, as well as facilitates the concrete application of these concepts to real-world situations. By centering the interrelationship of power, identity, and agency, this chapter ultimately equips participants with the necessary knowledge, skills, and awareness to interrogate gender bias and other manifestations of power and privilege in their practice and pursuit of leadership for social change.

4A: The Leadership Practices Inventory Through a Critical Lens

David M. Rosch

Objectives/Goals of Chapter

- Understand the significance of values and individual context in enacting the five leadership practices described in the Leadership Practices Inventory.
- Recognize how culture informs values and behavior in relation to the five practices.
- Identify how cultural biases affect the assessment of leadership effectiveness within the context of the five practices.

Critical Concepts: *ethnocentrism, privilege, social location, social perspective-taking*

> Chapter Overview

Over 3 million people have completed the Leadership Practices Inventory (LPI; Posner & Kouzes, 1988). This chapter examines the LPI through a critical lens, encouraging participants to reflect on the importance of context in understanding the behaviors that lead to effective leadership. Individuals will examine the inventory's history and foundational creation in modern, Westernized business and nonprofit organizations and how that context both informs and limits its use as a leadership development tool. The curriculum will subsequently describe how the LPI can be expanded and reconstructed with regard to diverse cultures and identities, especially examining the way cultural differences and societal privilege can weaken the validity of the LPI as a peer assessment tool. Participants will be challenged to examine their own values, behaviors, and goals for leadership development using the LPI, as well as privileges that may be inherent within them that influence understandings of leadership.

First, participants will be provided with two short excerpts—one adapted from Machiavelli's *The Prince* (1997) and one from Heider's *The Tao of Leadership* (1985)—that describe *effective leadership*. Each represents different values and contexts underlying suggested behaviors. Participants will then be asked to describe what effective leadership might look like in the context of the LPI practices using these guides within a short case study. Then, the facilitator will engage the participants in a discussion that compares and contrasts the behaviors listed. The first section should end with the facilitator describing the initial research context within which the LPI's authors worked in building their model with a short discussion about how this context both informs and limits the findings that were used in creating it.

Second, participants will examine cultural dimensions of leadership values and behaviors described in the Global Leadership and Organizational Behavior Effectiveness (GLOBE) study (House, Hanges, Javidan, Dorfman, & Gupta, 2004). Building on their discussion from the first section, participants will identify good practices for leadership-oriented behavior across each of these dimensions as well as how their identities as leaders can be expressed within the context of the LPI descriptors.

> Chapter Framework

This chapter is largely informed by initial studies conducted by Hofstede (1983) that examined cultural differences in management and decision making in organizations, and subsequent leadership-oriented research resulting from the GLOBE study (House et al., 2004). Hofstede initially categorized how cultural values inform our understanding of effective behavior in influencing others. This research resulted in a series of dimensions (e.g., power distance, uncertainty avoidance, individualism, long-term orientation) that govern cultural beliefs about how power should be exercised and accepted within a society. The GLOBE study emerged later and delineated which values and beliefs concerning effective leadership are most practiced across and within 62 separate international cultures. Both studies explicitly described the practice of leadership as culturally bound where *effective* leadership behavior is rooted in the values of a culture (Hofstede, 1983; House et al., 2004). This chapter examines the LPI and the implicit beliefs regarding effective leadership on which it is founded from a critical perspective.

> Curriculum Plan

The first session of the curriculum asks participants to examine the foundational roles that values and context play in determining *good* leadership behaviors, which is the focus of the five practices within the LPI. Participants are split into two groups: One is given an excerpt from *The Prince* and the other an excerpt from *The Tao of Leadership*. Each group will define the values of an effective leader implied by the readings. Then, based on these values, they will discern what describes good behavior within each of the five leadership practices. After each group has created their list of values and behaviors, they will come together to compare and contrast their lists highlighting how differences in values can lead to differences in behaviors across each practice. At the end of discussion, the facilitator should reveal the authors, writings, and historical contexts from which the excerpts were adapted. The session will end with a summary of the context in which the initial research was conducted to create the LPI and a discussion of how this context may have informed the makeup and description of each practice.

The second session begins with a short description of the GLOBE study and the nine dimensions of leadership behaviors informed by cultural values. After examining these dimensions and describing effective behaviors at the extreme ends of each dimension, participants will create a fictional LPI observer-assessment of an individual from the perspective of a peer who occupies the other end of each dimension (e.g., a highly individualistic person assessing the effectiveness of a collectivistic leader). Participants will also discuss the implicit values informing each dimension in the United States and how these values may affect one's perceptions of effectiveness of leaders who behave differently based on occupying different social locations along cultural spectrums. This curriculum is designed for 8 to 15 participants in approximately 105 to 120 minutes. However, larger groups can be accommodated by splitting into smaller groups during times of discussion or through assistance from additional facilitators.

❯ Activity 1—Leadership Readings

Participants will begin to examine the significance of context and values in determining how good (i.e., effective) leadership is described.

Learning Outcomes

- Examine perceptions of successful LPI behaviors in two separate contexts.
- Compare and contrast selected values espoused within *The Prince* and *The Tao of Leadership*.
- Reflect on the values on which perceptions of successful leadership behaviors rest.

Setting Up the Activity

Group Size: Open to any size group

Time: 25 minutes (15 minutes in small groups; 10 minutes of large-group discussion)

Methods: Assignment, group discussion

Materials: Copies of "Excerpt 1," "Excerpt 2," and "Excerpt Reflection" for each participant, flip chart paper or whiteboards/chalkboard, markers/chalk

Variations: Size of group can be increased depending on the number of facilitators on hand to help groups join together for intergroup "Compare/Contrast" discussions.

Directions

1. If participants are not already arranged, split them into small groups of four to eight people.
2. Assign each group one of the two reading excerpts (*The Prince* or *The Tao of Leadership*) and ensure that each participant has a copy of their assigned excerpt and a reflection handout ("Excerpt Reflection"). Note that you will want to omit the "Handout References" section that appears at the bottom of the handouts when you initially provide them to participants because they reveal the context of the writing.
3. Provide 15 minutes of group time for participants to (1) read their assigned excerpt, (2) individually spend up to 3 minutes

jotting down notes on the "Excerpt Reflection," and (3) discuss and complete the reflection as a group. You may wish to offer suggestions as necessary.

4. Once time has elapsed, join each small group with another group that was assigned the complementary reading. Ensure participants receive a copy of the reading they were not initially assigned. Provide these larger groups with 2 to 3 minutes to silently read their new excerpt. After time has elapsed or most individuals have completed the reading, share with the larger groups that their job is now to compare and contrast the behaviors each group came up with using a sheet of flip chart paper to summarize responses.

5. After 8 minutes of discussion, lead a 2-minute summarizing discussion that includes sharing the origin of each reading. Consider sharing the following:

- The Prince *was written by a counselor to the kings of Florence, Italy, in the 1400s and is a treatise on how to successfully govern—and remain in power—in that region during that time period.*

- The Tao of Leadership *was written by an American psychiatrist focused on alternative education practices in response to rising standardization in the 1980s.*

  Highlight the degree to which one's values serve as a foundation for what one chooses as *exemplary* leadership behaviors. Even within the constraints of an LPI category, significant variance exists related to what successful leaders do.

Debriefing Notes

Participants new to studying leadership might struggle to determine specific behaviors and values stemming from their assigned reading. You might need to ask more concrete questions to help facilitate their thinking (e.g., *Given what this author has said about valuing security while avoiding follower hate, how might they suggest leaders enable others to act?*).

Facilitator Notes

The Prince excerpt is adapted from the original text to increase relevancy to a broader audience. It comes from Chapter 20 of the book, which emphasizes building fortresses where princes could focus their power. The reading from *The Tao of Leadership* is an exact copy.

> Activity 2—Examining the Birth of the LPI

Participants will begin to reflect on aspects of privileged viewpoints taken into consideration during the construction of the LPI.

Learning Outcomes

- Understand the initial research utilized to create the LPI.
- Critically reflect on the representativeness of the LPI research sample.
- Examine how certain behaviors and leadership constructs may have been privileged or marginalized during the construction of the assessment tool.

Setting Up the Activity

Group Size: Open to any size group

Time: 10 minutes

Methods: Group discussion, presentation, self-reflection

Materials:"Birth of the LPI" handout (enough copies for each participant)

Multimedia: Show the LPI website and particularly the research page (optional) *The Leadership Challenge* (www .leadershipchallenge.com/research.aspx).

Variations: For groups larger than 15–20, split into smaller sets of at most 15–20.

Directions

1. Review the "Birth of the LPI" document paying special attention to the "Initial Data Collection" and "Creating the LPI" sections.

2. Provide participants with 2 to 3 minutes to individually reflect in writing in response to the questions provided within the handout.

3. Facilitate a short discussion within the group guided by the questions from the "Birth of the LPI" document. Start by asking individuals to share their thoughts and responses for Question 1 and help the group to synthesize their perspectives. After a few minutes, use the same process for Questions 2 and 3. Ensure that ample time is spent on Question 3, which focuses on practical reasons to critically examine the LPI from a cultural perspective. Depending on the comfort and knowledge level of participants, you should be prepared to raise the following questions to stimulate discussion:

   - Within Question 1: *How might working for a not-for-profit service agency be different from working for a large corporation? Or managing a church? Or coaching a little league team? Or guiding a social justice organization? How might the leadership behaviors necessary for success within these types of organizations differ?*

   - Within Question 2: *What do you think may be differences in the values of an organization like Verizon and a small, family-owned, local business? Or a community public library?* Note: If participants are unfamiliar with Verizon, ask the group to identify a larger organization they are familiar with for comparison.

   - Within Question 3: *Which organizations do you think were most represented by participants of management development seminars? Why? How do you think this type of representation may have affected how those participants (and the follow-up surveying of American MBA students) think about and describe effective leadership in their organizations?*

- Concluding Questions: *Given what we've discussed, how might the very development of the LPI result in biased perspectives? How might the dominance of certain organizational types privilege perspectives on leadership? Thinking more critically, consider who at the time, as it relates to social identity, was likely most represented in the research samples? How might this influence perspectives and practices of leadership that emerged in the study?*

Debriefing Notes

Depending on the statistical expertise of participants, it might be important to reinforce that just because *all* types of people were not represented within the initial study, it does not necessarily mean that the LPI is completely invalid as a measure of behavior—only that it might be placing a bias on the types of behavior on which it focuses. An important point for the group to consider is how the initial version of the LPI may have resulted in a different set of overarching themes than the current five practices if a broader representation of society were included.

Facilitator Notes

It is not within the scope of this activity to explain or discuss in great detail the statistical analysis required for psychometric survey building. If participants with some statistical training are interested in using the session to discuss this process, ensure the group is focused simply on the populations utilized for the initial survey construction.

› Activity 3—GLOBE Cultural Dimensions

Participants will learn about the nine cultural dimensions described within the GLOBE study, which are significant for understanding the importance of culture in describing good leadership behaviors.

Learning Outcomes

- Understand the nine dimensions of culture relevant to the practice of leadership described within the GLOBE study.
- Reflect on how leaders might define successful leader behaviors differently at opposite extremes within each dimension.
- Recognize how the national culture of the United States compares to other national cultures.

Setting Up the Activity

Group Size: Optimal size is 15–20 participants.

Time: 30 minutes

Methods: Activity, discussion, presentation

Materials: "Introduction to the GLOBE Study," "U.S. Scores on GLOBE," and "Key Points of the GLOBE Study" handouts

Variations: With more participants, allow additional time for small groups to discuss responses on the GLOBE handout prior to a large group discussion.

Directions

1. Begin by explaining that the GLOBE study is an international collaboration designed to investigate how culture is related to societal, organizational, and leader effectiveness.
2. Distribute the "Introduction to the GLOBE Study" handout and explain the nine cultural dimensions that have emerged as factors in defining how effective leader behaviors are described within a particular culture.
3. Either individually (for more advanced groups) or in small groups of three to four participants (for less advanced groups), invite participants to take 10 minutes to respond to the directions listed at the bottom of the document, which ask them to describe leader behaviors at each extreme of each dimension.
4. On the last page, invite them to consider the national culture of the United States, and take 2 minutes to hypothesize where

they believe the United States falls on each continuum. They can do this by placing an "X" along each line and noting why they chose their placements.

5. Once the handout is completed, distribute the "U.S. Scores on GLOBE" handout, which describes summary findings related to the United States.

6. Engage the larger group in a short (5 minutes) discussion to help participants summarize the salient differences between behaviors at each extreme and at different points within the spectrum of each cultural value. A key point to consider is that effective leadership behavior is often defined by the values of the culture in which the behavior is embedded, and that these values can shift from culture to culture. If you are newer to the GLOBE study, refer to and/or distribute the "Key Points of the GLOBE Study" handout.

Facilitator Notes

This activity is designed to summarize the GLOBE study and prepare participants for thinking about how cultural values place expectations on ideal leader behaviors. It is less important that participants understand the fine details of each cultural dimension. Although it is not the central focus of the discussion, you might help participants begin to think about the GLOBE study in the context of the LPI by occasionally asking questions such as this: *How might a low-assertiveness culture react to a leader who has been taught to Challenge the Process?*

> Activity 4—LPI Fictional Observer Assessment

Participants will (1) attempt to summarize how a peer might rate a leader within the Observer Assessment portion of the LPI in a setting where the two do not share similar cultural values with respect to the GLOBE study; (2) summarize privileged LPI behaviors within contemporary society; and (3) begin to define their preferred leadership behaviors.

Learning Outcomes

- Recognize how cultural values inform the perceived effectiveness of leadership behaviors.
- Reflect on the types of leadership behaviors privileged in contemporary society.
- Create a list of preferred LPI-oriented leadership behaviors.

Setting Up the Activity

Group Size: Optimal size is 15–20 participants.

Time: 40 minutes

Methods: Activity, discussion

Materials: "Peer Performance Evaluation" handout for each participant. If you would like to make U.S. culture a proxy for *contemporary society*, use the "U.S. Scores on GLOBE" handout for this activity.

Variations: With more participants, allow more time to get into small groups to discuss responses.

Directions

1. Distribute "Peer Performance Evaluation" handouts, along with LPI and/or GLOBE summary documents if deemed necessary.

2. Explain that all participants are members of a fictional culture that is *high* in power distance, assertiveness, and performance orientation, and *low* in institutional collectivism and in-group collectivism. This fictional culture:
   - Places a high value on leaders who are comfortable confronting others both inside and outside of their group with whom they disagree, and who act as if they are separate from and above most other group members.

- Emphasizes goal achievement as a central aspect of how one spends one's time and therefore places a low value on allocating resources equally, instead believing that those who work the hardest and achieve the most should get the most resources, regardless of their background or seniority within a group.

3. You might ask the group one to two questions to ensure understanding of this fictional culture. For example, you might invite participants to consider the mirror image of that culture: one in which leaders do not act assertively, are not separate from followers, treat them with fairness and kindness, and place a high value on equal sharing of resources and showing group pride.

4. Direct participants to the "Peer Performance Evaluation" document, and invite them to complete the first page for a hypothetical member of the second culture (keeping in mind that they are a member of the first culture).

5. After 10 minutes, facilitate a group discussion asking individuals to share their responses and reasoning behind their evaluations.

6. Based on their discussion, invite the group to complete the second page, where they rate LPI behaviors within each of the five leadership practices that might be privileged in contemporary society (you could use the "U.S. Scores on GLOBE" document referenced earlier as a proxy if you wish).

7. After 10 minutes, facilitate a group discussion asking participants to share their responses and reasoning behind their evaluations.

8. Direct participants' attention to the third page of the "Peer Performance Evaluation" document, which invites them to list LPI behaviors that would be a fit for them personally given their values and background. If participants have been working in small groups up until this point, it is important that they complete this part individually.

9. After 5 to 10 minutes of individual reflection, invite participants to discuss their responses with a partner. After 10 minutes of pair-and-share discussion, invite three to four participants to share in the larger group to help summarize. Remind the group to consider the following: *LPI behaviors are contextual; they are based on cultural and individual values; each leader must decide what behaviors within each of the practices are the best fit for them.*

› Conclusion

In each activity within this curriculum, participants critically engage with the LPI to consider how it can privilege specific behaviors. In particular, participants consider the significance of context and culture in defining successful LPI behaviors as well as leadership behaviors more broadly. The first half of the curriculum focuses on organizational context whereas the second half emphasizes culture. The curriculum ends with helping participants reconstruct the LPI and their own preferred leadership behaviors.

Handout 4.1: Excerpt 1

It has been the custom of new leaders, in order to lead with a greater sense of influence, to create distance and security between themselves and their followers. This allows them the ability to stabilize their role as a leader, especially against those who do not believe they should be in such a position.

This behavior has worked well in the past, but can also harm new leaders by sowing discontent among followers, especially within those who were not to be feared in the first place. Your security will not save you if your followers hate you. However, leaders never know when those who seek to take their influence away will arise.

Therefore, it would be best and safest for leaders to avoid having followers hate them, while at the same time building a sense of security that will leave them in power in the event of disagreement.

Adapted from: Machiavelli, N. (1997). *The prince.* New Haven, CT: Yale University Press.

Handout 4.2: Excerpt 2

The wise leader is like water.

Consider water: water cleanses and refreshes all creatures without distinction and without judgment; water freely and fearlessly goes deep beneath the surface of things; water is fluid and responsive; water follows the law freely.

Consider the leader: the leader works in any setting without complaint, with any person or issue that comes on the floor; the leader acts so that all will benefit and serves well regardless of the rate of pay; the leader speaks simply and honestly and intervenes in order to shed light and create harmony.

From watching the movements of water, the leader has learned that in action, timing is everything.

Like water, the leader is yielding. Because the leader does not push, the group does not resent or resist.

(Heider, 1985, p. 15)

Heider, J. (1985). *The Tao of leadership: Leadership strategies for a new age*. New York: Bantam Books.

Handout 4.3: Excerpt Reflection

How might your assigned author describe good leadership behaviors in the context of the five leadership practices within the LPI?

1. Model the Way

   _____

   _____

   _____

2. Inspire a Shared Vision

   _____

   _____

   _____

3. Challenge the Process

   _____

   _____

   _____

4. Enable Others to Act

   _____

   _____

   _____

5. Encourage the Heart

   _____

   _____

   _____

Given these behaviors and your assigned reading, what values do you think are found in the author's writing?

_____

_____

_____

Handout 4.4: Birth of the LPI

Initial Data Collection

- Surveyed hundreds of managers participating in management development seminars
- Sampled managers from companies that were either publicly or privately owned
- Conducted 38 follow-up interviews of middle- to senior-level managers in companies

Results

1. Model the Way
   - Set the example.
   - Plan small wins.
2. Inspire a Shared Vision
   - Envision the future.
   - Enlist the support of others.
3. Challenge the Process
   - Search for opportunities.
   - Experiment and take risks.
4. Enable Others to Act
   - Foster collaboration.
   - Strengthen others.
5. Encourage the Heart
   - Recognize contributions.
   - Celebrate accomplishments.

Creating the LPI

- The LPI and its survey items were initially created using thematic analysis from the interviews and qualitative surveys.
- The LPI was then tested and validated using responses from MBA students in the United States.
- Although the themes have never changed, individual survey items were modified as a result of tests with MBA students; subsequent testing occurred with thousands of managers and their subordinates participating in management development seminars conducted by the authors.

Questions to Consider

1. How might this context have informed the types of behaviors specified within each practice? Be sure to explain your reasoning.

_____

_____

_____

2. What types of values and leadership behaviors may be privileged given this context?

_____

_____

_____

3. What types of leaders may have been left out of the original analysis? How might this have affected the authors' analysis?

_____

_____

_____

Posner, B. Z., & Kouzes, J. M. (1988). Development and validation of the Leadership Practices Inventory. *Educational and Psychological Measurement, 48,* 483–496.

Handout 4.5: Introduction to the GLOBE Study

The Global Leadership and Organizational Effectiveness (GLOBE) study was initiated to focus on the role of culture in defining societal, organizational, and leader effectiveness. The research led to the creation of nine dimensions of culture that affect how people within that culture define leadership effectiveness.

Nine Dimension of Culture

1. *Power Distance*: The degree to which members of a collective expect power to be distributed equally
2. *Uncertainty Avoidance*: The extent to which a group relies on rules, processes, and leader proclamations to avoid unpredictability
3. *Humane Orientation*: The degree to which the group encourages its members to be fair, altruistic, and caring toward others
4. *Institutional Collectivism*: The extent to which the group encourages the collective distribution of resources
5. *In-Group Collectivism*: The degree to which the group encourages its members to display group pride and cohesiveness
6. *Assertiveness*: The degree to which group members are expected to be confrontational with other members
7. *Gender Egalitarianism*: The degree to which the group minimizes gender inequality
8. *Future Orientation:* The extent to which leaders should focus on delaying gratification while investing in the future
9. *Performance Orientation*: The degree to which leaders are expected to hold individuals accountable to performance improvement and quality

HOW MIGHT A LEADER ACT AT EACH END OF THE SPECTRUM?

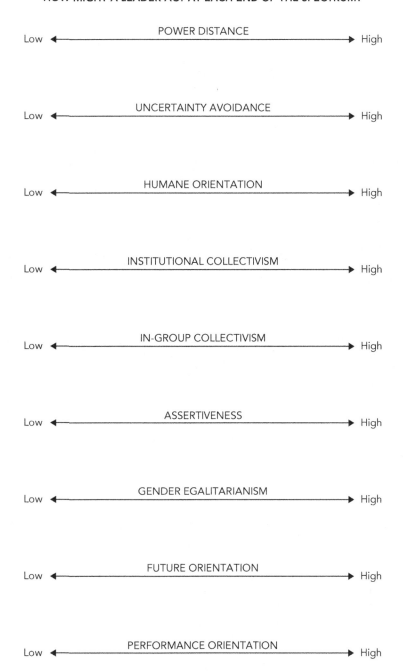

Along each dimension, where would you place the dominant culture(s) in the United States? Place an X along each line corresponding to the dimensions above.

Please explain the location of each X:

- Power Distance: _____

  _____

- Uncertainty Avoidance: _____

  _____

- Humane Orientation: _____

  _____

- Institutional Collectivism: _____

  _____

- In-Group Collectivism: _____

  _____

- Assertiveness: _____

  _____

- Gender Egalitarianism: _____

  _____

- Future Orientation: _____

  _____

- Performance Orientation: _____

  _____

House, R. J., Hanges, P. J., Javidan, M., Dorfman, P. W., & Gupta, V. (2004). *Culture, leadership, and organizations: The GLOBE study of 62 societies.* Thousand Oaks, CA: SAGE Publications.

Handout 4.6: Key Points of the GLOBE Study

- For cultures that value high *Power Distance*, followers expect leaders to be comfortable exercising power and holding themselves above followers. Low power distance cultures value leaders being seen in much the same way as followers but with an additional title. Cultures in the middle might accept leaders as needing to be held to different standards than followers but believe the same rule of law governs both groups.

- For cultures high in *Uncertainty Avoidance*, followers would expect leaders to have answers during times of discomfort or transition, while cultures on the lower end of the extreme may believe leaders with all the answers should not be trusted. Cultures in the middle might look up to leaders with a unique vision but expect followers to contribute to and improve it.

- Cultures high in *Humane Orientation* might expect leaders to spend time providing time and attention to members who are perceived as different from the majority, while cultures low in such orientation would likely expect leaders to expel such members. Within cultures outside of the extremes, leaders may be expected to provide members in need of support more of it, but still be expected to reinforce relatively rigid expectations for behavior and performance.

- High *Institutional Collectivism* societies expect their leaders to ensure all members receive the same resources, while societies low in this area would expect leaders to spend more time, energy, and resources on members that are deemed the most valuable. Societies somewhere in the middle might expect their leaders to provide all members a baseline of resource support while providing high-achieving members with more than the rest.

- Cultures high in *In-Group Collectivism* likely expect their leaders to be spokespeople for their organization and act with the belief that it is more important than others. Cultures low in this area might react to leaders that act in such a way as negatively biased and myopic. Cultures not in either extreme might expect their leaders to act as public supporters of their organizations while treating others with respect and fairness.

- Cultures high in *Assertiveness* might expect their leaders to overcome opposition—both from inside and outside the group—with a strong personality, while those low in this area would expect their leaders to consistently express politeness, patience, and respect toward those who object to the leader. Cultures somewhere in the middle might admire leaders who are adaptable in their short-term goals based on group opinion while remaining respectfully open about their long-term goals.

- Cultures high in *Gender Egalitarianism* might desire leaders who not only are balanced in terms of percentages from each gender, but also openly support the need for such balance, whereas those low in this area desire leaders who believe in strict gender-based roles. Cultures somewhere in the middle may expect their leaders to conform to traditional expectations while providing means for women to advance.

- Societies that value *Future Orientation* expect their leaders to be open about causing short-term pain for long-term gain, while societies low in this area look to leaders who provide quick-fix solutions to alleviate current discomfort. Societies in the middle might look to leaders who are work to advance long-term goals while recognizing that current pain cannot completely be ignored.

- Cultures that are high in *Performance Orientation* expect their leaders to serve as accountability experts seeking to reward and punish members based on achievement levels, while cultures low in this area might expect their leaders to treat everyone equally regardless of such achievement. Cultures not in either extreme might expect their leaders to provide extra support for underachieving members, while also providing special recognition to highly successful members.

House, R. J., Hanges, P. J., Javidan, M., Dorfman, P. W., & Gupta, V. (2004). *Culture, leadership, and organizations: The GLOBE study of 62 societies.* Thousand Oaks, CA: SAGE Publications.

Handout 4.7: U.S. Scores on GLOBE

Power Distance

U.S. culture scores <u>very low</u> in both valuing and practicing power distance between leaders and followers.

Uncertainty Avoidance

The United States scores <u>about average</u> compared to many countries on the degree to which leaders should provide answers at all times for their followers.

Humane Orientation

People in the United States believe leaders should be humane toward their followers to a <u>slightly greater extent</u> than most nations.

Institutional Collectivism

People in the United States score <u>below average</u> in the degree to which they believe resources should be distributed collectively.

In-Group Collectivism

The United States scores <u>relatively low</u> on the degree to which people believe group members should explicitly show in-group pride.

Assertiveness

People in the United States believe leaders should be <u>more assertive</u> than people in many other countries believe their leaders should be.

Gender Egalitarianism

The United States scores <u>highest</u> among all nations in believing in gender egalitarianism but falls far lower in comparison with the scores of other industrialized nations when it comes to practicing it.

Future Orientation

The United States scores <u>slightly above average</u> in the degree to which leaders are expected to plan and sacrifice for the future.

Performance Orientation

The United States scores <u>about average</u> in the degree to which they believe leaders should be held accountable to achieve.

House, R. J., Hanges, P. J., Javidan, M., Dorfman, P. W., & Gupta, V. (2004). *Culture, leadership, and organizations: The GLOBE study of 62 societies.* Thousand Oaks, CA: SAGE Publications.

Handout 4.8: Peer Performance Evaluation

Imagine you are part of a culture that would score *high* on power distance, assertiveness, and performance orientation, and *low* on institutional collectivism and in-group collectivism. How might you evaluate the behaviors of someone scoring on opposite ends of each spectrum (someone *low* on power distance, assertiveness, and performance orientation, and *high* on institutional collectivism and in-group collectivism) with regard to the LPI?

1. Modeling the Way

_____

_____

_____

Please explain your reasoning:

_____

_____

_____

2. Inspiring a Shared Vision

_____

_____

_____

Please explain your reasoning:

_____

_____

_____

3. Challenge the Process

_____

_____

_____

Please explain your reasoning:

_____

_____

_____

4. Enable Others to Act

_____

_____

_____

Please explain your reasoning:

_____

_____

_____

5. Encouraging the Heart

_____

_____

_____

Please explain your reasoning:

_____

_____

_____

Given the dominant culture(s) you evaluated relative to the GLOBE, what types of behaviors do you believe are privileged within the scoring of the LPI within contemporary society?

1. Modeling the Way

_____

_____

Please explain your reasoning:

_____

_____

2. Inspiring a Shared Vision

_____

_____

Please explain your reasoning:

_____

_____

3. Challenge the Process

_____

_____

Please explain your reasoning:

_____

_____

4. Enable Others to Act

_____

_____

Please explain your reasoning:

_____

_____

5. Encouraging the Heart

_____

_____

Please explain your reasoning:

_____

_____

Given your own values and background, what types of behaviors are a fit for you within the LPI model?

1. Modeling the Way

_____

_____

Please explain your reasoning:

_____

_____

2. Inspiring a Shared Vision

_____

_____

Please explain your reasoning:

_____

_____

3. Challenging the Process

_____

_____

Please explain your reasoning:

_____

_____

4. Enabling Others to Act

_____

_____

Please explain your reasoning:

_____

_____

5. Encouraging the Heart

_____

_____

Please explain your reasoning:

_____

_____

4B: Strengths-Based Leadership Through a Critical Lens: Valuing Social Identity and Power Dynamics in Strengths Facilitation

Amy C. Barnes

Objectives/Goals of Chapter

- Be able to challenge trait-based interpretation of strengths by exploring talents and strengths beyond participants' "top 5."

- Reflect on personal strength development to emphasize how strengths are a combination of innate ability, personal identity, and sociocultural influence.

- Understand the impact of social identity and systems of power and oppression on the use and application of strengths-based leadership approaches.

Critical Concepts: *agency, microaggressions, oppression, power, privilege, stereotype threat*

Chapter Overview

Since 2002, strengths assessments have become a common tool for helping learners gain a greater understanding of themselves as participants, leaders, and professionals. This is due in part to research and marketing efforts by the Gallup Organization and the creation of the StrengthsQuest program, which utilizes the StrengthsFinder instrument to help learners identify their top 5 strengths. Gallup's introduction of StrengthsQuest included a textbook, website, college educator training, and facilitator resources designed for use with college participants. This allowed for easy adoption of the assessment. At the same time, Gallup marketed StrengthsFinder to companies worldwide such as Best Buy, Target, and Nationwide, which began to use the tool in employee development. This reinforced the use of strengths-based approaches to personal and leadership development for participants preparing to enter or already in the workforce.

Strengths-based leadership development is a positive, appreciative approach to organizational dynamics and inter-group relations that emphasizes an understanding of both individual strengths and the strengths of others. Introducing this approach to participants has many benefits for leadership development, allowing participants to gain self-awareness and learn to appreciate how others might approach tasks in a group setting (Lopez & Louis, 2009). Additionally, strengths development requires that participants adopt a growth mind-set (i.e., the belief that your most basic abilities can be developed through hard work and dedication; Dweck, 2007).

Although there are many benefits to introducing participants to strengths-based development, the potential challenge of using an instrument like the Gallup StrengthsFinder is ensuring participants understand the complexity of strengths development beyond the brief assessment results. Significant concerns involve the misinterpretation by participants that their strengths are equivalent to traits or characteristics that are fixed parts of their personalities (especially if they are operating with a fixed mind-set or are developmentally more dualistic) as well as the danger of labeling others with negative perceptions or stereotypes associated with various strengths. For example, someone with Achiever as a strength might get labeled as a workaholic when, as defined by Gallup, an Achiever is someone who sets daily goals and has a constant drive for achievement (Clifton, Anderson, & Schreiner, 2001). In addition, from a training standpoint, participants are usually not asked to consider the implications of power dynamics, the effects of privilege and oppression, or how strengths definitions may be associated with negative stereotypes associated with social location. What may be lacking from most applications of StrengthsFinder or other strength-based assessments is a critical analysis of the instrument's use, the application of critical perspectives to strengths-based initiatives and programming, and/or current research efforts that incorporate these critical concepts.

> Chapter Framework

This chapter promotes a critical analysis of strengths-based leadership development and identifies activities, guided reflections, and small group discussions to help participants become more aware of the complexity of strengths development including the impact that social identity, privilege, and dominant structures can have on the way that individuals behave in group environments. Issues of structural domination and delimited agency (i.e., when an individual is in an environment where they feel marginalized) are likely not considered when strengths-based approaches are incorporated into leadership development curriculum. Structural domination is the consideration that there are historical, enduring patterns of thinking and behavior that favor the practices and rules associated with dominant groups (Ladson-Billings, 1998). Additionally, the application of a framework like critical race theory to the lens of strengths-based leadership allows facilitators to acknowledge that most environments where leadership is enacted are contexts where whiteness is positioned as normative and where everyone in that context is categorized based on that normative assumption (Ladson-Billings, 1998).

The basic premise of critical race theory is that racism is embedded in U.S. society, and because it is so pervasive, it is not always noticeable, especially in environments that are predominantly White. Critical race theorists expose instances of covert racism and microaggressions that exists in everyday situations (Ladson-Billings, 1998). In congress with the work of critical race theory, other critical and postmodern frameworks (e.g., multiple feminisms, queer theory, intersectionality, The Frankfurt School of critical social theory, Marxism) address the unique, yet entangled, forms of structural domination connected to social group memberships (e.g., ability, gender, religion, social class) including their manifestation in everyday lived experience (Dugan, 2017). The question then becomes, can participants from marginalized identities actively utilize their strengths in all contexts without encountering prejudice or stereotyping? Do manifestations of systemic oppression and normativity require those with marginalized identities to temper their natural talents and applications to leadership to navigate dominant environments? How can systems be restructured to redress these issues?

In addition to constraints imposed by environments where participants may encounter bias, it is important to consider that, historically, trait-based approaches to leadership development favored specific traits for leaders that were often derived from characteristics of White, Christian, cisgender, male, wealthy, able-bodied people in positions of power (Dugan, 2017). Even with the full list of possible strengths an individual can receive as results from the StrengthsFinder assessment, some of the strengths are likely more valued from a dominant cultural perspective by groups in power as effective leadership characteristics. It is important that participants do not walk away from a strengths-based curriculum thinking that they have the "right" strengths or the "wrong" strengths based on stereotypes typically attributed to leaders. It is also important that facilitators spend ample time helping participants feel that their strengths are valued within any given context. At the same time, this curriculum aims to make participants aware of how power dynamics or privilege may communicate to individuals from marginalized groups that their strengths are less valued. Throughout this chapter, participants are encouraged to consider ways in which structural domination often requires individuals to mask or alter the expression of strengths as a means to navigate dominant structures and belief systems.

> Curriculum Plan

The following curriculum connects strengths-based leadership to critical perspectives and provides participants with the opportunity to challenge dominant paradigms. Through critical self-reflection, small group discussions, and short case-study scenarios, participants will be challenged to consider the complexity of strengths development. In keeping with the spirit of the main text and the concept of reconstruction, this curriculum is designed to capitalize on the positive, affirming nature of strengths-based development while also considering context and the importance of understanding how power dynamics and dominant structures may be limiting for applying strengths in leadership processes.

This curriculum is designed to be implemented in one or two sessions, each ranging from 2- to 3-hours in length. However, it is assumed that participants have already had a basic introduction to their Gallup StrengthsQuest results and have a general understanding of how they tend to behave using their strengths in team settings. This can be accomplished through a 2- to 3-hour introductory strengths workshop where participants are informed about the basic philosophy of a strengths approach and are allowed time to process their results.

Note that it is essential that you are sufficiently trained to facilitate conversations around strengths-development if you are using the actual assessment tool. Gallup offers online education for educators who want to utilize strengths with participants. Visit the Gallup/StrengthsQuest website for more information (www .strengthsquest.com/home.aspx). Beyond official training through Gallup, it is recommended that you gain a strong understanding of how Gallup defines each of the 34 strengths, how the strengths interact with each other, and the ways in which leadership and power affect strength execution and development. There is a far greater chance that participants will leave a strengths workshop with the notion that strengths are fixed parts of their personalities (rather than behaviors that can be developed) if facilitators are not trained to process results beyond general awareness.

> Activity 1—Strengths Development Timeline

Through this activity, participants examine their strengths development, explore opportunities to extend this development through personal goal setting, and begin to view strengths development through a critical perspective. This lesson incorporates a short introductory discussion on the difference between a fixed and a growth mind-set, which is used to illuminate strengths as behaviors that can be continually improved. Participants are also challenged to consider how their social identities or societal systems of oppression and privilege may hinder or enhance the development of their strengths. Note that this activity utilizes results from the StrengthsFinder assessment (top 5 signature themes) but also asks participants to identify talents/strengths beyond those results. Additionally, this activity assumes that participants have already participated in an exploration of social location. In other words, this activity will ask participants to reflect on their strengths using a lens of identity. They should be able to articulate the identities that are most salient to them before starting this activity.

Learning Outcomes

- Understand the difference between fixed mind-set and growth mind-set.
- Identify how personal strengths develop over the course of life (incorporating past experiences, prior acquired skills and knowledge, and opportunities that enabled strengths development).
- Recognize how social location and oppressive structures affect strengths development.

Setting Up the Activity

Group Size: Open to any size group

Time: 90 minutes–2 hours

Training Method: Self-reflection, small group processing

Materials: Large paper/newsprint, writing utensils, computer/laptop, projector/screen, Internet

Multimedia: Conduct an Internet search for a graphic or video clip explaining the concept of *growth mind-set*. A quick search should generate several options.

Variation: Have participants share in pairs versus small groups to adjust the length of activity.

Directions

1. Begin the lesson with a quick overview of fixed and growth mind-sets. Show the video that you identified to illustrate mind-sets and lead a short discussion with the large group on differences between the two concepts. Ask participants to reflect on how this might influence strengths development (i.e., strengths development requires a growth mind-set).

2. Pass out pens and paper or markers and newsprint and provide participants with step-by-step instructions for timeline creation:

   - *Draw a line on your paper to represent the journey of your life to date.*

   - *You will be plotting your strengths development on the timeline. You must also plot three to five talents/strengths that you have beyond the top 5 strengths provided by the Gallup Strengths-Quest assessment.* Including strengths beyond the top 5 allows participants to realize that the strengths provided as results from the assessment are just a snapshot of their overall strengths and emphasizes the idea that strengths are not fixed traits.

   - *Write your top strengths in the top right-hand corner of your paper.* Ask participants to include eight to ten of their top strengths (both those from Gallup and the additional talents/strengths they brainstormed).

   - On the timeline, ask participants to indicate all of the experiences and lessons in life to date where they can see these strengths developed. Explain that there are no restrictions to what they might include because this is for personal reflection and they are the best judges of their strengths development to date. Offer suggested categories (e.g., experiences, mentors, family dynamics, learning opportunities). Creativity is encouraged in this activity, so they should depict the timeline of their life however makes sense to them personally. Note: Some participants may identify painful experiences from their past for their timeline because challenges can influence strengths development. Although it can be helpful to see how positive growth was a result of challenges, participants should be reminded that even though the room is a brave space, they are not required to share publicly.

3. Once participants complete their timelines, ask them to find another section of their paper or flip their paper over for an additional task.

   - Ask participants to consider how they wish to further develop their strengths.

   - Participants should make a list for each strength that includes experiences or learning opportunities that they hope to explore for their strengths development in the future. This allows them to see that strengths development continues and reemphasizes the importance of a growth mind-set.

4. Once timelines are finished, ask participants to spend time in small groups or with a partner sharing their work. Encourage them to help each other see connections in their strengths development and brainstorm ways to encourage future development.

   - After sharing, ask the large group for overall reactions to the following questions: *What did you learn about your-self from this activity and from sharing in your small group or with your partner? How do your lived experiences and the opportunities you have had in your life influence your strengths development?*

   - In processing the above question prompts, try to help participants see the connections between the strengths they identified at the beginning of the activity and how socialization and life experience have played a role in the development of those strengths. At this point, you want participants to see the connection of strengths to past experiences and help them understand that strengths development has been a combination of innate talents they were born with *and* experiences that have shaped their development to date. It might be helpful to point out that some experiences were positive and some may have been more challenging.

5. Let participants know that you want them to have one last discussion in their small groups. Pass out the list of Gallup's 34 strengths and short descriptions. Allow time to review the full list of possible strengths they could have received in their results. Have them reflect back on their timelines to consider again how their strengths were developed and pose these questions: *Are there other strengths on the list of 34 that you feel could have been in your top 5? If so, is there anything about your background and development that may have influenced those strengths not being as high on your list?* Give participants 5 to 10 minutes to reflect and discuss in their groups.

6. Next, remind participants that a significant learning outcome for this lesson is to use a critical perspective to evaluate strengths-based approaches to leadership. Ask participants to reflect briefly as a group on how they feel their strengths development may have been hindered or encouraged by their social location. Use an example to illustrate this, such as "As a girl growing up, I was assertive and constantly told that I should stop being bossy. Without that continuous lesson in what was appropriate behavior, I may have developed Command as a strength." Or "As a man, I was taught the importance of success and achievement and that likely influenced my strengths development as I have three executing strengths in my top 5 results." Encourage participants to consider how their social identity may have put them in environments where their strengths were supported or where they may have felt their strengths were less valued as a result of their identity.

7. Following the small group discussion, ask participants to reflect individually for a few minutes on the following: *How did your prior experiences documented in your timeline along with the experiences documented in the timelines of others from your group shape strengths development? In what ways did you see social identity intersecting with strengths development (both for yourself and for others in your group)? What was most surprising to you? In your*

opinion, how does looking at strengths through a critical lens affect your prior understanding of your results? It may be helpful to have individuals write responses down to be used as a prewriting exercise for the reflective journal assignment proposed later.

8. Lead a large group discussion in which you ask volunteers to share some of their small group discussions and personal reflection responses. You may need to offer a variety of examples to help guide participant thinking.

9. If this activity is facilitated in a classroom or with an otherwise continuously convening group, you might consider including a reflective journal assignment due the next time the group meets in which participants respond to the following prompts: *Go back to your timeline and review what you brainstormed during the activity. What are your reactions to the overall experience of reflecting on your strengths development? After sharing with others, what else would you like to add to your timeline that you left off? How do you think your social identity affects your strengths development?*

Facilitator Notes

Note that this activity may be particularly challenging for participants from dominant social identities because they may only see the positive ways their strengths development was encouraged and supported during their lifetime. It is also important to consider risks associated with participants from marginalized identities feeling tokenized based on how this activity is facilitated. Avoid forced sharing or asking individuals to speak on behalf of their broader social identity groups. Moreover, it is important that as the facilitator you provide examples from your own lived experience to encourage discussion. If you can identify ways that privilege influences your personal strengths development or how stereotypes and oppression have hindered your strengths development, participants may feel more comfortable sharing personal examples.

› Activity 2—Applying a Critical Social Theory Lens to Strengths Scenarios

In this activity participants apply critical perspectives to a variety of case studies to examine how power and privilege allow or disallow individuals to operate authentically within their strengths. Participants identify and name sources of power that contribute to oppression in each scenario and explore how to disrupt problematic situations and behaviors.

Learning Outcomes

- Understand how power and privilege allow or disallow individuals to operate authentically within their strengths.
- Identify ways to disrupt or intervene in cases where power and privilege are at play.
- Consider ways leaders can create environments where a strengths-based leadership approach can also support and celebrate a diversity of social locations.

Setting Up the Activity

Group Size: 10–30 participants; larger groups may need additional facilitators.

Time: 45 minutes to 1 hour (contingent on how many scenarios are used)

Methods: Dialogue, facilitated activity, mini-case studies

Materials: A copy of "Strengths Scenarios Worksheet" handout for each participant.

Directions

1. Host a refresher conversation on applying critical perspectives (refer to Chapter 2 of the main text for an overview). Ask participants the following question:

   - *How can an everyday situation be viewed through a critical perspective?* If participants struggle here, the following are useful strategies:
     - *How might you identify the ways in which stocks of knowledge are informing dynamics?*
     - *To what extent are dominant ideologies at play? Do interactions and/or actions of individuals and groups reflect hegemonic norms?*
     - *How are the dimensions of social location, and in particular social identity and power, influencing what is occurring?*

2. Divide participants into small groups of three to four people. Offer each group a scenario handout, explaining that the objective is to read the scenario and answer the guiding questions at the top of the worksheet.

3. After 10 to 15 minutes of discussion about the scenarios, return to the large group and share responses to the discussion prompts on the handout.

   - Guide the large group conversation so participants understand how power and privilege allow or disallow individuals to operate authentically within their strengths, and explore appropriate ways to disrupt problematic situations and behaviors (encourage both support for individuals in the scenarios along with ways to enact change systemically to prevent similar situations from occurring in the future). Guiding questions might include these:
     - *When leadership is examined through a critical perspective it includes the adverse impact of power, privilege, and dominant voices. What examples did you see in the scenarios of power*

and privilege and how did that affect the people who were attempting to navigate those issues?

○ *How did stereotypes have an impact on the people in the scenario and their ability to lead authentically?*

○ *How can we affect change in our own communities to broaden the conversation around strengths-based leadership?*

Debriefing Notes

At the conclusion of the two activities, it is important to create connections for participants. Consider assigning a reflective journal activity or providing time for reflection and discussion. Questions that could be used include these:

- *How do dominant structures affect an individual's ability to enact leadership using strengths?*
- *How can you ensure that your personal strengths development will include consideration of power and privilege?*
- *Although strengths development is important to understanding personal leadership and how teams interact, what are the limitations to a strengths-based approach to leadership development based upon critical perspectives?*
- *How do critical perspectives provide a better understanding of how privilege and power dynamics affect strengths-based leadership?*

⟩ Conclusion

This chapter was designed to help facilitators begin to apply a critical perspective to strengths-based leadership by integrating opportunities for critical self-reflection, dialogue, and the processing of strengths-based leadership scenarios into leadership development curriculum. These activities go beyond the traditional facilitation that typically accompanies a strengths-based curriculum using the StrengthsFinder assessment. It is important to note, however, that StrengthsQuest is not the only strengths assessment or approach that can be utilized for strengths development. StrengthsQuest is the focus of this chapter because it is already widely used. Greater attention to positive psychology concepts as a whole, intentionally linked with the critical perspectives covered in this chapter, is recommended when developing a more complex strengths-based leadership development curriculum.

Ultimately, the hope for this chapter is that participants will gain greater self-knowledge about the development of their strengths from a critical perspective. By introducing participants to another layer of complexity around strengths development (i.e., the impact of power dynamics and dominant structures), they are able to see not only how their personal strengths development has been influenced, but also how lived experiences may be empowered or constrained by a more traditional strengths development approach.

Handout 4.9: Strengths Scenarios Worksheet

Use the following questions to guide your discussion of the scenarios:

What is happening in this scenario? Using critical perspectives, what factors are at play? How is power influencing the actions of the characters? Are the individuals in the scenario able to act authentically using their strengths? Assuming you are in this scenario, how could you disrupt problematic situations and behaviors? Note that your role is defined in each scenario by your own social identity as the reader.

Scenario 1

Levi is an experienced trial lawyer whose strengths are Woo, Communication, Empathy, Includer, and Restorative. He has an excellent reputation and was just hired by you, the managing partner of a large, prestigious law firm. New partners are placed in mentorship relationships with existing partners, and Levi is paired with your most successful partner, Harvey. Initially, Levi and Harvey correspond via email to exchange details about a high-profile case that Levi will prosecute. When Harvey and Levi finally meet in person, Levi notes that Harvey appears confused at the sight of his cochlear implants. As a person with severe hearing loss, Levi has implants that allow him to hear and process speech. Later that day, Levi receives an email from Harvey expressing concern that he does not think Levi is ready to take responsibility for the lead prosecution with his largest client. Harvey asks Levi to observe the case instead. As a result, Levi approaches you with his concern that Harvey is sidelining him based on perceptions of his ability status even though he was hired because of his exceptional trial record.

Considerations to guide discussion:

- The purpose of this scenario is to encourage dialogue about ableism.
- Participants may want to defend Harvey and offer perfectly logical explanations (PLEs) for his behavior. They also might think Levi is overreacting and should not have complained. Additionally, they may say that Levi likely has a speech impediment because of his cochlear implants and that this could affect his communication style.
- To fully deconstruct the situation, ensure all participants understand the power and privilege at play. You may need to state that cochlear implants indicate no lack of ability on Levi's part. Rather, Harvey made an assumption regarding Levi's ability.
- Point out to participants that Levi was hired because of his excellent reputation and ask the students to reflect on his top 5 strengths. You might ask the following questions to spark conversation on reconstruction: *How are his strengths indicative of his potential success? How are Levi's strengths potentially contributing to stereotypes that are being assumed? How do dominant structures and norms within this organization contribute to assumptions regarding Levi's ability to communicate?*

Scenario 2

Devon is an African American male who works as part of a predominantly White project team at a large insurance company. His top 5 strengths are Adaptability, Responsibility, Futuristic, Strategic, and Arranger. He is known around the office as someone who takes frequent breaks, who likes to have water cooler conversations about the company's future, and who appears to be distracted, as coworkers see ESPN on his computer screen during work hours. By nature of this reputation, a few of Devon's fellow team members report to their supervisor their concerns that he is not getting his work done and is lazy. You are Devon's supervisor and you have consistently evaluated Devon on his performance across a variety of tasks and scenarios, and you know that Devon actually excels in all areas of production. Additionally, he has mentioned feeling scrutinized by his colleagues for his unconventional work style. Based on his strengths, you also know that he has an acute ability to adapt and flex his time in a way to accomplish the task at hand for the benefit of the entire organization's vision. At a leadership team meeting, one of the other managers who is White brings up the observations of Devon's "laziness" as a concern. You are caught off guard, but need to respond.

Considerations to guide discussion:

- This is a scenario about racism and racial stereotypes.

- Participants may react to this scenario defensively and provide PLEs as to why Devon's coworkers are upset with him. They might reflect on what they know about professionalism and appropriate office culture and criticize Devon's behavior because it does not align with dominant White, Western business norms.

- To deconstruct this scenario, participants should understand that Devon is being singled out because his work style is different from the dominant culture. His coworkers who are critiquing his work are making assumptions and operating under racist stereotypes. You can also prompt this discussion if you feel that it will challenge students to think differently. Help participants consider how the scenario may have played out differently if it were a White male. *Would his peers have complained?*

- Participants should consider Devon's top 5 strengths and the fact that his performance evaluation reflects that he is highly capable and accomplished in his work. Point out that Devon's Adaptability strength is potentially being viewed negatively and his Responsibility strength is not being given enough weight in the critique by his colleagues. Here are several questions you could ask to spark conversation on reconstruction: *How do his strengths help him to be successful? How are his strengths potentially contributing to the racial stereotypes that are being assumed? In terms of organizational culture, how could Devon's work style be something to admire rather than to critique? If he is contributing to the overall goals of the organization, why does it matter how he gets his work done? How might you as the supervisor work to alter systemic racism and the implicit bias playing out in the scenario?*

Scenario 3

Elena is the CEO of a midsized nonprofit organization responsible for providing scholarships and educational training programs for low-income students who want to go to college. Her top 5 strengths are Analytical, Belief, Strategic, Maximizer, and Focus. She has earned a degree in organizational leadership and was appointed to this role unanimously by the board. They are pleased with her work so far in expanding the services of the foundation into the most financially needy and resource-starved areas in the state. The board decided to establish a new grant program that will be awarded to teachers based on the test scores of their participants—the higher the scores, the greater the dollar amount awarded. The board has asked Elena to promote the incentive grants to a group of local community leaders. Elena is strongly opposed to this program. She feels it won't serve participants well in the more disadvantaged areas of the community, including the low-income neighborhood where she grew up. She shares her concerns with one of the board members who she has grown to trust but feels that her feedback is dismissed as she is encouraged to redirect her energies into convincing the community leaders that this philanthropic gesture is for the best. Frustrated, she turns to you, her mentor, for advice.

Considerations to guide discussion:

- The focus of this scenario is classism, observed in Elena's frustration with a grant program that will benefit schools in neighborhoods with more resources.

- Participants may focus on meritocracy and may come from the perspective that all students have the same opportunity to do well on the tests. Participants may critique Elena and question her opinions because they are based on her personal experience/emotional connection to where they grew up rather than data. They may say she is overly sensitive because this is her neighborhood. Participants may identify sexism at play here as well (as her board is dismissive of her concerns and they may assume the board is predominantly male). Try to steer the conversation toward classism.

- For deconstruction, consider these questions: *Why is Elena's role as a CEO not valued in this discussion? Why is her background coming into question here? If she were from an affluent part of town, would the board have taken her concerns more seriously? Has she been allowed to change classes?* If the group is struggling, it might be appropriate to interrogate the power dynamics at play based upon her background coming from a lower socioeconomic class. *Why does she have less social capital with her board?*

- To reconstruct the scenario, encourage participants to consider turning their attention to her strengths and her prior experience as her lens for critiquing the program (rather than her emotional connection). *How can her strengths help her be successful in this role? How does lack of consideration of her strengths contribute to the stereotypes at play?*

Scenario 4

Hassan is the chief nursing officer at a large hospital. His strengths are Harmony, Connectedness, Positivity, Consistency, and Includer. Over the past 10 years he has developed a positive reputation within the profession and among the staff at the hospital. Recently, he hired a new director of Nursing Services, and the two finalists, Regina and Jacob, were both internal candidates. Jacob was ultimately hired. Two weeks later, Hassan learns that the female candidate filed a formal complaint through HR stating that she was denied her promotion because, despite her being the most qualified candidate, Hassan allowed his religious beliefs as a Muslim to favor hiring a man over a woman in the hiring decision. Hassan calls you, his trusted professional colleague from another local hospital, to get advice on how to respond.

Considerations to guide discussion:

- This scenario is about religious bias and assumptions/stereotypes made about Hassan's leadership decisions based upon his Muslim faith.

- Participants may focus on the sexism in this scenario rather than the religious bias. You may need to help students separate the two issues. It might be helpful to ask participants to generate a few stereotypes that relate broadly to religious difference or Islamophobia to frame the discussion. Remind them that their ability to generate the stereotypes does not mean that they believe in the stereotypes themselves (you might consider having students write these on a note card to turn in and be read by the facilitator).

- Some questions to spark discussion might include these: *In Western societies, why are Muslims subject to greater scrutiny? What stereotypes are being placed on Hassan in this scenario? What is the impact of making an assumption based on a religious affiliation?*

- To spark reconstruction, ask participants to consider Hassan's strengths. *How might his 5 relationship-building strengths come into play in a hiring process? How do his strengths help him to be successful in this role? How does lack of consideration of his strengths contribute to the stereotypes being assumed?*

- Encourage participants to consider that Hassan could feel misunderstood because his strengths indicate that he would be thoughtful and considerate of all candidates. Also, consider his positive reputation. If participants are stuck on the religious assumptions, ask them to consider how they live out personal faith traditions.

Scenario 5

Sandra is the community relations director for the mayor's office and has been asked to convene a diversity task force because of recent concerns raised at a town hall meeting about a lack of minority-owned businesses. Her strengths are Maximizer, Connectedness, Input, Deliberative, and Relator. Sandra is excited for this opportunity to act genuinely in her strengths since her leadership role sometimes prevents her from being her genuine self. At the first meeting made up of members from various constituencies, she attempts to create personal connections among group members, but the members seem confused and reluctant to share. Later, she approaches you, a trusted colleague whom she knows well, and asks about what happened. You tell her that several members of the group have the perception that she is dominant and overbearing from her previous roles in the office. This feedback frustrates Sandra because, as her strengths show, she is approachable, understanding, and interested in getting to know the team to ensure the success of the group. Her frustration is coupled with the fact that this is not the first time this has happened: employees have made assumptions before about her demeanor because she is an African American woman in a leadership role. She wants to process her next steps with you.

Considerations to guide discussion:

- This scenario is about racism and sexism. It is about the complexity of intersecting identities and how both racism and sexism may be at play.

- Participants may think Sandra is "pulling the race card" in expressing her concerns. They may think that Sandra is unaware of how she comes across to others and that perhaps she is more dominant than she thinks. Participants may also want to stay in the realm of sexism and should be pushed to consider the intersectional nature of this scenario.

- To facilitate deconstruction, consider these questions: *How do common stereotypes about women have an impact on this scenario? How do common stereotypes about African American women affect this scenario? How would those stereotypes affect Sandra's ability to be a leader in this setting? If Sandra were a White woman with relationship-building strengths, would she be described as dominant and overbearing?*

- To reconstruct the scenario, ask participants to consider Sandra's strengths. *How do her strengths help her to be successful? How are her strengths potentially contributing to the stereotypes that are being assumed because of normativity?*

Final Reflection:

If participants push back with other possible scenarios, it may help to acknowledge that the PLEs could be occurring. However, lead participants to consider why they are not engaging with the scenarios as they were intended, and challenge them to reexamine the purpose of this activity: to deconstruct and reconstruct these scenarios considering power, privilege, and social identity. Also, encourage students to consider how systemic oppression and dominant norms affect individuals. You may ask the following: *Why is there pushback from the group about engaging in the possibility that racism, sexism, and so on are at play here? What do these scenarios highlight that feels uncomfortable? Why does it matter that we build our awareness of our implicit biases when we consider leadership and strengths?*

4C: Emotionally Intelligent Leadership Through a Critical Lens

Paige Haber-Curran

Objectives/Goals of Chapter

- Understand emotional intelligence and connect it to critical perspectives.
- Explore and apply the three facets of emotionally intelligent leadership (EIL).
- Assess one's own EIL facets and capacities across inclusive and exclusive contexts.

Critical Concepts: *critical self-reflection, microaggression, oppression, patriarchy, power, privilege, social identity, social perspective-taking*

> Chapter Overview

Over the past 20 years the concept of emotional intelligence has gained attention in both popular and academic literature (Bar-On, 2006; Goleman, 1995; Mavroveli, Petrides, Rieffe, & Bakker, 2007; Salovey & Mayer, 1990). Emotional intelligence encompasses personal competence and social competence through "the ability to monitor one's own and others' feelings and emotions to use the information to guide one's thinking and actions" (Salovey & Mayer, 1990, p. 189). Research suggests that more so than IQ, technical expertise, or advanced degrees, emotional intelligence is a significant factor contributing to an individual's leadership performance and success (Goleman, Boyatzis, & McKee, 2013). Aligned with progressive thinking on leadership development, emotional intelligence can be learned and developed, and it is linked to leadership (Goleman et al., 2013).

Emotionally intelligent leadership (EIL) integrates concepts of emotional intelligence with contemporary thinking on leadership. The model approaches leadership as a process with a goal of effecting positive change that involves both interpersonal and intrapersonal competence (Shankman, Allen, & Haber-Curran, 2015). EIL encompasses an intentional focus on three key facets: consciousness of self, consciousness of others, and consciousness of context. Across the three EIL facets are 19 capacities that equip individuals with the knowledge, skills, perspectives, and attitudes to achieve desired leadership outcomes (Shankman et al., 2015). The purpose of this curriculum plan is to introduce and critically examine the concept of emotional intelligence and the EIL framework, connect these concepts to critical perspectives, and facilitate opportunities for participants to apply the concepts to their experiences.

> Chapter Framework

This chapter connects the concept of emotional intelligence and the EIL framework to critical perspectives. The critical perspectives examined highlight the complexity of human interaction and underlying dynamics that can affect individuals, relationships, and leadership processes. Critical concepts such as microaggressions, oppression, patriarchy, power, privilege, and social location are examined in conjunction with the emotional intelligence and EIL frameworks. The concepts of critical self-reflection and social perspective-taking are integrated into activities in the curriculum as key skills for developing EIL.

› Curriculum Plan

This curriculum introduces the concept of emotional intelligence and the EIL framework as explored through the lens of critical perspectives. In the first activity, participants engage in storytelling and discussion to explore emotional intelligence. The second activity introduces participants to EIL and includes self-assessment and social perspective-taking partner activities to help apply the concepts. The following curriculum plan is designed to be implemented over two sessions—the first activity for approximately 90 minutes, and the second for approximately 2 hours. Although segmented sessions are optimal for the curriculum to allow ample processing and recentering time, the activities can also be facilitated consecutively as an extended workshop or training. Additionally, Activity 2 could be split into multiple sessions.

› Activity 1—Stories on Emotional Intelligence

Participants are introduced to the concept of emotional intelligence and share personal stories on unsettling interactions in which they or another person did not readily display emotional intelligence. Participants then connect these stories to critical perspectives associated with microaggressions, oppression, patriarchy, power, privilege, and social identity.

Learning Outcomes

- Understand the concept of emotional intelligence and how it influences human interaction.
- Identify a personal story reflecting a lack of emotional intelligence.
- Apply critical perspectives to personal stories and the stories of peers.

Setting Up the Activity

Group Size: Open to any size group

Time: 85 minutes

Methods: Dialogue, presentation, reflection, storytelling

Materials: Whiteboard/chalkboard, markers/chalk, handouts

Variations: Instead of personal stories, provide brief unsettling
interaction case examples.

Directions

Prior to the Activity:

1. Display the following quote:
   - *I've learned that people will forget what you said, people will
     forget what you did, but people will never forget how you made
     them feel.* —Maya Angelou

2. Create a handout with the following critical perspective
   concepts:
   - *Microaggression*: The subtle and/or unintentional actions,
     symbols, or language used to project inferiority onto a target
     social group
   - *Oppression*: The exercise of power with malicious and cruel
     intentions of subjugation
   - *Patriarchy*: The presence of systematic, gender-based
     oppression in which males are centered as the good, the
     powerful, and the moral agents of society
   - *Power*: The ability to influence or control; usually con-
     nected to the systematic privileging or oppression one expe-
     riences based on their social location and social identities
   - *Privilege*: Unearned advantages and social power inherited
     by an individual because of their social location
   - *Social Identity*: A facet of an individual's identity connected
     to social group membership (e.g., race, class, gender, ability)

3. As the facilitator, identify a personal story that you wish to
   share about an unsettling situation. Your story should be about

a situation when you were negatively affected by someone's limited display of emotional intelligence. Select a situation in which someone had a formal leadership role or some other source of power. Ideally, the situation should connect to one of the critical perspective concepts just identified. As an alternative, you can share a story about when *you* struggled with emotional intelligence and the impact this had on others or on the leadership process; a story in which you were the one who did not readily display emotional intelligence has the possibility of demonstrating more vulnerability, which can be a powerful way to connect with participants and facilitate deeper sharing.

During the Activity:

1. Begin the session by displaying the Maya Angelou quote. Ask participants what the quote means to them. Allow 5 minutes for participants to share their perspectives.

   - Spend 10 minutes connecting this quote to the concept of emotional intelligence. First, explain that this quote (and likely their responses to the quote) relates to the concept of emotional intelligence. Ask participants what they think emotional intelligence entails and gather responses from a number of participants. Then, share this definition: *Emotional intelligence is "the ability to monitor one's own and others' feelings and emotions to use the information to guide one's thinking and actions"* (Salovey & Mayer, 1990, p. 189). Explain that emotional intelligence includes an intrapersonal dimension (i.e., self-awareness and self-management) as well as an interpersonal dimension (i.e., social awareness and relationship management). Share that one's ability to influence the feelings and emotions of others is powerful and can influence relationships and leadership processes. Further, explain that when people have a leadership position associated with power and authority, they have a responsibility to manage relationships in a way that empowers others rather than brings them down.

2. Share your personal story about an unsettling interaction. Note how the situation affected you personally (e.g., feelings, emotions, thoughts, action) as well as the relationship and/or the leadership process. Take no more than 5 minutes to share the story.

3. Ask participants to break into small groups of three to four. Allow 20 minutes for participants to share a similar story by providing these instructions:

   • *In your groups, allow each person to share a story of an unsettling interaction they had with someone in a leadership setting when someone—either they or the other person—did not readily display emotional intelligence. Share how this influenced them, their relationship, and the leadership process. The other group members can ask questions to better understand the situation. Monitor your time to be sure each group member has an opportunity to share.*

4. Explain that oftentimes unsettling situations have underlying dynamics and issues at play that make their impact more complex than the mere human interaction. Pass out the handout of critical concepts and explain what they mean. Ask for clarification questions about the concepts. Then, revisit the story you shared and explain how it connects to one or more of the critical concepts; further, explain how examining your unsettling situation through the lens of these concepts highlights the complexity of human relations and the interplay of numerous dynamics that have the ability to significantly affect a person individually, relationships, and the leadership process. Allow 10 minutes for this activity.

5. Ask participants to return to their small groups and spend 15 minutes connecting their stories to the critical concepts.

Encourage participants to apply these concepts to their own stories as well as ask questions of others in their group to see how these concepts apply. For example, a participant may discuss differences in social identities or perceived privilege that may have been at play during the unsettling situation. Or, a participant may connect their personal experience to power dynamics that were at play in the situation.

6. Spend the last 20 minutes facilitating a debriefing. Return to the handout and ask for volunteers to briefly share an example for each critical concept. Then ask: *How, if it all, did examining your unsettling situations through the lens of these critical concepts shift your understanding or perspective of the situations?* Build off participants' responses, affirming their perspectives and challenging them to think more critically as needed.

7. Conclude by reemphasizing the power of human interaction and how situations like the ones shared in this activity, where someone struggles with emotional intelligence, may be reflective of underlying dynamics and larger issues of privilege and oppression. How people choose to interact with others, therefore, has power implications whether there is conscious awareness of it or not.

Facilitator Notes

Participants may have a hard time applying the critical concepts to their personal examples. The personal example that you share is critical in helping participants understand how these concepts can apply. If you think participants will have a hard time with this portion of the activity you could instead provide brief unsettling situation case examples to consider. The stories being shared may be sensitive for some participants and may evoke a range of emotions. Thus, you may want to begin with preparing the group for these conversations by setting ground rules for confidentiality, respecting others, and withholding judgment.

Activity 2—Considering Context, Self, and Others

Participants are introduced to the three facets of emotionally intelligent leadership (EIL): consciousness of self, consciousness of others, and consciousness of context (Shankman et al., 2015). Participants will examine each alongside one of the critical perspective concepts and their experiences.

Learning Outcomes

- Understand EIL.
- Demonstrate perspective-taking skills to consider aspects of inclusive/exclusive contexts.
- Apply critical perspectives to EIL.

Setting Up the Activity

Group Size: Optimal size is 30 participants or less.

Time: 110 minutes

Methods: Discussion, hands-on interaction, presentation, reflection

Materials: "Emotionally Intelligent Leadership Self-Assessment" (one copy per person), slide deck with definitions, computer, projector/screen, two different color sticky notes (three notes per color per participant), whiteboard/chalkboard, markers/chalk, writing utensils

Variations: For more than 30 participants, the sticky note activity can be replaced with a group discussion and brainstorm or a small group discussion with reporting back to the large group.

Directions

Prior to the Session:

Create a slide deck to display the following definitions. Create one slide with the first three terms all together, and then create individual slides for each of the additional terms.

- *Consciousness of context*: Awareness of the setting and situation; it's about paying attention to how environmental factors and internal group dynamics affect the process of leadership.

- *Consciousness of self*: Awareness of your abilities, emotions, and perceptions; it's about prioritizing the inner work of reflection and introspection, and appreciating that self-awareness is a continual and ongoing process.

- *Consciousness of others*: Awareness of the abilities, emotions, and perceptions of others; it's about intentionally working with and influencing individuals and groups to affect positive change.

- *Critical self-reflection*: The learning process of becoming aware of one's own meaning perspectives, assumptions, and biases that guide mental tasks and enacted behavior.

- *Social perspective-taking*: The process of suspending one's frame of reference (i.e., values, assumptions, perspectives) to see the world through the eyes of another as they might see it through their set of values, assumptions, and perspectives.

- *Displaying empathy*: Being emotionally in tune with others; it's about perceiving and addressing the emotions of others. Emotionally intelligent leaders place a high value on the feelings of others and respond to their emotional cues.

During the Session:

1. Introduce the model of EIL. Explain that the foundation of the model is emotional intelligence, which was the focus of the first activity. Share the three facets of EIL by displaying the slide with the three definitions (i.e., consciousness of

context, consciousness of self, consciousness of others). Ask participants to note key words within the definitions that stick out to them. Share that the model emphasizes each of these facets as necessary for effective leadership. This should take approximately 5 minutes.

2. Project the definition of consciousness of context and ask a volunteer to read it aloud. Explain that this facet involves awareness of dynamics that happen within a group (i.e., the EIL capacity of analyzing the group) as well as the larger context and environment outside of a group (e.g., social, cultural, economic, and political forces; the EIL capacity of assessing the environment). Solicit examples of each (i.e., internal and external dynamics and forces). Examples could include group dynamics or whose voice is valued in the group (analyzing the group) or external societal or political trends (assessing the environment). Connect examples to applicable critical concepts such as microaggressions, oppression, patriarchy, power, privilege, and social location. As an example, the voices most often heard or valued in a group could relate to the critical concepts of privilege and power; and alternatively the voices less often heard or valued in a group could relate to the concepts of patriarchy or oppression. Explain that these critical concepts can exist within groups as well as from the external environment. Share any personal examples, such as a time you experienced these critical concepts at play in an organization you were part of or how external factors reflecting these critical concepts affected your organization. Spend approximately 10 minutes on this portion of the activity.

3. On the whiteboard/chalkboard, write "Inclusive Context" on the left side and "Exclusive Context" on the right side. Explain that some contexts can be inclusive, welcoming, and empowering, and some can be exclusive, uninviting, and disempowering. Note that most environments have characteristics of both. Then, pass out three sticky notes of

each color to each participant. Instruct participants that on one color they should write characteristics of an inclusive context and on the other color characteristics of an exclusive context. They should write one word or phrase per sticky note so they have three characteristics for inclusive contexts and three characteristics for exclusive contexts. Once participants complete this, they should put them up on the board under the respective categories of Inclusive Context and Exclusive Context. Allow 10 minutes.

4. Ask for six volunteers. Assign three volunteers to organize and sort the Inclusive Context sticky notes and three volunteers to organize and sort the Exclusive Context sticky notes. Instruct them that they should sort the sticky notes into common themes looking for patterns in characteristics. They can also set aside outliers or sticky notes about which they have a question. While they are doing this, ask the remaining participants to form groups of two or three and to share examples of inclusive and exclusive contexts they have experienced. Allow 10 minutes for the sticky note sorting and small group sharing.

5. Once the volunteers have completed their sorting, ask them to report themes and patterns they identified. They may also note any outliers or sticky notes for which they have questions. Facilitate a brief discussion about these common patterns and themes. Then, solicit examples from the rest of the group of inclusive and exclusive contexts they have experienced. Conclude the discussion by sharing that there is a range of contextual factors that we should consider and be aware of that may empower and include individuals and disempower or exclude others, sometimes even simultaneously. Revisit the critical concepts touched upon earlier in the activity. Allow 15 minutes for this.

6. Project the definition of consciousness of self and ask a volunteer to read it aloud. Next, project the definition of

critical self-reflection. Explain that self-awareness is an ongoing process that requires learning to become aware of your perspectives, your assumptions, and your biases and recognizing how they influence your thought process and behaviors. Explain that we often just go through the motions without critically reflecting on how we make meaning of situations. Explain that critical self-reflection is a learned skill and is central to effective leadership. Spend approximately 5 minutes on this.

7. Pass out the "Emotionally Intelligent Leadership Self-Assessment" handouts. Explain that across the three facets of EIL are 19 capacities. Let participants know that through engaging in critical self-reflection they will assess themselves on the three facets and 19 capacities. To do this, ask participants to identify two different contexts. One context should be an inclusive one and the other should be exclusive. Ask them to write those specific contexts (e.g., the name of an organization) at the top of each of the columns on the right hand side of the self-assessment. Acknowledge that some of their self-assessment ratings may be the same or different across the two contexts. Provide participants with 10 minutes to complete the self-assessment.

8. Once the participants complete the self-assessment, facilitate a discussion on how the different contexts affected, or did not affect, their self-assessed scores. Discuss the significant positive or negative impact a context can have not only on a group, but also on an individual. Ask participants why they think some contexts are inclusive for some individuals and exclusive for others. As you facilitate, connect the discussion to critical concepts such as social location, privilege, and oppression. Explain that a key aspect of leadership is influencing and creating contexts that are inclusive and equitable. Project the definition of consciousness of context once more and ask participants what they think is missing from this

definition. Emphasize that leadership involves more than just awareness of contextual dynamics and forces, but also the courage and ability to influence these contexts to be more inclusive and equitable. Spend approximately 10 minutes on this portion.

9. Project the definition of consciousness of others, and ask a volunteer to read the definition aloud. Then, project the definition of the EIL capacity of displaying empathy. Explain that this is a core foundation of the consciousness of others facet and of the EIL capacities. Explain that to effectively display empathy, one must be able to engage in social perspective-taking. Project the definition of social perspective-taking. Explain that like critical self-reflection, social perspective-taking involves acute awareness into who we are in terms of our perspectives, biases, assumptions, and values and how this influences how we make meaning of a situation. Social perspective-taking builds off of one's ability to be critically self-reflective and requires the ability to set aside one's frame of reference to deeply understand others and see the world the way they see it. Empathy and social perspective-taking are key for developing meaningful relationships and working effectively with others. This should take approximately 10 minutes.

10. Ask participants to find a partner with whom they may have differing perspectives, experiences, or worldviews. Encourage them to partner with someone who they do not know well. Ask each pair to take turns sharing a leadership challenge they have faced. While one person is talking the other person should listen and engage in social perspective-taking. The partner should seek to understand the individual; the individual's perspectives, values, feelings, and experiences; and what it may be like to be in that person's shoes in the situation. The participants should *not* try to analyze, assess, provide suggestions, or fix the other person's challenge. Rather, they

can ask probing questions to better understand the person's frame of reference. Allow 15 minutes for this.

11. Once sharing is complete, spend 10 minutes debriefing. Begin by asking participants what it was like to attempt to set aside their frame of reference to empathize with their partner and understand their frame of reference. Ask participants why this is an important skill for leadership and how they can apply this to their leadership experiences and relationships. To conclude the activity, project the slide with the definitions of the three facets of EIL (i.e., consciousness of context, consciousness of self, consciousness of others) and revisit the model to wrap up. Share that this framework is useful for critically assessing oneself and for engaging effectively with others and across contexts.

Facilitator Notes

Participants may have a difficult time identifying inclusive and exclusive contexts. This could be due to limited awareness, limited life experiences, or a reluctance to share. If this is the case, you could provide examples or ask them to imagine being in two different organizations: one in which they felt included and one in which they felt excluded.

› Conclusion

This chapter was designed to facilitate critical engagement with the concepts of emotional intelligence and the EIL framework. Through a range of interactive pedagogical strategies, participants learn about emotional intelligence and EIL, apply critical perspectives to the model, and use these perspectives to frame reflection and engage in self-assessment. By applying critical concepts to the models and to participants' experiences, leadership is viewed through a more complex lens.

Handout 4.10: Emotionally Intelligent Leadership Self-Assessment

Emotionally intelligent leadership (EIL) promotes an intentional focus on three facets: consciousness of self, consciousness of others, and consciousness of context. Across the three facets are 19 capacities that equip individuals with the knowledge, skills, perspectives, and attitudes to achieve desired leadership outcomes. Assess yourself using the following symbols across each dimension:

✓– (poor)   ✓ (satisfactory)   ✓+ (excellent)

	Context 1	Context 2
Consciousness of Self: Awareness of your abilities, emotions, and perceptions		
Emotional Self-Perception: Identifying emotions and their impact on behavior		
Emotional Self-Control: Consciously moderating emotions		
Authenticity: Being transparent and trustworthy		
Healthy Self-Esteem: Having a balanced sense of self		
Flexibility: Being open and adaptive to change		
Optimism: Having a positive outlook		
Initiative: Taking action		
Achievement: Striving for excellence		
Consciousness of Others: Awareness of the abilities, emotions, and perceptions of others		
Displaying Empathy: Being emotionally in-tune with others		
Inspiring Others: Energizing individuals and groups		
Coaching Others: Enhancing the skills and abilities of others		
Capitalizing on Difference: Benefiting from multiple perspectives		
Developing Relationships: Building a network of trusting relationships		
Building Teams: Working with others to accomplish a shared purpose		
Demonstrating Citizenship: Fulfilling responsibilities to the group		
Managing Conflict: Identifying and resolving conflict		
Facilitating Change: Working toward new directions		
Consciousness of Context: Awareness of the setting and situation		
Analyzing the Group: Interpreting group dynamics		
Assessing the Environment: Interpreting external forces and trends		

Adapted from: Shankman, M. L., Allen, S. A., & Haber-Curran, P. (2015). *Emotionally intelligent leadership for students: Facilitation and activity guide.* San Francisco, CA: Jossey-Bass.

Chapter 5: Theories of Production and Effectiveness

5A: Style Leadership Through a Critical Lens

Daniel M. Jenkins, Amanda B. Cutchens, & Corey Seemiller

Objectives/Goals of Chapter

- Understand the various styles that individuals possess as leaders.

- Increase awareness of and assess contextual influences affecting the decisions leaders make about style.

- Recognize how critical concepts influence leadership perspectives about style.

Critical Concepts: *critical self-reflection, power, social justice*

❯ Chapter Overview

Recognizing the context in which leadership takes place and the assumptions individuals bring to their roles as leaders is important to understanding the complexities of being an effective leader. Bennis (2009) wrote, "We must master context if we are to solve our own problems, let alone societal ones, and to do that we must first examine it" (p. 7). Leaders must consider a myriad of situational variables, including organizational culture, social systems of power, and personal assumptions that can influence leadership styles and decision making. This curriculum plan helps participants explore how context and perspective can challenge leadership effectiveness.

By engaging in a brief activity designed to draw attention to the importance of context, participants will identify multiple factors that arise from a singular issue, value the many styles that leaders possess, and assess a context for which styles are most effective in a given situation. Following that activity, participants will take part in a demonstration intended to discuss the assumptions individuals bring to their roles as leaders and how those assumptions affect style and behavior. Afterward, participants will better understand how concepts like power and influence may impact leadership perspectives as well as be able to identify the different leadership styles suggested by Blake and McCanse (1991).

> Chapter Framework

The theoretical framework informing this curriculum is anchored in critical leadership. According to Jenkins and Cutchens (2011), leading critically is the application of critical thinking skills to decisions about leadership actions in different situations. It is constructivist in nature because the actor must take into account prior experiences and knowledge before making decisions. In practice, critical leaders maintain an awareness of context in each situation, evaluate the implications of their decisions and their assumptions in making them, and take informed action (Jenkins & Cutchens, 2011). Viewing leadership through a critical lens can help leaders be more effective as they adapt to both changing circumstances and the different behaviors and attitudes of their constituents. Note that the concept of leading critically presented here defers from the application of critical perspectives as it does not necessarily address concepts related to critical social theory such as stocks of knowledge, ideology/hegemony, or social location.

Critical perspectives offer an additional lens to leading critically through consideration of other factors that influence leadership styles and effectiveness. Power and influence are two elements that affect the ethical decision making of leaders. Many leaders accrue power by making others dependent on them for resources, or they derive power from capitalizing on an opportune moment. The level of power a leader possesses in these situations affects the style in which they lead and the amount of influence they have over others. The tactics a leader uses to then exert that influence can vary significantly. For example, Adolf Hitler was a leader who came to power amid various situational variables that included capitalizing on a vision of hope for the war-torn people of Germany. Yet, he used that power to institute an autocratic leadership style and implemented undue pressure as a tactic to influence many people to do unspeakable things. In contrast, Dr. Martin Luther King Jr, was a leader who also rose to power by capitalizing on a vision of hope, but instead, he used his power to institute a collaborative style of leadership and made an inspirational appeal to all individuals that peaceful protest was the path to racial equality. When we consider these two iconic leaders, we observe how leadership styles vary. This curriculum draws on the concepts of power and influence to explore their impact on leadership style and effectiveness.

> Curriculum Plan

This curriculum reviews style theories of leadership to provide participants with an understanding of how context influences leader and leadership effectiveness. Through the use of visceral pedagogy (i.e., teaching that centers on emotional reactions and deep feelings), Activity 1 positions the power of context in leader effectiveness as a baseline for the remaining activities. Through the use of a critical style protocol, Activity 2 offers participants an opportunity to critically reflect on scenarios from their organizations, consider their assumptions about the issue, and analyze the challenges therein through a critical leadership style framework.

The curriculum should be implemented over one session, ranging from 60 to 75 minutes. Optimally, Activity 1 is utilized to introduce and set a foundation for the importance of context, whereas Activity 2 provides a foundation for analysis and discussion about the intersections of leadership styles with contextual influences, assumptions, and decision making.

> Activity 1—The Value of Context

This activity highlights the importance of context in leadership through a simple demonstration of how one set of styles is not universally effective in every leadership setting and that different situations require different leadership styles (Hersey & Blanchard, 1969).

Learning Outcomes

- Identify multiple contexts that can exist from a singular issue.
- Value the variety of styles that individuals possess as leaders.
- Assess a context to determine which styles are most effective.

Setting Up the Activity

Group Size: Open to any size group

Time: 10 minutes

Methods: Group discussion, metaphor

Materials: One of each: ballpoint pen, marker, crayon, dry erase marker, pencil

Directions

1. Begin by holding up the ballpoint pen and ask the group what the pen would best be used for. Have participants either raise their hands or shout out answers. They will likely say things like signing documents, taking notes, and so on.
2. Then, hold up the marker and ask the group what it would be best used for. They will likely say things like making signs, marking through text, and so on.
3. Repeat this process for the pencil, dry erase marker, and crayon.
4. Then, ask participants which is the best writing utensil. Some might say a particular writing utensil, but many will probably ask "The best for what?"

Debriefing Notes

Immediately process the activity by asking the following questions:

1. *What does this activity have to do with leadership?* Explain that what they assessed in making their determinations about what these writing utensils would be best for included considering the context. For example, using a marker to do math might not be as effective as doing math with the pencil. Explain that the writing utensils are metaphors for the diversity of leadership styles one can use in a particular situation. Each situation calls for a different style to be most effective, just as certain writing utensils are best for particular situations.
2. *What is an example of a leadership style that would be valuable in one setting but not another? In what setting would this style be most valuable and in what setting might it not be as valuable?* It may be helpful to refer participants to Chapter 5 of the main text as a refresher on leadership style theory.

    End by sharing that what is valuable or essential in one context may not be in another, and that to maximize a situation, leaders must assess the context and act in accordance with it.

Activity 2—Exploring Assumptions About Style Leadership Through Contextual Decision-Making

This activity explores how attitudes, beliefs, and assumptions may influence leadership styles through critical self-reflection and small group discussion.

Learning Outcomes

- Understand how assumptions about leadership affect leadership style.
- Understand how concepts like power and social identity influence leadership perspectives.
- Identify the different leadership styles suggested by Blake and McCanse (1991).

Setting Up the Activity

Group Size: Open to any size group

Time: 45–60 minutes depending on length of debrief

Methods: Critical self-reflection, small and large group discussion

Materials: "Critical Style Protocol Worksheet" handout, paper, writing utensil

Variations: Consider having participants complete the "Critical Style Protocol Worksheet" prior to the session.

Directions

1. Have participants complete the "Critical Style Protocol Worksheet" in advance of the session or designate

independent reflection time at the start of the activity to complete it (10–15 minutes).

2. Divide participants into three-person small groups to discuss reflections from their worksheets. Ask each person in the group to summarize their analysis of effective and ineffective leaders (approximately 5 minutes). The two other group members should then engage in a discussion using prompt questions from the "Critical Style Protocol Worksheet" to examine connections to style theory as well as to underlying assumptions.

3. Debrief this activity in the large group.

Debriefing Notes

Process the activity by asking the following questions in the large group:

- *How do you think leadership styles are influenced by a leader's assumptions? What stocks of knowledge might these assumptions draw upon?*

- *What type of assumptions about leadership do you think authoritarian or autocratic leaders hold? Democratic? Laissez-faire?*

- *Are there situations in which you believe any of these styles of leadership can be effective? Give some examples.*

- *How do you think power influences leadership style?*

- *Think about the leader you labeled "effective" versus "ineffective." How might leadership styles and behaviors be received differently based on various social locations and/or the power differentials of the leader?*

- *How do social systems of power and privilege influence the enactment of style-based approaches to leadership as well as how they are received? In what ways may social identities shape both the enactment of and responses to this? How might the styles of leadership as described in Chapter 5 of the main text be applied and enacted differently based on both environmental context and social location?*

Facilitator Notes

This activity draws on a number of elements present in Chapter 5 of the main text related to leadership style theory (Dugan, 2017). Initial questions in the "Critical Style Protocol Worksheet" are designed to explore overarching style (i.e., authoritarian or autocratic, democratic, and laissez-faire) and their implications for power dynamics. If this does not come out during the debriefing session, make certain to prime participants' thinking accordingly. Additionally, it is useful to consider how social systems of power, privilege, and oppression can be applied to style-based approaches to leadership to more fully understand potential disconnects between perceived style and enacted style in organizational contexts.

> Conclusion

Leaders make myriad assumptions about the contexts in which they lead. Consequently, the styles leaders choose and the decisions they make are enhanced through the application of a critical lens. Activity 1 focuses on the contextual elements of leader decision making and stresses that leadership styles are not universally effective. Instead, we learn that different situations require different leadership styles for effectiveness and that critical leaders must maintain an awareness of context. Through critical self-reflection, Activity 2 focuses on how attitudes, beliefs, and assumptions influence a leader's style. Specifically, this activity provides opportunities for participants to openly share perspectives about power and social justice through personal contexts, to cross-examine small group members through the protocol provided, and to question assumptions about leadership and style through a critical lens.

Handout 5.1: Critical Style Protocol Worksheet

Part I: Think of an effective or successful person in an organization you are currently a part of; provide an alias for that person: _____

1. What does this leader do that contributes to their effectiveness?

   _____

   _____

   _____

2. How does this leader act?

   _____

   _____

   _____

3. Describe one detailed, illustrative example of this leader's effectiveness. Make sure to outline the situation, parties involved, issue(s) at hand, and the decision(s) the leader made.

   _____

   _____

   _____

   _____

   _____

Part II: Think of an ineffective or unsuccessful person in an organization you are currently a part of; provide an alias for that person: _____

1. What does this leader do that contributes to their ineffectiveness?

   _____

   _____

   _____

2. How does this leader act?

   _____

   _____

   _____

3. Describe one detailed, illustrative example of this leader's ineffectiveness. Make sure to outline the situation, involved parties, issue(s) at hand, and the decision(s) the leader made.

_____

_____

_____

_____

_____

Part III: After you have completed Parts I and II, find two other people with whom to share. After each person in your trio shares, please examine the following ideas and assumptions—separately for the person in Part I and Part II—from their responses:

1. What assumptions do you feel your peer holds about the situation and leader?

_____

_____

2. From your perspective—evaluating your peer's description of the situation—what kind of behaviors/actions and attitudes does your peer seem most drawn to? What perspectives seem to be most influential to them?

_____

_____

3. Considering the critical concepts of power and influence, what perspectives seem to shape your peer's opinion?

_____

_____

4. Which parts of the situation do they feel most strongly about?

_____

_____

5. What assumptions about leadership actions and decision making does your peer hold?

_____

_____

6. What kind of leadership do you think they believe to be most effective? Consider the leadership styles (i.e., indifferent, accommodating, controlling, status quo, sound, paternalistic, opportunistic) suggested by The Leadership Grid presented in Chapter 5 of the main text (Dugan, 2017).

_____

_____

5B: Critical Perspectives on Situational Leadership Theory: Does Considering Situational Context Foster Inclusivity?

Amy C. Barnes

Objectives/Goals of Chapter

- Understand biases that may exist when evaluating follower behavior, especially when considering power dynamics.
- Identify ways in which personal narratives can disrupt situational leadership analysis, especially when influenced by social identities and stereotypes.
- Recognize how leaders can engage in meaningful analyses of situations in which dominant narratives may be the norm.

Critical Concepts: *bias, microaggressions, normativity, oppression, power, privilege*

Chapter Overview

Situational leadership theory, developed initially in 1969, focuses on a managerial grid that leaders are encouraged to use to assess the maturity level of followers to appropriately tailor feedback and coaching (Hersey & Blanchard, 1981). It helps leaders assess the commitment levels of followers and provides recommended interventions that are intended to be developmentally appropriate. The simplistic nature of the model has contributed to its success and widespread use. However, without sound research to support the claims set forth by the approach (Dugan, 2017), a common critique is that situational leadership does not adequately account for the nuances that exist in individual coaching relationships. Further, from a critical perspective, the model does not consider the impact of power dynamics, how underrepresented social identities navigate these dynamics, or how the theory contributes to maintaining dominant norms in the workplace. When applying critical perspectives to situational leadership, dominant narratives are challenged as the authoritative standard and leaders are encouraged to consider how bias can unfairly advantage those with privilege and power.

Chapter Framework

This chapter addresses the potential gaps that exist in applying situational leadership to contexts that may include power dynamics, various social identities, or a setting in which dominant narratives are the norm. Through the lens of critical perspectives, it becomes apparent that situational leadership does not account for power dynamics, especially those that exist based on social stratification. Multiple critical and postmodern frameworks (e.g., critical race theory, queer theory, multiple feminisms) situate oppression as normative in U.S. society and oppression is perpetuated through both social relationships and institutional structures that provide unearned privilege to some while constraining others (Dugan, 2017).

This chapter highlights how stereotypes and microaggressions, two ways in which dominant norms are operationalized, can significantly impact the agency of individuals. The term *microaggressions* emerged from literature on critical race theory. They are defined as "brief and commonplace daily verbal, behavioral, and environmental indignities, whether intentional or unintentional, that communicate hostile, derogatory, or negative racial slights and insults to target a person or group" (Sue et al., 2007, p. 273). The concept of microaggressions is frequently extended beyond just race to other social identities with those from underrepresented groups often enduring this covert form of oppression due to limited power to confront behaviors directly in organizational contexts. The impact of these often-ignored forms of bias can be significant and include emotional distress, the perpetuation of stereotype threat, physical health problems, and lower work productivity and engagement due to mental distress (Sue, Lin, Torino, Capodilupo, & Rivera, 2009). Microaggressions can also have negative consequences for those with privileged identities, harming relationships and incurring personal and organizational costs. For example, White people present when microaggressions occurred experienced lowered empathic ability, dimmed perceptual awareness, and lessened compassion for others (Spanierman, Armstrong, Poteat, & Beer, 2006). The significant impact that microaggressions have on the experience of all individuals is an important consideration within leadership contexts where power and privilege are ever present. These understandings of structural oppression and microaggressions guide the content of this chapter.

> Curriculum Plan

The following curriculum guides participants through various contexts in which applying situational leadership may fall short of fully understanding leadership dynamics because of a lack of consideration for power and dominant structural norms. The activities encourage participants to consider how situations of leadership involve more than just the maturity levels of followers or the commitment levels of employees. When accounting for privilege and power, the contexts within which leadership occurs become much more complex than the situational leadership model is able to explain.

Guided reflection will help participants consider a time when their biases may have caused implicit assumptions about a situation or context, thus leading to an oversight of another person's experience. Individual reflection and digital storytelling will help participants recall past situations in which their personal narratives were not fully considered in a context where power dynamics existed. Lastly, participants will be asked to consider how applying situational leadership may lead to unintentional oppression and bias by a leader or manager. This curriculum is designed for one session lasting 2 to 3 hours or two sessions each lasting approximately 60 to 90 minutes.

❯ Activity 1—Situational Leadership Storytelling

This activity provides participants with an opportunity to reflect on a previous experience while considering situational leadership. Special attention is given to both benefits and limitations of the model. Participants are encouraged to consider the implications of various social identities as they relate to their personal experiences.

Learning Outcomes

- Understand elements of situational leadership in the context of one's personal life.
- Be aware of the influences of social identities, privilege, and power on leadership experiences.

Setting Up the Activity

Group Size: This is an individual activity, followed by sharing time in small groups.

Time: Completed as homework a week before the session. Explanation of the assignment requires 30 minutes. Processing occurs in a separate session.

Training Method: Group processing, self-reflection

Materials: Computer and Internet access, video-editing application (e.g., iMovie, Movie Maker)

Multimedia: Computer for presentations (1 per small group), Internet

Variations: If the setting for this activity is not a class, time can be spent working in teams and groups to develop stories and map out a plan for the digital story. Participants could use cell phones or tablets to record each other or be given time to record a video responding to prompts.

Directions

1. A week ahead of small group discussions, give participants the following homework assignment to prepare for the next session. Participants should use digital media to tell a story based on the prompt that appears in Step 3. The narrative should include the typical elements of a story, such as setting, character(s), problem, and resolution, in additional to answering the requirements of the prompt. Creating a digital story includes narrating the story in which images highlight the story components. If digital storytelling is not feasible, video blogs or even written assignments may be substituted. For more information on digital storytelling, simply search the Internet; many examples are available. One digital storytelling resource can be found through EDUCAUSE (https://net.educause.edu/ir/library/pdf/ELI7021.pdf).

2. If needed, provide a quick review of situational leadership while reviewing the homework assignment. Ask participants

to reflect silently on experiences in which situational leadership has been at play.

3. Ask participants to reflect on the following prompt making notes of the sequence of events:

   • *Tell us about a time when you were directed, coached, supported, or delegated by a supervisor in a way that did not work best for you. How did this make you feel? What was happening that made that the wrong approach for you or made it challenging? What was the outcome of this situation? How, if at all, did power dynamics impact your ability to ask for what you needed in this situation? Were social identities at play that influenced the experience on either or both sides? If so, what and how?*

4. Participants should prepare a 1- to 2-minute digital story recounting their experience, including all of the reflection prompts and elements of storytelling just covered.

5. At the next meeting, participants are placed in small groups in which they will take turns sharing their digital stories and discussing the following questions about what they have learned about situational leadership based on the digital storytelling activity:

   • *What common themes emerged in the group discussion about situational leadership?*

   • *Identify and discuss the ways in which systemic oppression, unearned privilege, bias, and/or dominant narratives affected the scenarios that were shared.*

   • *What new information do you possess that may change your views of situational leadership in the future?*

❯ Activity 2—Visualization Activity

This mini-lesson and large group activity introduces situational leadership in an applied setting. Participants explore the consequences of this model by visualizing a scene and examining an example of it in a larger context to illustrate the imperfect understanding one has when making judgments based on limited or contextual information.

Learning Outcomes

- Understand the principles of situational leadership.
- Analyze the utility of situational leadership.
- Understand how to apply its merits and critiques in future leadership experiences.

Setting Up the Activity

Group Size: Open to any size group

Time: 10–20 minutes (5–10 minutes for review, 5–10 minutes for discussion)

Methods: Group processing

Materials: Computer, image, projector/screen

Multimedia: Computer to show image, projector/screen, online resources regarding visualization:

- "POSE + REVOK on the Huffington Post" (http://jonathanlevinegallery.com/?method=Blog.NewsDetail&EntryID=7D630A0C-D9FF-98A8-89DD2D9B841B315C)
- "How Painting Can Transform Communities" (www.ted.com/talks/haas_hahn_how_painting_can_transform_communities?language=en)

Directions

1. Begin this activity with a review of situational leadership (see Chapter 5 of the main text).
2. Ask participants to articulate the consequences, both positive and negative, of the theory. As facilitator, you will not share

your perspectives until the end of the visualization activity and discussion.

3. Ask participants to close their eyes and envision the following scene:

   - *Imagine a run-down street and an adjoining alleyway. Look around; what do you see? What buildings surround you? What does it sound like? [PAUSE.] Now, envision a group of four similarly dressed people of multiple races. You notice that these people are wearing matching clothing with visible spray paint cans in their hands. Where do you think they are heading? What do you think they are planning to do?*

4. Ask participants to share what they envisioned; have them describe their surroundings, the people, and the activities. After participants share their responses, show the community image mural and story that aligns with the visualization. There are multiple online resources regarding visualization that can be used for this portion of the activity. You might consider using the story on the Jonathan Levine Gallery website titled "POSE + REVOK on the Huffington Post" (http://jonathanlevinegallery.com/?method=Blog.NewsDetail&EntryID=7D630A0C-D9FF-98A8-89DD2D9B841B315C). You can also use the TED talk, "How Painting Can Transform Communities" (www.ted.com/talks/haas_hahn_how_painting_can_transform_communities?language=en).

5. Ask participants to share their reactions and the activity's tie to situational leadership:

   - *How (dis)similar were your images to those of the community mural story? How so?*
   - *What does this indicate about the implicit biases you hold and/or stocks of knowledge that inform your thinking?*
   - *How does this tie to situational leadership?*

6. Conclude the activity by asking participants to describe the positive and negative consequences of situational leadership. Additional questions to prompt discussion might include these:

- *What assumptions did you make about the situation prior to having all the details revealed?*
- *What contributes to an individual's interpretation of a particular situation?*
- *How do power, privilege, and stereotypes affect personal interpretations of situations?*

    Note: Ensure participants understand the following points about the activity during discussion:

- Situational leadership has its merits in allowing managers/leaders or individuals to broadly make quick assessments of a situation and take a prescribed action.
- Those using situational leadership as a lens attempt to take into consideration the momentary experience of their followers/employees.
- However, this momentary consideration often does not consider the fullness of one's experience, leaving the opportunity for misunderstanding and mistreatment.
- Much like what happened with the image created during the visualization exercise, situations often appear only one way on the surface. As leaders/managers/individuals, we may not understand how our implicit biases shape our perception of what is occurring in any given situation. Therefore, it is critical to see the full picture before making final judgments or decisions.
- As explicitly applied to situational leadership, it is imperative that the leader seek to understand the experiences (e.g., identities, backgrounds, prior work-related situations) of followers before making a decision on how to best lead them.

7. Ask participants if they have any final comments or questions.

❯ Activity 3—Managing Situations Through a Critical Perspective

Through this activity, participants examine the application of situational leadership to a manager and employee relationship. In the scenario, one managing style appears best for the task at hand. Participants will be asked to apply situational leadership with baseline information and brainstorm questions to pose as a supervisor. To further this lesson, additional information will be provided about the personal narrative of the individual to further complicate the basic application of situational leadership. The additional information seeks to highlight the limitations of situational leadership when all factors are not considered, especially when that includes personal characteristics and/or social identities. Participants will have an opportunity to reconstruct the scenario using a more inclusive adaptation of situational leadership and discuss how this changes the supervisor/supervisee relationship.

Learning Outcomes

- Be able to apply situational leadership to a case scenario.
- Recognize the influences of social identities and oppressive structures when using situational leadership.
- Identify questions and approaches to complement the traditional use of situational leadership.

Setting Up the Activity

Group Size: Open to any size group

Time: 60–90 minutes

Methods: Small group processing of case scenarios

Materials: Case scenarios, illustration of situational leadership (Chapter 5 of the main text)

Directions

1. Begin with a quick overview of situational leadership including what approaches are applicable for the task at hand (described in Step 2). Emphasize the supervisee's readiness (competence and commitment levels) as an important piece of information for the manager's decision-making process.

2. Provide participants with the following scenario. Ask them to plot a course of action as if they were in the role of manager in their small groups using questions outlined in Step 3.

    As a manager of an engineering plant, a few months ago you had a new project to complete and you needed to choose a project manager. The project required high technical skill to help create the newest part for an automobile. Kimberly, an African American woman, was your most skilled worker and had been with the plant for 8 years. Kimberly showed great initiative assisting with other projects in the plant, even with projects she was not assigned. Kimberly recently emphasized in meetings her desire to make this particular plant the most reliable, safe, and efficient plant in the region. Based on this information, you selected Kimberly to be the new project lead. You were confident in her abilities, her high level of commitment, her work ethic, technical skill, and initiative. Kimberly accepted the task and led a team that consisted of all men, most of whom were in their first year or two with the company.

    Kimberly and the team worked for 2 months on the new automobile part, and a few days ago she presented it to the management team. The part was completed on time, but it did not meet the desired outcomes related to efficiency or technological innovation that the leadership of the company emphasized at the onset of the project. Additionally, you noticed that Kimberly did not seem happy about the outcome, although she was trying to stay positive. Based on informal rumors about the project, you heard that Kimberly lacked organization and may have been overwhelmed with the new role. You request a meeting with her to process the outcomes of the project. Prior to the meeting, you consult your handbook on situational leadership from a recent training you attended. You realize that at the start of the project, you chose a delegating style of leadership because of Kimberly's high commitment and high competency from past experiences. After seeing the result of the project and hearing the informal rumors, you fear that maybe you have an inaccurate perception of Kimberly and have used the wrong situational leadership style to manage her. Perhaps you should have used a coaching or directing style. You are unsure of how to proceed given the information you have and your training.

3. Split participants into small groups. Ask them to take on the role of Kimberly's manager. Tell them that they need to prepare for this meeting with Kimberly. Provide time for participants to discuss the following questions:

   - *As Kimberly's manager, do you have all the information you need to properly debrief the situation?*
   - *If not, what questions would you ask to get the full picture of what happened with Kimberly's team?*
   - *How was situational leadership helpful in assessing Kimberly's needs as an employee, and how may it have been detrimental to the beginning of this situation?*

   Allow 10 minutes for groups to discuss the questions and then debrief as a larger group. Spend time on the second question regarding additional questions or insights that they would like to have about Kimberly and what happened in the situation.

4. Once participants share their questions, provide the following details to the scenario that were not previously known: *As Kimberly's supervisor, you become aware of additional information or reflect on prior information that you had not considered. You also have an opportunity to talk with Kimberly.*

   - *This was the first time Kimberly led a project team and the first time a woman has led a group in the plant's history.*

- *Kimberly was promoted quickly due to her talent and hard work (although this is not always perceived to be the reason by her male peers; most believe that she has been given promotions because of a need to increase diversity at the plant).*
- *The new project team consists of all men, the majority of whom are White and one of whom has been reprimanded for derogatory and sexist remarks toward women in the past.*
- *During the project, a fellow team member pulled Kimberly aside after her introduction to the team and commented, "You are really articulate. You don't see that often from people like you. I am excited to work for you on this project."*
- *Ben, a team member, tweeted out over his personal account, "My new project lead does not know how to manage. Here we go again. #unorganized."*
- *Kimberly asked for input and collaboration for the new auto-mobile part, something she expresses might have contributed to people thinking she was not visionary or organized. Her team seemed to tune her out when they had group meetings and they often made excuses when there was a need to stay late to help her with the project. She expressed feeling a sense of tension in the room and a general unwillingness to go above and beyond.*
- *Kimberly implied that she felt as though she was never given a chance. She felt that maybe that was because she was a woman leading a group of men or because of racial dynamics (she referred to several occurrences of microaggressions).*

5. Use the following questions as a basis for conversation on how situational leadership is limiting or can be more inclusive especially in the scenario with Kimberly:

- *How does this new information change the scenario and/or your course of action? Do you have any personal biases that are contributing to your reflection on the scenario? How can you interrupt those biases?*
- *How does this information affect your approach to supervising Kimberly? How does situational leadership apply to this case?*

What aspects of the case are missed as a result of applying situational leadership?

- *For managers, how is the situational leadership grid (see Chapter 5 of the main text) helpful, and how is it potentially limiting?*
- *How do social identities and underlying biases influence what information is known or provided in a workplace? How does this impact your ability as the manager to pursue the best course of action?*

Facilitator Notes

This activity needs to be segmented. After each progression, you should pause to address the scenario at that point. If participants begin to jump ahead, caution them to base their answers, questions, or decisions only on the information at hand. Additionally, during the critical reflection questions at the end be sure that participants are making connections between this scenario and the chapter framework that highlighted the impact of dominant structures, microaggressions, and privilege. It is important that participants can apply concepts from a critical perspective to contexts where structural inequality is present.

⟩ Conclusion

This curriculum plan was designed to help participants understand how the quick diagnosis of followers using situational leadership may be limiting in its application. When originally developed, situational leadership was an improved approach over earlier leadership theories that rarely considered the needs of followers. However, when viewed with a critical lens, situational leadership may omit perspectives from multiple and intersecting social identities and oversimplify a prescribed leadership approach based upon limited knowledge of the complexity of an individual's experience. Furthermore, empirical research largely discredits the utility and validity of situational leadership (Dugan, 2017).

Omitting personal experiences, especially those related to social identity, oppression, or microaggressions, and power dynamics from the diagnosis of situational leadership, could lead to individuals feeling further marginalized. By framing the discussion of situational leadership with a critical perspective, leaders validate that individuals often have distinctly different experiences in situations in which the dominant culture is the norm. Leaders who employ a more critical approach to this theory honor the existence of personal narratives, challenge power dynamics that could be oppressive, and expose how organizations and leadership contexts can often unfairly advantage those with privileged social identities.

5C: Path-Goal Leadership Theory: Four Leadership Styles and Situational Factors

Matthew Sowcik & Clinton M. Stephens

Objectives/Goals of Chapter

- Understand House's (1971) path-goal leadership theory.
- Comprehend the four leadership styles and situational factors fundamental to path-goal theory.
- Recognize assumptions and biases that shape perception and ways to apply this knowledge to understand path-goal leadership styles.

Critical Concepts: *assumptions, bias, critical self-reflection, locus of control*

> Chapter Overview

As an area of study, the term *leadership* continues to be defined and redefined. Part of the reason for the lack of clarity concerning a common definition is that our perception of leadership changes based on a number of factors including context, issues, situational factors, and individuals involved. However, most current definitions of the term leadership have some reoccurring themes. One example of this is Perruci's (2011) definition, which states leadership is "the process by which leaders and followers *develop*

241

a relationship and work together toward a goal (or goals) within an environmental context shaped by cultural values and norms" (p. 83).

Within Perruci's (2011) definition are a few generally accepted themes concerning leadership. The first of these is that leadership is a process. Since leadership is a process, it is not solely based on the characteristics or traits of a leader, but instead driven by the relationship between leader and follower. Within this process the second general theme of leadership emerges. Leadership happens between two or more people who influence each other while working toward a goal (or goals). The process of leadership is influenced by both the relationship between leader and follower and the goal(s).

The final theme found in Perruci's (2011) definition is that leadership occurs within an environmental context. The context in which leadership occurs can have a unique influence over the individuals involved and the overall process. These general themes of leadership are also the key drivers of House's (1971) path-goal theory of leadership. This theory emphasizes the important role a leader plays in the process of selecting a leadership style that would motivate a follower to achieve their goals. The relationship that is established between leader and follower and the leadership style that is selected are both direct results of situational factors inherent in the follower and the environment.

> Chapter Framework

Path-goal theory, utilizing the key tenets of expectancy theory (Vroom, 1964), suggests a leader's role is to establish a path for followers to achieve their goals, ensure followers receive desired rewards when they achieve goals, and provide support, direction, and removal of roadblocks along the way. As leaders interpret the needs of followers and adapt their leadership style based on both these needs and the contextual variables of a situation, there is an opportunity for the leader's bias to influence the process. In fact, one poignant criticism suggests, "Because the scope of path-goal theory is so broad and encompasses so many different interrelated sets of assumptions, it is difficult to use this theory fully in trying to improve the leadership process in a given organizational context" (Northouse, 2013, p. 132). It is these "assumptions" that prompt us to consider path-goal theory from a critical perspective. More specifically, this provides an opportunity to engage in critical self-reflection because "central to the process of critical reflection, then, is the recognition and analysis of assumptions" (Brookfield, 1990, p. 177).

"Critical self-reflection uncovers and deconstructs inconspicuous beliefs, perceptions, and experiences" (Terhune, 2005, p. 144). As an inquiry-based process, critical self-reflection challenges the validity of our assumptions and provides a deeper awareness of perceptions, knowledge, beliefs, and biases. In most cases, these assumptions and biases are not in the forefront of one's thoughts. However, through critical self-reflection the individual is more aware of their thoughts and actions. When an individual's perceptions are challenged, their thoughts, actions, and ultimately the habits that drive their behavior, are also challenged.

Brookfield (1990) proposed three interrelated phases that drive critical self-reflection. The first phase is "identifying the assumptions that underlie our thoughts and actions" (Brookfield, 1990, p. 177). In this phase, questions about "what happened" and "what assumptions were made that lead to the thoughts and actions" are contemplated. In phase two, the individual "scrutinizes the accuracy and validity of these assumptions in terms of how they connect to, or are discrepant with, our experience of reality (frequently through comparing our experiences with others in similar context)" (Brookfield, 1990, p. 177). The chapter debriefing questions encourage participants to scrutinize their assumptions and compare their perceptions to others in the group. In the final phase, one "reconstitutes these assumptions to make them more inclusive and integrative" (Brookfield, 1990, p. 177). Participants will engage in reflection around questions that ask them to consider, "What are their new interpretations of the experience?" "What have they learned about their leadership/followership assumptions?" and "How will the insights garnered from the exercises inform their leadership in the future?"

> Curriculum Plan

The two outlined activities engage participants in practicing, observing, and analyzing the four different leader behavior styles and the situational factors influencing leadership. For each activity, it is expected that individuals already have a working knowledge of path-goal theory (see Chapter 5 of the main text). The activities are designed to deepen a participant's understanding of path-goal theory. You can use one of these activities independently or both activities simultaneously. The two activities are presented in increasing depth of learning per Bloom's taxonomy (Bloom & Krathwohl, 1956).

The first activity engages participants in practicing the four leader behaviors through a game of Rock-Paper-Scissors. Through four rounds, participants are assigned and enact directive, participative, supportive, or achievement-oriented behaviors. This familiar game is a great platform to illuminate several of the limitations present in path-goal theory. In addition, this activity challenges participants to address some of their personal biases and assumptions as they make decisions throughout the activity. The second activity explores path-goal theory in participants' daily lives. Participants invest a week looking for and recording the four leadership behaviors they observe. These two lessons are flexible in duration. Each can fill a 60-minute period or flex from 20 minutes to 90 minutes in length.

> Activity 1—Learning Path-Goal Theory Through Rock-Paper-Scissors

This activity provides participants with an opportunity to observe different elements of path-goal theory. Each of the scenarios is set up to emulate the different environments, follower characteristics, and leadership styles that are essential in path-goal theory.

Learning Outcomes

- Understand the basic dynamics of path-goal theory.
- Enact the different leadership styles depending on the follower and environment.
- Reflect on how the different styles in path-goal theory influence outcomes of a task.

Setting Up the Activity

Group Size: Open to any size group

Time: 35 minutes (20 minutes for rock-paper-scissors, 15 minutes debrief)

Methods: Discussion, peer interaction, simulation game

Materials: "Strategic Rock-Paper-Scissors Game Play" handout

Directions

1. Place participants in groups of two or three. Ask the teams to select a team leader.
2. Explain to those who do not know the rules of the game that
   - Two opposing players will each make a fist with one hand and hold the other open, palm upward.
   - At the same time, the two opposing players will tap their fists in their open palms—once, twice, and on the third time, each will form their fist into one of three shapes:
     - A *rock* (by making a fist with their hand)

- o A sheet of *paper* (by holding their hand flat with the palm down)
- o A pair of *scissors* (by extending their index and middle fingers and holding them apart).
- Individuals who play *rock* will win against players who play *scissors*. Individuals who play *scissors* will win against players who play *paper*. Individuals who play *paper* will win against players who play *rock*.

3. Let the groups know that all the team members of one team will pair up against all the members of an opposing team and compete in a rock-paper-scissors tournament (if there is an uneven number, have one of the team leaders observe). Individuals are to keep a running total of their victories over a 5-minute period. Once the 5 minutes are complete, the team leader will ask each individual team member for their number of victories. The team leader will then combine the individual wins from each player on their team for one total team score. The team with the most number of total wins is the winner.

4. Prior to starting the tournament, have the *teams* count off in fours. Provide the team leader with the following information that corresponds with the number of their team:
   - *For the teams that counted off "**1**" (Directive)*: Tell the team leader (and instruct them to tell the team) that only the team leader will decide what each individual on the team will play, every time, without input from the other team members. This means that after each throw the team member must check in with the team leader on what to throw next.
   - *For the teams that counted off "**2**" (Participative)*: Tell the team leader (and instruct them to tell the team) that they will be deciding together on what each of them will play every turn. A collaborative approach should be taken to make decisions on what to play next.

- *For the teams that counted off "3" (Supportive)*: Tell the team leader (and instruct them to tell the team) that neither the team leader nor the team will make a decision on what to throw. The team must play the following throws in this order:
  - **Rock-Paper-Scissors-Scissors-Paper-Rock-Rock-Paper-Scissors** (repeat pattern from this point). Tell the team leader to overly support the team and make statements like (but not limited to), "That's okay, we will definitely win next time!" or "We are doing great!"
- *For the teams that counted off "4" (Achievement Oriented)*: Tell the team leader that they should hand out the "Strategic Rock Paper Scissors Game Play" sheet to all the members on their team. Explain to the team leader that because the team has received "insider information" about how to win the game, that they will be held to a higher standard. Let the team leader know that they will need to win at least 75% of their throws to win against another team.

5. Ask if there are any questions. Once all questions are answered, begin the game. After 5 minutes, ask team leaders to add the individual victories for a total team score. Declare a victor and then rearrange teams so that each participant can play on a different team. Continue to switch every 5 minutes. End the competition once you have reached 20 minutes. At the end, ask team leaders to count all the victories they had over the other teams.

6. Debrief and review the following questions:
   - *What process did your team go through to select a leader (describe the experience)? Why do you think that particular individual was selected? What factors contributed to that individual being selected? What influence did this leader have on the game? If another individual on your team was selected to be the team leader, how would they have influenced the game? What personal biases/assumptions did you have that shaped*

how you selected a team leader? Were implicit leader prototypes at play?

- *What path-goal leadership style was your team leader demonstrating in the role play? How could you tell? What were the instructions your leader/team was given and how does that correspond to the path-goal leadership style? What influence did this style have on your rate of success or failure?*

- *As a team leader, did the leadership style that you were asked to use reflect how you usually like to lead? If not, how did it make you feel to lead in this particular way? Prior to starting the competition, did you assume this leadership style would work/fail? Why was this your assumption? How did your assumption change (or stay the same) through the exercise? As a member of the team, could you tell that this style was comfortable/disconcerting to your team leader? Why or why not?*

- *What do you think were the advantages to being lead the way you were in the exercise? What were the disadvantages to this style? How did the different styles make you feel during the competition?*

- *What impact did the way you were led have on the game? Why did certain teams have more wins/losses than other teams? Initially, if you were asked which leadership style would be most effective, what would have been your answer? After playing the game, which styles of leadership were most effective?*

- *How did you or others on your team make decisions on what to throw next? How was this decision influenced by previous experiences? What assumptions did you make about your competitor that influenced what you decided to throw next? Were your assumptions more often correct or incorrect? If you had a chance to play the same people again, would you change the way you competed?*

- *Knowing that one of the teams had a "Strategic Rock Paper Scissors Game Play" sheet that was "insider information" about how to win the game, how does it feel to know they had an advantage over you? Did you know about this advantage during the game? Would you have liked to know about the advantage? If you knew about the advantage, how would you have played the game differently? Do you think you would have won more games if you had the sheet prior to playing?*

- *Besides the leader's style, what elements (environment or the team members) influenced your team's success?*

Facilitator Notes

Since one of the driving tenets behind path-goal theory is the incentivizing of tasks to motivate followers, adding a layer of incentive would be ideal. One recommendation is to provide points/credit for each team victory the group has at the end of the competition (e.g., if a group has one victory at the end, they would receive five total points). If the team won all four rounds they would receive 20 total points. These points can then be applied to a paper or a test during the semester. Be sure to let the teams know ahead of time about the point structure and that the team leader will be determining how the points will be distributed.

Additionally, it is important to assess at the beginning of the game if those who are participating have played the game previously. This is important for a number of reasons:

- Those who have not will need more time to go over the directions.
- You may be interested in having a few practice rounds.
- There may be a cultural assumption that this game is played around the world. That is not true and in certain parts of the world this is not a well-known game.
- It may come as a surprise to those who have played this game that others in the class have never played the game. Once again, this would be a valuable debriefing point to make if you do have individuals who have not played previously.

⟫ Activity 2—Path-Goal Theory Spectator

This section of the curriculum builds on participants' prior learning of path-goal theory and invites them to observe it being practiced in their daily lives. The critical self-reflection and meaning-making nature of the activity challenges participants to increase their observation of leaders' behaviors while making their own meaning from the observations.

Learning Outcomes

- Apply knowledge of path-goal theory to future leadership experiences.
- Be able to recognize and critique the behaviors of leaders in their life.
- Assess their leadership behavior choices in the context of learned biases and assumptions.

Setting Up the Activity

Group Size: Open to any size group

Time: Introduction (10 minutes), Observation (7 days), Debriefing (20–40 minutes)

Methods: Peer discussion, journaling/tracking, reflection

Materials: Paper and writing utensil for introduction activity; a copy of the "Path-Goal Theory Spectator" handout for each participant

Directions

1. *Pre-knowledge check:* By now participants should be knowledgeable of leader behaviors in the path-goal theory and be able to differentiate directive, supportive, participative, and achievement-oriented behaviors.

2. Invite participants to consider a particularly salient experience with a leader from the past week and to record it on their paper with a descriptive phrase or two.

3. Next, ask participants to classify the experience using path-goal theory:

   D = Directive

   P = Participative

   S = Supportive

   A = Achievement-Oriented

4. Pose each of the following questions and pause for participants to write their responses. Ask participants to respond about the leader behavior they chose and classified.

   - *What evidence did you observe that supports this classification?*
   - *What were the outcomes on follower motivations?*
   - *If you were in the leader's role, based on what you know about path-goal theory, how would you have handled it?*

5. Next, invite participants to share responses in small groups of two to four people. Welcome participants to assist with one another's responses when they are unsure. Allow about 2 minutes per participant.

6. Walk around and listen for the classifications (i.e., D, P, S, A) participants used. Be prepared to help clarify questions and responses.

7. Next, invite participants to volunteer to report out in the large group. Ask for two examples for each leader behavior (i.e., D, P, S, A). For each example, ask participants to share their responses to the three questions. Congratulate participants on coming up with good examples of where they have observed path-goal theory in practice.

8. Pass out the "Path-Goal Theory Spectator" worksheet. Inform participants that over a week-long period, they should continue observing leader behaviors and record their observations on the worksheet. Participants need not

answer all three questions, just one of the three questions per observation—but they should have a mix of all three responses by the end of the week.

9. Ask them to write in one observation for today and answer one of the questions. This practice helps them depart with a worksheet already started.

10. Ask what questions they have that you can address to help them be successful.

Debriefing Notes

After one week of observing leader behaviors, the participants will return with their completed worksheets. If time permits, participants will benefit from 5 minutes of sharing the highlights from their observations with a peer. Additionally, it would be beneficial to pose the following questions:

1. *Did anyone suggest a different classification for one of your examples or did you recommend a different classification for another participant's example? What assumptions and perceptions exist that allow you and others in the class to classify an example the same? What are the different assumptions and perceptions in place that lead to different classifications?*

2. *After reflecting on the example and hearing from others on classification and outcomes of follower motivation, would you have handled the situation differently? What assumptions did the leader make that prompted them to handle the situation with that particular leadership style? Knowing what you know now, what information do you have that would encourage you to lead differently?*

3. *Did you observe more participants' examples in any of the leadership styles and few examples in other styles? Why do you think this is the case? Why did this happen? What factors contributed to these patterns? What (if any) is the significance of this pattern?*

4. *How might our culture, gender, race, age, and other characteristics of social location affect the way we classify leadership behaviors? How do these unique dimensions of identity have an impact on the way we perceive the outcomes experienced by followers?*

5. *How might our social location shape the way we lead/follow others? What inherent biases and/or assumptions did you have when examining the leaders around you?*

Facilitator Notes

Sometimes examples cluster to two or three styles with few examples of one style. If this occurs be prepared to share examples so participants see a strong representation for each.

- *Directive*: "When I got lost finding my sister's new home, I called her and she stayed on the phone talking me through the drive."
- *Supportive*: "My director told me to finish the TPS report by the end of the month and let her know if I needed any help."
- *Participative*: "In this group project the team facilitator asked everyone what areas of the project they wanted to work on most."
- *Achievement-Oriented*: "I am the fundraiser for a nonprofit group and the chair person told me we needed to raise $10,000 in six months."

Additionally, it is important to anticipate that some participants will struggle with finding multiple observations each day. Remind them that many sources are appropriate for their observations from current events in the news to interactions with their family members.

Conclusion

This curriculum engages participants in practicing, observing, and analyzing the four leader behavior styles and situational factors affecting leadership. At the completion of each activity, participants will develop a deeper comprehension of path-goal theory and be able to apply the theory in their leadership. Although there are numerous theories available to examine leadership, you may find House's (1971) path-goal theory of leadership a useful framework to discuss critical self-reflection in the leadership process. Designed to teach House's theory, this curriculum provides participants with concrete examples, heightens their scrutiny of their environment, and challenges their previously held perspectives of effective leadership styles.

Handout 5.2: Strategic Rock-Paper-Scissors Game Play

- Rock-Paper-Scissors is not simply a game of luck or chance. There is always something motivating your opponents' actions. There are techniques you can use to win.

- In "rookie" or pedestrian matches (i.e., where there is no prior experience), most new (or inexperienced) players will select rock as their first throw. Rock is perceived as strong and forceful, so individuals tend to fall back on it. You should select paper as your first throw to have the best chance of winning.

- Look out for the same throw twice. In Rock-Paper-Scissors, if your opponent throws the same throw twice, you can safely eliminate that throw and guarantee yourself at worst a stalemate in the next game (e.g., if your opponent throws paper twice, then statistically they are more likely to throw rock or scissors. Logically, your best throw would be rock since you will either win or draw).

- Tell your opponent what you are going to throw and then actually throw what you said. They may not believe you are bold enough to throw what you said you were going to throw.

- Having difficulty deciding what to throw? If your opponent lost the last throw, you should try the throw that would have lost to your opponent's last throw. If a player loses a round by playing scissors, then rock is more likely to be thrown the next time. If you know this you can play paper.

- Still having trouble figuring out what to throw? Statistically, scissors is thrown the least amount of times. So when in doubt, go with paper.

Adapted from:

Walker, D., & Walker, G. (2004). *The official rock paper scissors strategy guide*. New York: Simon & Schuster.

Wang, Z., Xu, B., & Zhou, H. J. (2014). Social cycling and conditional responses in the Rock-Paper-Scissors game. *arXiv.org preprint arXiv:1404.5199*. Retrieved from http://arxiv.org/pdf/1404.5199.pdf

Handout 5.3: Path-Goal Theory Spectator

Observations of the Path-Goal Theory

Leader Styles

Identify at least three examples of leader behavioral styles that you observe. Label each one as:

D = Directive, P = Participative, S = Supportive, or A = Achievement-Oriented.

Interpretation

For each of the observed behaviors answer the following three questions:

a. What evidence did you observe that supports this?

b. What were the outcomes on subordinate motivation?

c. In the leader's role, how would you have handled it?

Monday	1. 2. 3.	
Tuesday	1. 2. 3.	
Wednesday	1. 2. 3.	
Thursday	1. 2. 3.	
Friday	1. 2. 3.	
Saturday	1. 2. 3.	
Sunday	1. 2. 3.	

6A: LMX Theory Through a Critical Lens: Exploring the Impact of Power and Privilege

Natasha Chapman & Benjamin Brooks

Objectives/Goals of Chapter

- Introduce leader-member exchange theory as a prescriptive and descriptive model that centers on the recognition of in-groups and out-groups in organizations.
- Critique the leader-making process and the role of agency, power, and privilege in negotiating roles and developing in-groups and out-groups in organizations.
- Interrogate underlying assumptions concerning social identity, normative behavior, rational decision making, and the impact of bias on access to power and privilege.

Critical Concepts: *agency, bias, capital, discrimination, marginalization, power, privilege*

Chapter Overview

Leader-member exchange (LMX) theory proposes that leaders or managers develop different relationships with their subordinates, and the qualities of these relationships are divided into an in-group (higher quality) and an out-group (lower quality; Roberson & Block, 2001). Initially, studies of LMX were

257

descriptive and directed toward the ways in which the leader-member exchanges affected organizational performance (Graen & Uhl-Bien, 1995). These studies suggested that high-quality exchanges between leaders and followers resulted in positive outcomes that benefited the leader, the follower, and the organization. More recently, the focus of LMX has been on the leader-making process and "emphasizes that leaders should try to develop high-quality exchanges with all their subordinates" (Northouse, 2013, p. 182).

Although LMX theory emphasizes high-quality exchanges, a limitation of the theory is its failure to explain how one goes about creating relationships marked with a high degree of mutual trust, respect, and obligation (Dugan, 2017). Some scholars suggest that subordinate initial performance and competence are critical to the developmental process, whereas others argue that managers should rely on controlled processing (i.e., consciously aware, effortful, intentional, in-control) rather than automatic processing (i.e., unintentional, involuntary, occurring outside awareness) to reduce the use of stereotypes (Roberson & Block, 2001). Roberson and Block (2001) inferred that theorists have traditionally ignored the influence of demographics on LMX and believed the role of demographic factors, such as race or ethnicity, on the process was small. However, the authors opined that recent work around similarity-attraction and social categorization theories infer that the demographic effects on LMX are inevitable (Roberson & Block, 2001).

Chapter Framework

There are two dominant theoretical perspectives that can help to explain supervisor bias toward targeted groups in organizations or the workplace (Roberson & Block, 2001). The first, *social categorization*, implies that "individuals perceive others based on social category membership, designating some as in-group members (like me), and others as out-group members (not like me). This categorization process is a fundamental aspect of thought and occurs naturally" (Roberson & Block, 2001, p. 260). Social categorization also attributes stereotypical characteristics to groups and individuals that serve as frameworks for interpreting behavior. Individuals seek information that confirms their expectations while discounting information that contradicts this framework. This behavior provides a way of preserving in-groups and out-groups. Positive behaviors of in-group members are attributed to internal factors and negative behaviors are attributed to external factors. The opposite applies to out-group members.

A second perspective is *similarity-attraction*, which suggests that individuals are more attracted to those who are similar to themselves. Similarity on variables such as socioeconomic status, demographics, and attitudes increases interpersonal attraction and liking and affects communication, turnover, and performance rating. "Research has also demonstrated in-group biases in evaluations of performance, allocation of outcomes, and the provision of help and assistance" (Roberson & Block, 2001, p. 262).Both theoretical perspectives, similarity-attraction and social categorization, demonstrate the degree to which similarity makes individuals more attractive to the group and gives them more influence among group members (Hogg, 2001).

Although these perspectives suggest the presence of both explicit (i.e., obvious) and implicit (i.e., hidden) biases, behaviors stemming from explicit bias in organizations and the workplace are most often illegal or culturally/socially inappropriate. Thus, this chapter highlights the role of implicit bias in the designation of in- and out-group membership. Implicit Association Tests (IATs; Greenwald, McGhee, & Schwartz, 1998) tap into hidden, or automatic, stereotypes and prejudices that evade consciousness and will be utilized as self-evaluative tools for participants to interrogate the role of social categorization and social identity in the leader-making process. Participants will also recall personal experiences to examine the role of social categorization, similarity-attraction, and social identity in the formation of in-groups and out-groups.

> Curriculum Plan

This curriculum explores the basic tenets of LMX while interrogating its underlying assumptions concerning individual social identity, group normative behavior, rational decision-making processes, and the potential impact of bias on access to power and privilege. LMX theory is a unique approach to the study of leadership in that it centers the interaction between leader and follower (i.e., the dyadic relationship), and there is a large body of research on the benefit of a strong relational bond between leader and follower in terms of outcome achievement and professional advancement, adding credence to its prescriptive dimensions. The descriptive nature of the theory further recognizes that people segment into groups based on some shared identity or purpose, and, in hierarchical societies, some groups manifest more power than others.

LMX is limiting in that it fails to fully consider how larger social schemas—ranging from societal influence on unconscious bias to organizational norms—affect one-on-one relational bond formation in terms of access to bond formation and an explicitly prescriptive set of guidelines for developing that bond. This curriculum involves multiple sessions that embrace the positive descriptive and prescriptive components of LMX while critiquing its limited theoretical scope, potential pitfalls, and the disregard of contextual realities inherent in creating equal access for all followers to form dyadic partnerships with a leader.

The curriculum should be implemented over two sessions, each approximately 90 minutes in duration. Segmented sessions are preferable as the first session establishes much of the theoretical framework of LMX and helps individuals place their lived experiences within the descriptive elements of LMX. The second session takes participants through a process of self-examination concerning bias and behavior that many individuals, at least at first, reject because of the perceived negative connotation toward the self the exercise elicits. Processing and recentering time is needed after each session for participants to fully appreciate the nature of LMX, how their brains process and use information, and how these two concepts are related.

> Activity 1—Going Back to High School

This section introduces and explains the central tenets of LMX through small group and large group dialogues and lecture. The identity politics of high school cliques is used as a mechanism for understanding the phenomena of in-groups, out-groups, and dyadic partnerships, and for determining the potential benefits of group membership and leader-follower collaboration. The activity will gradually challenge participants to uncover potential criticisms of LMX tied to concepts of social identity, groupthink, access, agency, and bias through an examination of participants' lived experiences in high school.

Learning Outcomes

- Understand LMX as a descriptive and prescriptive model of leadership that centers on the recognition of in-groups and out-groups in organizations.
- Examine and critique the leader-making process and the role of agency, power, and privilege in negotiating roles and the development of in-groups and out-groups.
- Assess the potential for groupthink in the leader-making process.

Setting Up the Activity

<u>Group Size</u>: Open to any size group

<u>Time</u>: 90 minutes

<u>Methods</u>: Dialogue, lecture, reflection, potential to include multimedia

<u>Materials</u>: Computer, projector/screen, audio, Microsoft Office Suite (or equivalent), Internet access (optional), whiteboard/chalkboard, markers/chalk (optional), blank paper (one per participant), writing utensils

<u>Multimedia</u>: Consider using film clips set in high school that demonstrate relatable and pertinent social scenarios. Sample films include *Remember the Titans*, *Mean Girls*, *Clueless*, and *The Breakfast Club*.

<u>Variations</u>: If the group size is small (5 to 10 participants), remain intact for the entire session. If the group is larger, optimal results are achieved by breaking into smaller groups of four to five participants for the dialogue phase.

Directions

1. Begin the activity by informing participants that they will be taking a trip back to high school. Place your participants into groups of four or five. Ask them to consider a series of increasingly specific questions about the social schemas of their high schools, their social identities and social location within their high schools, and how group memberships or alienation contributed to issues of power, privilege, and self-concept. Note that the approach has participants unpack concepts related to the theory before introducing it. Doing this places the theory in a real-world context instead of trying to apply a real-world context to a theory. This helps with the accessibility of the theory to learners not yet well-versed in it. If you are working with individuals who already have a strong theory background, you may want to alter this plan to best fit

learner needs. Prompts and questions can be tailored as appropriate for your participants, but should include the following:

- *Name and define as many cliques (i.e., social groups predicated on a shared interest) from your high school as you can remember. Describe the nature of these groups including a discussion of the social hierarchy of the clique.*
  - *How did one gain entry into a clique? Were there any rites of passage one had to go through to confirm membership?*
  - *How did one rise in power or authority within a clique? How was leadership passed from one member to another?*
  - *Were any cliques more powerful or influential in your high school? How did they gain that power and influence? How did they affect students who were not in those cliques?*
- *What clique(s) were <u>you</u> a part of in high school? How did you become a member? If you rose to a position of power, how did you gain that power? How did you use that power?*
- *Did you ever see a person rejected from membership in a clique or were you ever rejected from membership? Why did this occur? How did group membership or alienation impact your view of yourself in relation to your social environment?*

  Have participants consider these questions individually and then discuss with small groups. Monitor and engage with the small groups as appropriate. Ask probing questions to elicit specific recollections about high-school experiences.

2. After 15 to 20 minutes in small groups, hold a large group dialogue based on the prompt questions. Be cognizant that some sensitive information may be shared. Be empathetic and nonjudgmental. The total exercise should take approximately 30 minutes.

3. Transition from the large group dialogue into an LMX discussion/lecture that should take 25 to 30 minutes in its entirety. LMX has some unique visual markers (see Chapter 6 of the main text), so it may be beneficial to create a visual guide to assist in participant understanding. Explain the core

descriptive dimensions of LMX, including in-groups, out-groups, dyadic relationships, and the uniqueness of this theory's focus on the interaction between leader and follower.

- Discuss research findings that link strong leader-follower bonds to improved leader and follower psychological well-being, outcome achievement, effectiveness, and career advancement.
- Explain the prescriptive component of LMX, most notably Graen and Uhl-Bien's (1991) leader-making process, including a discussion of the three phases of relational development: stranger, acquaintance, and partnership. Allow time for participants to ask questions to make sure they understand the theory.

4. Transition the conversation to applying relevant topics to LMX including stocks of knowledge, ideology/hegemony, social location, and any of the tools of deconstruction and reconstruction (*Note*: Chapter 2 in the main text provides useful content for this conversation). This dialogue should take between 20 to 30 minutes depending on the amount of explanation required to establish participant comfort with each aforementioned concept. Specifically, ask participants to use information and examples they provided in the high school clique dialogue to validate and critique LMX. Prompts and questions can be tailored as appropriate for your participants, but should include these:

- *How do you feel about this theory?*
- *How does this theory and its descriptive and prescriptive components relate to your lived experiences?*
- *Given what we've explored related to social identity and location, intersectionality, power, and privilege …*
  - *What are the potential problems with LMX? Can everyone be a part of the in-group? Is there anything wrong with not wanting to be a part of the in-group and should this negatively impact advancement?*

- *Does everyone have equal access to the in-group? What are some potential reasons why everyone might not have equal access?*
- *Is there any potential downside to everyone being in the in-group?*

5. Introduce or reiterate through this conversation the concepts of groupthink, proximity bias, and in-group bias and their deleterious effect on individual self-concept, privilege, and performance outcomes.

6. Conclude with a general discussion of what the participants believe can be done to offset the potentially negative effects of leading using an LMX approach given that there are some well-substantiated, positive indicators associated with its use. This concluding dialogue will serve as a priming exercise for the next activity.

Debriefing Notes

The conclusion of this section of the curriculum is designed to ensure a basic understanding of LMX and its descriptive and prescriptive elements. In addition, this section recaps potential areas of critique of LMX, notably around social identity, social location, privilege, bias, and groupthink, which will be more intimately explored in the next session. As a reminder, this session does include the sharing of personal experiences tied to identity, and therefore it should be tailored to the developmental readiness of a group. Use professional judgment in the solicitation of sharing personal experiences throughout the debriefing process.

Facilitator Notes

It is important to note that this activity may be challenging for participants who reflect on potentially psychologically damaging memories tied to identity during high school. Put another way, kids can be cruel. Some participants may be unready to name or discuss facets of their identity or to share self-concept damaging memories. As the facilitator, use caution in pushing individuals to reveal and discuss sensitive components of their identities too quickly.

› Activity 2—Implicit Association Tests: Homework and Reflection Paper

Implicit bias refers to the way people unconsciously, and often unwillingly, exhibit bias toward others. These hidden biases are rooted in various aspects of life but should not be mistaken for conscious or explicit bias and preferential treatment that is generally prohibited in many laws and cultures. Significant literature evidences the reality of implicit bias and describes the ways institutions such as education, the judicial system, and healthcare are influenced by these unconscious attitudes (Dugan, 2017). One of the most commonly used inventories for testing implicit bias is the Implicit Association Test (IAT; Greenwald et al., 1998). Participants will complete three computerized IATs in preparation for this activity. Participants will also complete a reflection paper describing their reaction to their results to initiate meaningful dialogue during the forthcoming activity. The reflection paper can be optional, and there are alternatives to using the IAT computerized test.

Learning Outcomes

- Understand implicit bias and the distinction between these hidden biases and explicit bias.
- Identify and explore personal implicit biases toward others.

Setting Up the Activity

Group Size: Individual activity

Time: IATs will take 15–20 minutes each.

Methods: Individual reflection, self-assessment, writing

Materials: Computer, Internet access

Multimedia:

- "Project Implicit: Preliminary Information" (https://implicit .harvard.edu/implicit/takeatest.html)
- "Project Implicit: Origins and Measurements with the IAT" (https://implicit.harvard.edu/implicit/demo/background/ posttestinfo.html)

Directions

1. Announce that the next activity requires that participants complete an assignment before beginning Activity 3. Share the following instructions with participants:

    - *Go to "Project Implicit: Preliminary Information" and click on "I wish to proceed" at the bottom of the page.*
    - *Complete the Race IAT, a Gender-related IAT, and one more IAT of your choosing. Record or print your results. Each test will take 15 to 20 minutes.*
    - *Go to "Project Implicit: Origins and Measurements with the IAT" and read the brief description. Click on the FAQ and browse content if you would like to learn more about the research tool and implicit bias prior to Activity 3.*

2. Ask participants to write about their results in a brief reflection paper (two pages) expressing their reaction to results and how the information assessed might be applicable to leadership.

3. Encourage participants to come to Activity 3 prepared to discuss their findings.

Facilitator Notes

One alternative to taking the computerized IAT is to use a paper format. Another alternative is to simply provide a series of verbal prompts for participants to reflect on as described in "Managing Unconscious Bias: Your Workplace Advantage" (Theidermen, 2014). For example, you may ask the participants to write down the first thought that comes to mind when they encounter the member of another group (e.g., a single mother with three children, a person who smokes cigarettes, a native New Yorker). Ask participants to consider the immediate generalities that enter their minds. Additional prompts include *What do you do when you learn that an individual does not conform to your first thoughts? Is the source of your bias reliable? How many people do you actually know who conform to your biases?* (Thiedermen, 2014)

Activity 3—Understanding Implicit Bias

This section of the curriculum builds upon Activity 2 and introduces participants to IATs (Greenwald et al., 1998) as tools for understanding the presence of implicit attitudes and stereotypes to examine the implications of bias on one-one-one relational bond formation.

Learning Outcomes

- Understand the distinction between explicit and implicit attitudes and bias and consider the ways in which these biases disadvantage marginalized groups and individuals in the leader-making process.
- Learn techniques that help de-bias perceptions and improve interactions.
- Explore strategies to minimize factors that prohibit marginalized individuals from obtaining the benefits and advantages associated with in-group status.

Setting Up the Activity

Group Size: Optimal group size is from 5 to 25 participants given sensitivity of content.

Time: 90 minutes

Methods: Dialogue, lecture, reflection

Materials: Computer, projector/screen, audio, Internet access (optional), whiteboard/chalkboard, markers/chalk (optional), participants' IAT results and reflection papers

Multimedia: Note that both of these resources are optional.

- *Testing for a Hidden Racial Bias* (www.nbcnews.com/id/ 18122831/ns/dateline_nbc/t/testing-hidden-racial-bias/# .VP4SWU9THcs)
- *Managing Unconscious Bias: Your Workplace Advantage* (Theidermen, 2014) (www.workplaceanswers.com/managing-unconscious-bias-webinar-thank-you/)

Directions

1. Begin this activity by setting participation guidelines. You may have already set expectations or guidelines in previous sessions that you can refer back to here.

2. Explain that the focus of this session is to continue previous conversations on LMX centering on factors that prevent individuals and groups from benefiting from in-group status and effectively negotiating to the partnership stage in leader-making. More specifically, factors related to social identity and location, social categorization, and explicit and implicit biases will be the focus.

3. Ask participants to find a partner and share their reactions to their IAT results by responding to the following questions:
   - *What were your initial feelings while taking the IATs?*
   - *What was your reaction when reviewing your results?*
   - *To what extent were your results expected or surprising? Why?*

4. Bring participants back to the large group and walk through each question together encouraging individuals to share responses when comfortable. Throughout this discussion participants may reveal questions or criticisms about the inventories or their results. You may decide to use your time to elaborate on Project Implicit and the IATs at that point or inform the group that you will spend more time describing the inventory and the process shortly. Note that a majority of the session time may be spent here. Be cognizant that sensitive information may be shared and act empathetically and nonjudgmentally.

   - If you decide to elaborate on Project Implicit, share that it was created by psychologists to develop hidden bias tests—called *IATs*—to measure unconscious, or automatic, biases. Address any questions about the tests. It may be useful to review the FAQs on the Project Implicit website or, if time allows, show one or both of the following: *Testing for Hidden Racial Bias* or *Managing Unconscious Bias: Your Workplace Advantage* (Theidermen, 2014).

5. For supplemental purposes, an Internet search of videos using the terms *unconscious bias*, *hidden bias*, or *implicit bias* will also pull up materials related to specific topics or current events such as *Trayvon Martin and Implicit Bias: A Discussion with Drs. N. G. Berrill and Isaiah Pickens* (www.youtube.com/watch?v=jXSFaEVDU3A).

6. After debriefing, introduce the concept of implicit bias. Address the following:

   - *The ability to quickly and automatically categorize people is a fundamental quality of the human mind* (Teaching for Tolerance, n.d.).
   - *Categories give order to life, and every day we group other people into categories based on social and other characteristics. This is the foundation of stereotypes, prejudice, and—ultimately—discrimination* (Teaching for Tolerance, n.d.).

- *People can be consciously committed to equality and deliberately work to behave without prejudice, yet still possess hidden negative prejudices or stereotypes* (Teaching for Tolerance, n.d.).

- *Hidden biases can reveal themselves in action, especially when a person's efforts to control conscious behavior weaken under stress, distraction, realization, or competition* (Teaching for Tolerance, n.d.).

- *Hidden biases are related to discriminatory behavior in a wide range of human interactions, from hiring and promotions to choices of housing and schools* (Teaching for Tolerance, n.d.).

7. Provide examples of the impact of implicit bias in our everyday lives such as these:

   - *"Studies have found that school teachers clearly telegraph prejudices; so much so that some researchers believe Children of Color and White children in the same classroom effectively receive different educations"* (Teaching for Tolerance, n.d., para. 20). *Similar results are noted with regard to students with disabilities and LGBTQ students* (Crumpacker & Vander Haegen, 1987; Shapiro, 1999).

   - *"A now classic experiment showed that White interviewers sat farther away from Black applicants than from White applicants, made more speech errors, and ended the interviews 25% sooner"* (Teaching for Tolerance, n.d., para. 20).

   - *Those who showed greater levels of implicit prejudice toward, or stereotypes of, Black or gay people were more unfriendly toward them* (Teaching for Tolerance, n.d., para. 20).

8. Once participants have a better understanding of implicit bias, cover the following:

   - *Why do you think this topic is relevant to leadership?*

   - *How does this impact the way we lead? How we make decisions? Our behaviors and attitudes toward others?*

   - *How does implicit bias specifically relate to the previous session on LMX? Why does understanding implicit or unconscious bias matter in the formation of in-groups and out-groups? What are the implications for leader-making?*

- *Can you think of examples of the role implicit bias has had on the development of group formation in your leadership experiences?*
- *What can you do about unconscious stereotypes and prejudices?*
- *Describe strategies to de-bias perceptions and improve interactions with others.*

Debriefing Notes

Taking the IATs and discussing results in a public setting can be daunting. Again, it will be important to use caution in pushing individuals to reveal and discuss their IAT results—this activity does include the sharing of personal experiences and may reveal personal attitudes that are even surprising to the participant themselves. Use caution to tailor the conversation to the developmental readiness of the group and continue to use professional judgment in the solicitation of personal experiences throughout the debrief. It may be helpful to remind participants that discovering and facing biases should not make them feel ashamed or fearful. In attempts to de-bias perceptions and improve interaction with others, it is important and necessary to first uncover implicit bias to work toward the elimination of bigotry and discrimination.

> Conclusion

This chapter was designed to guide participants through a developmentally sequenced curriculum that provides a comprehensive understanding of LMX while interrogating its underlying assumptions concerning individual social identity, group normative behavior, rational decision-making processes, and the potential impact of biases on access to power and privilege. Through personal reflection, self-assessment, group dialogue, and lecture, participants were challenged to learn a unique leadership theory that is descriptive, prescriptive, and positively supported by extensive research while also uncovering and interrogating the theory's many concerning elements related to intersectionality and social identity.

Through this theoretical interrogation, participants, with facilitator support, experience potentially psychologically difficult tasks to better understand biases they may not have been aware of and the impact of those biases on decisions and behaviors that may have undermined the types of interpersonal exchanges that LMX is attempting to produce. The activities presented in this chapter further enhance the development of participants' critical lenses. Specifically, these activities encourage a deeper understanding of how leadership is influenced by the changing nature of identity. It provides a platform to interrogate how identity is affected by the world around us and how identity can inform even the most basic of interactions we have with others.

6B: Team Leadership Through a Critical Lens

Adam Goodman

Objectives/Goals of Chapter

- Understand leadership and decision making in teams.
- Reflect on experiences to understand why some teams succeed and others fail.
- Recognize how power, privilege, and social identity influence team dynamics.

Critical Concepts: *critical self-reflection, power, privilege, social identity, stocks of knowledge*

› Chapter Overview

This curriculum is premised on the assumption that people typically have mediocre experiences working with teams, including with a few teams that have failed. It also assumes that people may be able to point to a few teams that they would describe as "high performance," but without critical thought as to why a particular team experience was so positive. Achieving effective teamwork matters because it can help teams make good decisions and reduce, but not eliminate, the risk of failure. Accordingly, this curriculum helps people identify effective and ineffective teamwork for themselves, others, and for the team as a whole. However, there is no single formula for team effectiveness or success because different teams take different paths and have different experiences. At its most fundamental level, this is because teamwork is a behavioral activity that involves people. As a result, teams often struggle, particularly to overcome mediocrity and bad habits. Some teams break down and then become successful. Others do not overcome their self-imposed hurdles.

A team's success or failure often depends on whether trust is present among members, healthy conflict is understood and embraced, each team member is committed to team success over individual needs, and whether the team is accountable—especially in achieving results (Lencioni, 2002). Culturally, teams also need to create a psychologically safe environment, one where people know that their ideas are welcome (Edmondson, 2012). This requires team members, especially leaders and facilitators, to empower others rather than seek control; ask questions rather than provide answers; and focus on flexibility rather than adherence to ideas, doctrines, or rules (Edmondson, 2012). In other words, sharing power, having an open mind, and disrupting privilege matter when building effective teams. This curriculum explores team phenomenon with a more intentional and critical lens by helping individuals identify effective and ineffective teamwork for themselves, others, and for the team as a whole.

> Chapter Framework

Teams generally prefer to get right to work on the project they have been given. This is unwise. In hindsight, many teams trace their failure(s) to not having shared expectations and specific ground rules. Instead, teams should start with the question "How will we work together?" not "What is the right answer to the project?" Setting shared expectations, checking for effective teamwork, and making adjustments along the way are also essential. The exercises that follow do just this. They are built from best practices that are commonly found in industry; they help teams reduce risk by identifying typical teamwork problems at the individual and team levels and by offering a process for solving those problems.

The bottom line is that teamwork affects project quality. However, success is not guaranteed because teamwork is a human activity as much as it is about getting work done. Teams commonly falter because people focus on team mechanics such as task delegation and project management while ignoring more foundational issues such as power, trust, healthy conflict, and decision rights. For example, teams may publish a schedule, but members do not feel accountable for adhering to it. Interestingly, teams that start effectively often improve from there. Teams that struggle tend to know that they are struggling, but they often fail to address their problems and performance worsens. Simply put, this curriculum challenges people to think and work together differently than is typical of most people's experiences with teams. It is intended for teams that have a project or longer mission that they are about to undertake.

The critical perspectives applied to this chapter are predicated on the fact that nearly every aspect of team processes is manifest as a result of stocks of knowledge (see Chapter 2 of the main text for full details; Dugan, 2017). These deeply rooted ways of interpreting the world inform how we engage with others in and outside of team experiences. Stocks of knowledge are in turn shaped by social identity and historical social forces and manifest in the context of systems of power and privilege. When team leadership is examined through this lens, the focus shifts to recognizing and addressing how social histories and structures shape the unique differences, perspectives, and approaches each person brings to a team.

Curriculum Plan

This curriculum is designed to equip participants with tools to use for future team leadership experiences. As such, each activity is more of a preview of team processes when engaging in collective group work. Adapted from an online leadership portal (Goodman, Wolff, Bockenfeld, Tiedeman, & Kim, 2010), the curriculum helps people learn how to reliably and repeatedly work with others in a collegial manner. It does not provide ready answers to simple questions that can be applied in a formulaic manner, nor will memorization of facts or models aid team success. Instead, success depends on each person's ability to …

- Think critically
- Ask great questions
- Understand, synthesize, and commit to the team's charter
- Be prepared to express themselves in a concise and effective manner
- Challenge and play well with teammates, the team's sponsor(s), and other stakeholders
- Identify and commit to improving specific individual and team development goals
- Recognize and value the unique perspective and approach to leading each member brings
- Acknowledge the roles of power, privilege, and external social forces on individual and collective agency
- Diagnose and overcome indifference, freeloading, and signs of failure

This curriculum consists of three sessions: a team charter that should be written before work begins on team projects; a mid-project review that should be conducted at a logical midpoint during projects, typically after a significant milestone has been completed; and an after-project review that should be conducted when the projects end. Sessions begin with individual homework followed by exercises conducted by the full team. In general, the team charter requires individual homework time of 20 minutes and 60 to 90 minutes of team time. Activities 2 and 3 each require 10 minutes of time per team member and 45 minutes of team time.

❯ Activity 1—Team Charter Exercise

This is a structured exercise for teams to discuss each person's past experiences with teams, build on those experiences by identifying principles for why some teams fail and others succeed, and develop a charter to govern team conduct.

Learning Outcomes

- Identify behaviors (or absence of behaviors) that contribute to team success and failure.
- Recognize social contexts that contribute to or hinder contributions to team efforts.
- Learn how to produce a team charter that describes a collective agreement for how to work together.

Setting Up the Activity

Group Size: Open to any size group. Optimal small group sizes are 4 to 12 people per team.

Time: Individual homework (20 minutes), team exercise (60–90 minutes).

Methods: Group discussion, self-assessment, reflection

Materials: Whiteboard/chalkboard for each team, writing utensils

Directions

1. Each person prepares brief, written responses to each of the following questions *prior* to the actual team experience:
   - *What is an example of team failure, ideally one that you experienced?*
   - *What behaviors, by their presence or absence, caused the failure?*
   - *What is an example of team success, ideally one that you experienced?*
   - *What behaviors helped bring about the team's success?*
2. The team experience begins with the full team discussing each person's homework responses and working together to produce a single document addressing the following:
   - *Why do some teams succeed and others fail?*
   - *What might this team do to maximize the likelihood of success?*
   - *What might this team do to minimize the likelihood of failure?*

   Note that answers to the second and third questions are not necessarily the inverse of each other. For example, a list for maximizing success might include "offering as many new ideas as possible," and minimizing failure might include "speaking up when I disagree with someone on the team." This is also an excellent opportunity to raise themes such as accountability, conflict, empowering others, equity, self-awareness, self-reflection, shared commitment, power, and trust by posing questions such as these:
   - *How do status, title, power, and privilege affect accountability and decision making among team members?*
   - *What is the difference between equity of commitment and equality of contribution?*
   - *What types of team dynamics would enable people to feel that they are psychologically safe to contribute ideas and work?*

- *What role does self-awareness and self-reflection play in team-work? What are the differences between being self-aware and self-reflective?*
- *How do people build and maintain trust with each other? In what ways can social identity assumptions and biases, stocks of knowledge, and/or ignorance of particular social histories and systems result in team conflict and, ultimately, eroded trust?*

3. Tell your participants that as a team, they need to write a team charter. The charter sets out a team's collective agreement about how people will work together, standards for excellence, and how people will respond to gaps in individual and team performance. Although there is no set formula for team charters, it will typically answer the following questions:

- *What is the mission?*
- *What will success look like?*
- *What specific objectives does the team need to reach for success? By when?*
- *What roles are needed within the team, and who will fill those roles?*
- *What resources (e.g., people, time, financial, processes) does the team need?*
- *What is the context of the team's work? Who sponsored the team and what is known about that person's (or team's) expectations?*
- *How will the team allocate power and authority? For example, who has authority to make what decisions? What decisions can individuals make? What decisions can be made by smaller work teams? What decisions does the full team make? If power is abused, what steps will be taken to address and resolve this? What stocks of knowledge inform how power and authority are understood?*
- *How will the team define healthy conflict? What stocks of knowledge inform how healthy conflict is understood? What value does the team place on conflict? How will the team resolve conflict when it occurs?*

- *How will the team build and protect psychological safety on the team? What stocks of knowledge inform how psychological safety is understood? What do members on the team need to experience such safety?*
- *How will the team know when it has achieved genuine agreement on the charter?*

Facilitator Notes

Great team charters set specific expectations for quality and responsibility. For example, many would agree with the statements "We want to reach our goals," or "We want to be the top team." Similarly, members might agree "Everyone should come to each team meeting prepared to contribute." Great; those are goals. However, they do not specify how these goals will be measured along the way. How do members know whether mediocre or excellent work takes place when work is turned into the team or during team discussions?

Teams should change charters as they learn about habits that aid or impede team effectiveness. It is essential that the entire team meet together to make these changes. Often, teams find it useful to review the charter on a regular basis, typically after the first two weeks and then at least once each month thereafter. Although teamwork is an essential part of any great team, it must be complemented with effective project management. A simple project planning tool is to document "What, When, and Who?" What work needs to be done? When does the work need to be done? Who is responsible for making sure the work gets done?

❯ Activity 2—Mid-Project Review

This review provides teams with an evidence-based, uniform method with which to evaluate each member's performance. Members identify how they can improve their teamwork and the team identifies three changes for its charter.

Learning Outcomes

- Understand the impact of individual performance on team dynamics.
- Identify areas of growth and change to enhance overall team effectiveness and behavior.

Setting Up the Activity

Group Size: Open to any size group. Optimal small group size is 4 to 12 people per team.

Time: Individual homework (20 minutes), team exercise (60–90 minutes)

Methods: Group discussion, self-assessment, reflection

Materials: Whiteboard/chalkboard for each team; writing utensils

Directions

1. Prior to the actual team experience, have each participant evaluate each team member's performance, including their own, by briefly commenting on each member. Comments to consider include examples of the way(s) in which individuals aided or impeded the team, and/or ideas for how people can improve their teamwork abilities.

2. Have each participant assign a point value to the overall contribution made by each team member including the one they made. The total points awarded across all team members should equal 100.

3. Then have each participant provide notes about the overall team by responding to each of these questions (Note that these comments are not a substitute for observations about individual team members):

   - *What went well for the team?*
   - *What could the team have done better?*
   - *What should the team do differently based on what has been learned?*

This is a useful opportunity to revisit critical perspectives from the Team Charter Exercise. As a reminder, these are commonly accountability, conflict, empowering others, equity, psychological safety, self-awareness, self-reflection, shared commitment, power, and trust. Have participants consider questions such as the following:

- *How did status, title, power, and privilege affect accountability and decision making among team members?*
- *Are any stocks of knowledge influencing how the team works together? If so what? How would you characterize the influence of these stocks of knowledge?*
- *Were there issues building and maintain trust with each other?*
- *How were the needs and voice of all members heard and attended to throughout the project?*

4. Have your participants rate their agreement with the following statement: *I am satisfied with how my team is doing overall.* Have them use the following scale: *Strongly Disagree, Disagree, Neither Agree nor Disagree, Agree,* or *Strongly Agree.* Finally, invite participants to consider their individual experience on the team given what they observed and articulated at the team level. Questions could include these:

- *How did you experience the team process?*
- *How did you experience psychological safety as a member of the team?*
- *How did you feel affirmed? Not affirmed?*

The team experience begins with the group collectively assisting each individual member to identify one important and specific gap to close. Teams should have an honest discussion about each person's performance, one at a time. The person being discussed begins by asking others about their performance and what they see as possible gaps or areas of growth. Repeat the process so that every person both receives feedback and shares feedback for each member.

Note that it is tremendously important that teams first revisit their Team Charter as a set of ground rules to use to engage in this exercise. Discussing individual performance from an organizational standpoint can be sensitive and can potentially trigger deep insecurities, tensions, or reactions to team dynamics. Moreover, the integration of social dynamics into this process only increases that sensitivity. In particular, group recognition of biased or offensive behaviors that resulted in an erosion of psychological safety and trust for members of the team should be handled with tremendous care. Tone is important and participants should use "I" statements focusing on their own feelings when providing feedback (e.g., "I felt invisible when you ignored my suggestion but seemed to listen to all of the suggestions coming from men").

Furthermore, participants receiving feedback should work to avoid entrenchment in defensive stances. This includes listening and only asking questions to clarify the feedback being given rather than refuting it. The reality is that this can improve their behavior. Team members should approach this conversation as they would with a trainer they have hired to improve their physical fitness and not as people who are there to prove themselves (See the "Facilitator Notes" section for additional tips on how to deliver feedback).

5. Have participants identify potential changes that will improve the team's performance. The team reviews its charter and discusses the following questions:

- *Did the team use a project plan? If so, in what ways has it helped?*
- *What are the weak spots in either the plan or its execution?*
- *Did the team have specific expectations for quality and responsibility? What expectations did the team set for psychological safety and trust? Can members still state those expectations? What were the gaps between the team's expectations and the actual execution?*
- *What is one example of effective teamwork from the project? From a leadership perspective, what aided the team's success?*

- *What is one example of ineffective teamwork from the project? From a leadership perspective, what caused failure to happen?*
- *What practices, routines, or habits should the team stop because they are ineffective or create problems?*
- *Is there an idea or two that really aided the team's work?*
- *Is there an idea or two that, on reflection, would have significantly aided the team's work had it been put into action?*

6. Based on discussion of these questions, *what are 2 or 3 specific changes in the team's behavior that it will implement for the next part of the project?*

Facilitator Notes

Below you will find tips on how to assist participants in giving and receiving feedback.

- *Giving Feedback*: Apart from "I felt" statements, another effective structure for sharing feedback is to say, "When you did X, this was the effect on me and my experience with the team."
- *Feedback Challenges*: Honest conversations often challenge teams to …
  - Address problems that exist so that members overcome their fear of doing so
  - Encourage each other for the good of the work
  - Set clear and shared expectations for each person's participation
- *Receiving Feedback*: People need to be invited to express themselves without worry and to avoid the temptation to respond. The person being discussed should sincerely listen to others' ideas about what gaps can be addressed. People will be overly polite and less honest at the first sign of defensiveness, diminishing the opportunity to receive honest insights. Useful questions to ask often include these:
    - *If I understand you correctly, you perceived me as doing … ?*

- *What actions did I take that led you to that conclusion?*
- *Help me understand what I did that contributed to you thinking that?*
- *What could I have done differently?*
- *What was it about my words/tone/action/body language/decision that worked or did not work?*
- *How could I communicate better in the future?*
- *If you had one piece of advice for me, what would it be?*
- *What is the one skill that you think I should work on?*
- *What can I do to improve your experience on the team?*

> Activity 3—After Project Review

This review provides teams with an evidence-based, uniform method with which to evaluate each member's performance. Members identify how they can improve teamwork next time they are on a team and also identify three behaviors that each person believes are important for effective teamwork. Note that the format is similar, but not identical, to the mid-project review.

Learning Outcomes

- Recognize best practices for delivering and receiving feedback from team members.
- Identify habits that promote effective teamwork and are useful in teams' interactions.

Setting Up the Activity

Group Size: Open to any size group. Optimal small group size is 4 to 12 people per team.

Time: Individual homework (20 minutes), team exercise (60–90 minutes)

Methods: Group discussion, self-assessment, reflection

Materials: Whiteboard/chalkboard for each team, writing utensils

Directions

1. Prior to the actual team experience, have participants evaluate each team member's performance, including their own, by briefly commenting on each member. Comments to consider include examples of the way(s) in which the participant aided or impeded the team and/or ideas for how the participant can improve teamwork abilities.

2. Have each participant assign a point value to the overall contribution made by each team member including themselves. The total points awarded across all team members should equal 100.

3. Have each participant provide notes about the overall team by responding to each of the following questions (note that these comments are not a substitute for observations about individual team members):

   - *What went well for the team?*
   - *What could the team have done better?*
   - *What should the team do differently based on what has been learned?*

4. This discussion provides a useful opportunity for participants to revisit critical perspectives from the team charter and the mid-project exercises. As a reminder, these themes are commonly accountability, conflict, empowering others, equity, psychological safety, self-awareness, self-reflection, shared commitment, power, and trust. Have participants consider questions such as these:

   - *How did status, title, power, and privilege affect accountability and decision making among team members?*
   - *Did any stocks of knowledge continue influencing how the team worked together? If so what? How did this influence the team?*
   - *How were equity of commitment and equality of contributions managed?*

- *What types of team dynamics did you implement to ensure people felt they were psychologically safe to contribute ideas and work? How effective were they?*
- *How did the team engage in self-reflection and self-awareness?*
- *How did people build and maintain trust with each other? Were there issues building and maintaining trust?*

5. Have participants rate their agreement with the following statement: *I am satisfied with how my team did overall.* Use the following scale: *Strongly Disagree, Disagree, Neither Agree nor Disagree, Agree,* or *Strongly Agree.*

6. The team experience begins with the group working collectively to help each member identify one important and specific gap to close. During this portion of the curriculum, this team exercise has only one step, which should be facilitated exactly the same as in Step 4 of Activity 2. Teams should have an honest discussion about each person's performance, one at a time. Be sure to reference the note included in that step and apply the same level of care and sensitivity during this iteration of the discussion process.

7. The final element of this activity involves a follow-up homework assignment. Have participants identify up to three specific changes to the team charter that would have improved the team's performance. Ask them: *What are two to three behaviors that future teams should use?*

> Conclusion

These exercises provide members and facilitators with a routine method for helping people learn from their experiences and about how they work with others to produce a shared outcome that would not be possible through the accomplishments of a single individual. As with any process that requires change, success is not assured. Teams often find that their work can produce multiple possible right answers (as well as multiple possible wrong answers). With so much change and uncertainty, teams need to find ways to reduce risk. Because teamwork is fundamentally a behavioral process, it is difficult for members to define and understand their expectations for each other. It is equally difficult for members to understand the ways in which they individually aid and impede success. Team members often want to focus all of their work on the project that they have undertaken. However, they should begin by first reaching a shared understanding of the behaviors, constraints, expectations, and resources at their disposal. As work proceeds and as the project ends, members need to take time to evaluate, refine, and make this thinking more specific.

Chapter 7: Theories of Transformational Leadership

7A: Transformational Leadership

Marilyn J. Bugenhagen

Objectives/Goals of Chapter

- Understand transforming and transformational leadership theory facilitating an awareness of power and influence dynamics.
- Identify foundational tenets of transforming and transformational leadership and interactions when considering social location.
- Recognize the possibilities and challenges of transforming and transformational leadership in the context of stocks of knowledge and ideology.

Critical Concepts: *authority, ideology, power, social location, stocks of knowledge*

Chapter Overview

Transforming and *transformational* leadership are vibrant terms used across the study of leadership. Yet, through critical perspectives, they become less heroic and more focused on the influence of the reciprocal relationships between leader/followers. Burns (1978) first employed the term *transforming*, a verb, to *describe* leadership as a mutually reciprocal process between leader/followers that uplifts "one another to higher levels of motivation and morality" (p. 20). This reciprocity is described as the fusing of power bases available to both follower and leader in "mutual support for a common purpose" (p. 20). The ability to motivate one another around a common purpose for the collective good fosters strong moral and ethical engagement.

Alternatively, *transformational*, an adjective, is presented *before* the word *leadership*. It implies related to or involving transformation, which, as a noun, describes a thorough or dramatic change in form or appearance. Transformational leadership theory provides a view of the leader as one who engages in particular behaviors and actions with followers to promote a change in followers' performance for the purpose of organizational goals and outcomes. Although this includes an individualized approach to develop the follower, the leader is focused on inspiring followers for the vision and mission of the organization's goals as the ultimate end.

Although most literature credits Burns's *Leadership* (1978) as introducing transformational leadership, he was not the first to expound on the transforming potential of the leader/follower relationship. Burns (1978) followed Downton's (1973) introduction of transformational leadership in *Rebel Leadership*. Burns characterized the relationship between politician and citizen as one of exchange leading to mutual satisfaction: the political leader would bring the interests of the electorate to bear on decisions to uplift society in a way that promoted social change and "higher levels of motivation and morality" (Burns, 1978, p. 20). This reciprocity serves as an important distinction associated with Burn's transforming leadership. In the mid-1980s, Bass, an industrial psychologist, expanded the reciprocal nature of the leader/follower dyad to include transformational and transactional behaviors within the leader/follower exchange process. Although transactional behaviors are widely viewed as activities of management, transformational behaviors are thought to uplift the follower to higher levels of effectiveness and satisfaction enhancing the overall good of the organization. This presents a paradox of the transforming versus transformational leader. This dynamic of moral motivation for service, as posited by Burns (1978), shifts to an organizational concept focused on the follower uplifting the organization's goals over any individual goal in Bass's (1985) work.

› Chapter Framework

From a critical perspective, *transforming* leadership resists the tradition of granting sole authority to positional leaders and reimagines leadership as the potential for shared responsibility, collaboration, and development. *Transforming* leadership has the potential to be *transformational* precisely because the relationship between leader/followers is mutually constituted. Kegan (2009) stressed that meaning-making is transformation (i.e., "What forms, transforms," p. 44) and serves as an important component in the development of this leader/follower relationship. In the quest for shared meaning and commitment among leaders and followers, how information is received and prioritized matters as well as how that information becomes part of the sense-making of the relationship. When the follower/leader relationship moves from leader as "hero" to coleadership (Alvarez & Svejenova, 2005) or shared leadership (Pearce & Conger, 2002), we begin to see the reciprocal process in action. Leaders uplift followers and followers uplift leaders, creating a shared focus on higher motivation and morality. This partnership requires a complexity of mind rather than a position of dominance over a group.

Critical perspectives offer an inroad to developing the complexity of mind necessary for transforming leadership, which requires individuals to explore the stocks of knowledge that inform their understanding of leaders, followers, and power dynamics. It also necessitates the exploration of ideology and how strong differentiations between leaders and followers as well as the situating of development as primarily in service of organizational goals likely reflects dominant norms that reinforce the authority of positional roles. Finally, the complexity of mind that cultivates transforming leadership requires us to explore issues of social location and how varying identities groups may experience and manifest transforming leader behaviors.

> Curriculum Plan

This curriculum provides participants with an exposure to information as well as evidence that conflicts with potentially flawed beliefs and models of transformational and transforming leadership. Activities will guide participants through a process of questioning their understanding that is likely to take time, patience, and creativity in order for them to develop a deeper understanding of leader authority and leader/follower reciprocity for leading. The following curriculum plan may be implemented over four sessions, each ranging from 1 to 2 hours. Although segmented sessions are optimal for the curriculum to allow ample processing and reflection, the sessions may also be facilitated consecutively as an extended workshop or training.

> Activity 1—Transformational Leadership

The focus of this activity is on understanding transactional and transformational leadership, which sets up the leader/follower relationships of authority and power. Participants' experiences of leadership may challenge the appeal of transformational leadership.

Learning Outcomes

- Identify elements, nuances, and challenges of transformational leadership.
- Understand preferences for engaging in certain leadership behaviors.
- Adopt a critical lens toward transformational leadership that considers social identity.

Setting Up the Activity

Group Size: Open to any size group

Time: 60 minutes

Methods: Dialogue, lecture, reflection

Materials: Projector/screen, Chapter 7 of main text and supplemental readings on transforming leadership (e.g., Burns, 1978, pp. 20–21 and pp. 68–72 and/or Bass & Riggio, 2005, Part II)

Variations: Self-assessment of transactional and transformational leadership behaviors could be provided prior to the activity. Note that paper and electronic versions of the Multi-Factor Leadership Questionnaire can be accessed by visiting: www .mindgarden.com.

Directions

1. Begin the session by explaining the learning outcomes and activities. Explicitly state that the first activity will explore transformational leadership versus transforming leadership.

2. Overview the primary components of transformational and transactional leadership referring to Chapter 7 of the main text as necessary.

3. Engage participants in a dialogue about their experiences with the component parts of the theory. Most participants will gravitate to the transformational components despite the fact that longitudinal research demonstrates that contingent

reward (i.e., transactional) is also highly effective (Avolio & Bass, 2004). The exchange of work for reward is motivating for a majority of people. During the dialogue consider the following prompts:

- *What immediate reactions do you have to the terms transformational and transactional? What emotions do they conjure for you? Attempt to connect any emotional responses to specific life experiences that inform your reactions to the terms.*

- *How and to what extent might reactions to the concepts of transformation and transactions be a function of stocks of knowledge? What "recipes" are you holding that shape your reaction?*

- *What are the potential benefits of considering transaction and transformation not as binary concepts, but ones that coexist? What implications might that have for leadership?*

4. If you had participants complete one of the suggested assessments, engage them in a dialogue about this next. Inquire about their reactions to each of the transformational behaviors. The goal is to problematize reactions to the concepts of transaction and transformation to increase complexity of meaning. Consider the following questions:

- *How do transactional behaviors of leaders positively or negatively impact followers? How effective do you think contingent reward maybe in the leader/follower relationship?*

- *To what extent might transformational behaviors (e.g., idealized influence) reinforce "leader as hero" views and, in turn, authority dynamics? How?*

- *How might transformational behaviors provide an "uplift" in motivation and morality that would be mutually beneficial to followers and leaders rather than just be in service of organizational goals?*

5. Conclude by asking participants to examine how ideology and social location may aid in deconstructing their understanding of transformational leadership. Have them consider these questions:

- *How might transformational leadership reflect a dominant ideology? What values, assumptions, and myths might it reinforce (e.g., leadership as inherently positive, view of leader as hero, leaders knowing what is best for follower development)? How might ideological assumptions play out in the component parts of transformational leadership?*

- *How might social location influence how one experiences or practices transformational leadership? How might followers be influenced by the leader? How might leaders be influenced by the follower? How can followers and leaders work together to shift thinking about the relationship?*

- *How does considering the social identities of leaders and followers influence transformational leadership practice? How might inclusion or exclusion occur in the use of transformational leadership? Can members of traditionally marginalized social identity groups (e.g., women, People of Color) enact the four factors and have them received in the same way as those from dominant groups?*

- *What is the role of power and authority in transforming the ways of making meaning in organizations? How could returning to Burns's transforming leadership reflect critical perspectives and aid in reconstruction?*

Debriefing Notes

The process of coming to understand transformational and transactional leadership provides a starting point for connecting to participants' prior knowledge and experiences. As participants become more aware of their "discourse" with the concepts through a critical perspective, they may push back on whether or not the critical perspective is distorting a perfectly healthy way of leading. Leaders often believe they use their authority for the good of the organization. Chapter 7 brings an awareness of the possibility that good intentions may not be enough (Dugan, 2017). The best intentions of leaders may be viewed as an abuse of authority. Furthermore, traditional leader/follower relationships can exclude, promote injustice, or promulgate the primacy of organizational outcomes. The ability to balance the distribution of power and authority through a discussion of critical perspectives will be important to creating a deeper understanding of this chapter.

Facilitator Notes

Be aware that participants who have more experience to draw upon may overtake the conversation or become self-proclaimed experts. Tapping into everyone's experiences, no matter how much experience they have, may be worth exploring.

> Activity 2—Transforming Leadership

The focus of this activity is on understanding transforming leadership and reciprocity in the leader/follower relationship. Through the readings and tapping into participants' prior experiences, participants will create a shared definition of transforming leadership.

Learning Outcomes

- Identify elements, nuances, and challenges of transforming leadership.
- Understand the concept of transforming leadership along with characteristics and hallmarks of leaders/followers engaging in reciprocity.

Setting Up the Activity

Group Size: Open to any size group

Time: 60 minutes

Methods: Dialogue, lecture, small and large group interaction

<u>Materials</u>: For each group: one sticky flip chart page, markers, color coded sticky dots

Directions

1. Begin the session by explaining the learning outcomes and activities. Explicitly state that this activity will explore transforming leadership.

2. Overview the key tenets of transforming leadership differentiating it from transformational leadership. Refer to Chapter 7 of the main text as necessary.

3. Split into groups of five. Provide flip chart page and markers to groups. Tell participants: *You have 15 minutes to create a list of the characteristics of transforming leadership.* Encourage groups to refine their list to no more than 10 characteristics.

4. After 15 minutes, have each group share and hang their flip charts for viewing. Engage in a dialogue about similarities and differences among the lists. Next, create a new flip chart combining the characteristics into a master list. Give each participant five sticky dots. Tell them: *Place one dot per characteristic you believe is a component of transforming leadership.*

5. Tally the dots to make a final list of characteristics. Lead a discussion on the final list encouraging participants to connect to the session's readings. Have them consider the following questions:

   • *What made the list that surprises you? What didn't make the list that surprises you? How might the list have looked different had the instructions been to focus on transformational instead of transforming leadership?*

   • *What considerations related to stocks of knowledge, ideology, and social location addressed in the discussion of transformational leadership also merit conversation here?*

   • *Are there ways in which characteristics reflect dominant or heroic leader prototypes? To what extent can the characteristics listed be enacted by members of varying social identity groups and be received similarly?*

6. Instruct small groups to reassemble and construct a final list of characteristics of transforming leadership for use in a later activity.

Debriefing Notes

This session was a significant step in understanding the differences between transforming leadership and transformational leadership. Transforming leadership engages leaders and followers in a reciprocal process in which power is diffused and authority is distributed as mutual development occurs.

> Activity 3—Transforming Relationships

Engage participants in viewing one of the suggested films to bring to life and contribute to a greater understanding of the elements of transforming leadership.

Learning Outcomes

- Identify elements, nuances, and challenges of transforming leadership in a historical account through film.
- Understand transforming leadership and the characteristics and hallmarks of leaders and followers engaging in reciprocity as depicted in the film.

Setting Up the Activity

<u>Group Size</u>: Small groups of three to five people or an individual activity

<u>Time</u>: 30–55 minutes depending on the activity plus time for viewing the film

Methods: Video, reflection, small group interaction

Materials: DVD player, screen, audio, online film guides that provide educational teaching tools such as *Teaching with Movies* (www.teachwithmovies.org/index.html).

Multimedia: The following films offer strong connections to activity content and are presented in order of best representations: *Lincoln* (2012): 2 hours, 30 minutes; *Invictus* (2009): 2 hours, 14 minutes; *Gandhi* (1982): 3 hours, 11 minutes; *Iron Lady* (2011):1 hour, 45 minutes

Variations: Participants could watch the selected film prior to the session, taking notes on prompt questions. Alternatively, this could be completed prior to the session. Finally, the recommended films all focus on formal leaders rather than group processes. This is to showcase content that allows participants to trouble, rather than sidestep, formal authority. You could, however, use films in which there is no formal authority, such as *Selma* (2014) or *Lord of the Rings* (2001–2003).

Directions

1. Assign a film and provide prompt questions on which participants should take notes:
   - *Moral Leadership*: Focus on values and ethics for a "good society" whereby people feel shared responsible for the good of one another.

     What values were represented by different characters in the film? How did the characters experience dilemmas associated with maintaining and acting on their values? What constituted shared values for the common good in this film?
   - *Motivation for Leadership*: The desire to lead and be led for higher purpose of the society over self-interest.

     Describe a scene where a character(s) displayed a motivation to a higher purpose beyond self-interest. In what scenes did a character struggle with their motivation for leading or being led?

How did others respond to the struggle for motivation? What seems to erode motivation (consider stocks of knowledge, ideology, social location, power, and authority)?

- *Transforming Leadership:* The ability to lead and be led in a way that lifts one another up for the higher purpose of society.

  How did the leader or the led struggle with the "hero as leader" concept? Were there changes in the way the leader/followers created an understanding about the purpose for leading? What struggles for understanding did you see between leaders and the led? Was there a resolution to the struggle, or did it maintain some sort of tension in the leader/follower relationship? How did the leader view their role in creating understanding about the higher purpose and what might have been their inner struggle in the film? How did the followers create meaning out of the struggle as portrayed in the film? In what ways was reciprocity between leaders and followers evident? Were there explicit examples of behaviors that cultivated this?

- *Critical Perspectives:* An approach, in this case in studying leadership, that addresses issues of stocks of knowledge, ideology/hegemony, and social location.

  In what way did power dynamics influence the course of events in the film? How did power flow between and among characters in the film? How was that power used or not used in leader roles and processes? Were there ways in which stocks of knowledge influenced leadership events or relationships? What ideologies were at play and how did they shape the ways in which characters engaged with leadership? How did social location influence the manifestation of leadership? To what extent was social location explicitly named as an influence on leadership? What elements of exclusion and inclusion were apparent in the film? How do leaders and the led work through these concepts? What interventions do leaders or followers take when exclusion or inclusion occurs? To what extent do the interventions succeed?

2. Begin by explaining the learning outcomes and activities. Share that the focus of this session is examining how relationships unfold in the practice of transforming leadership.

3. Create small groups of three to five participants. Ask groups to engage in a dialogue around the question prompts in Step 1. The goal is to identify themes across their interpretations. It may be helpful to identify two to three scenes to play during the session to focus conversation.

4. Reconvene as a large group to consider the following questions:
   - *How is this movie instructive about the nature of leader/follower relationships? What challenges emerge in attempting to engage in transforming leadership? What specific behaviors advanced transforming leadership? What detracted from it? What is the value added for integrating considerations associated with critical perspectives?*

❯ Activity 4—Reciprocal Relationships

Engage participants in identifying the concepts of power, influence, reciprocity, and influence dynamics in transforming leadership. Participants consider power takeovers, resisting power, and the importance of shared leadership.

Learning Outcomes

- Identify elements, nuances, and challenges of transforming leadership in practice.
- Recognize how leader/follower dynamics are manifest.

Setting Up the Activity

<u>Group Size</u>: Open to any size group

<u>Time</u>: 60 minutes

<u>Methods</u>: Dialogue, lecture, reflection

<u>Materials</u>: List of transforming leadership characteristics from earlier activity

<u>Multimedia</u>: Projector/screen, *Leadership and Followership: What Tango Teaches Us About These Roles in Life* video (www.youtube .com/watch?t=1&v=Cswrnc1dggg)

Directions

1. Begin the session by explaining the learning outcomes and types of activities.

2. Ask participants to gather in their small groups and make sure they have the transforming leadership characteristics lists that they created in Activity 2 with them. Ask the groups to discuss the specific roles of leaders and followers in engaging in transforming leadership. What are the necessary behaviors and responsibilities of each?

3. Introduce the video, explaining that through tango dance, and the role of the two dancers, participants can begin to understand the dynamics of power, influence, reciprocity, shared leadership, and individual dynamics. View the video (7 minutes) and lead a discussion about power, including resistance, influence, reciprocity, and shared leadership. Have participants consider the following questions:

    - *How was power exhibited between the leader and the led in this video? What happens when the follower resists the power asserted by the leader? What attempts at influence did you view as the leader attempted to lead? What resistance did you see from the follower to the leader's attempt to lead? How did a mutual reciprocity of give and take become possible?*

    - *How might the dance of leading, and being led, result in a shared responsibility for leadership? What interventions do you see that apply to establishing this type of reciprocal relationship?*

4. Conclude the session with a dialogue on what it would be like to be in an organization where transforming leadership

was practiced. Encourage participants to explore the pros and cons as well as ways in which transforming leadership can be reconstructed to better address critical perspectives (i.e., stocks of knowledge, ideology/hegemony, social location).

> Conclusion

This chapter was designed to guide participants through how they think about leadership and the impact of their prior knowledge and experiences on the change that can occur from understanding a concept from different perspectives. Through self-assessment tools, personal reflection, group idea generating and sharing, and large group processes, participants were challenged to explore the topics of transformational and transforming leadership to come up with a shared understanding. Participants' applications of critical perspectives allow for deeper identification of the reciprocal relationship between leaders/followers. As participants gain a deeper understanding of the complexity of these concepts, they can begin to explore personal ways of making meaning of their experiences in organizations. They may begin to challenge their own ways of leading and begin to think about the role of power and influence in leadership.

7B: Servant Leadership Through a Critical Lens

Richard A. Couto

Objectives/Goals of Chapter

- Situate the historical context of the rise of servant leadership in the context of leadership studies, especially as compared to other U.S. social movements.
- Reexamine the inspiration of servant leadership using Hesse's *The Journey to the East* (1956).
- Recognize how servant leadership may relate to and be applied in organizations.

Critical Concepts: *agency, critical self-reflection, efficacy, normativity, social location*

> Chapter Overview

The publication of Greenleaf's *Servant Leadership* in 1977 and Burn's *Leadership* in 1978 marked a paradigmatic shift in the study of leadership. Both works emphasized values and, although they remained leader-centric, brought followers into the leadership process. Often unnoticed is that both works come from origins in a disappointment that the democratic promise of the 1960s did not result in greater democratic transformation. Both scholars cited mediocrity as the reason for the shortcomings of democratic aspirations of the 1960s. For Burns, it was intellectual mediocrity: we do not know enough about the nature of transforming leadership. Greenleaf pointed to institutional mediocrity: our institutions were not doing as much as they could with their resources to achieve their social purposes. Greenleaf pointed to two institutional culprits of mediocrity: low levels of trusteeship (i.e., everyone takes responsibility for the mission of an institution) and the shift of primary responsibility to a single chief executive. Greenleaf's grand purpose in writing was to increase institutional excellence by providing people within institutions (e.g., schools, churches, businesses) with the motivation and agency to act as their trustees. The slow but surest means of reducing mediocrity, he opined, was "a process in which able, honest, serving people prepare themselves to lead and accept the opportunity to lead when offered" (Greenleaf, 1977, p. 149).

Chapter Framework

Since the publication of Greenleaf's (1977) original work, servant leadership has been utilized in organizational settings as a means to inspire a connection to organizational values and as a model for how selfless, values-based leadership can positively impact others. This positive, selfless interpretation often leaves servant leadership difficult to critique. A basic assumption of the theory is that of shared power and flat structures. Yet, as an organizational reality this may not be possible, especially given systems laden with dominant power structures. Additionally, the idea that servant leadership positioned service-oriented leadership as a novel approach fails to give credit to leadership occurring within social movements prior to Greenleaf's work. Traditional views of leadership give significant credit to Burns and Greenleaf for transforming the ways in which we understand leadership often without acknowledging that these ways of leading have long been in place and evident in social movements and activism.

In the spirit of shared power and selflessness espoused through the tenets of servant leadership, we must consider important critical questions around the inclusiveness of servant leadership.

> Curriculum Plan

This curriculum first centers on Greenleaf, his explanation of servant leadership, and the historical context within which servant leadership was popularized. The curriculum then examines the book that Greenleaf claims inspired his concept of servant leadership, *The Journey to the East* (Hesse, 1956). A deeper, more critical reading of Hesse's book suggests that there is much more to it than Greenleaf's summary. The process of examining the main character's aspirations and failures, and understanding of the true nature of servitude provide a platform for critical self-reflection. The activities within this chapter lead participants to reflect on their organization's goals, their trusteeship of them, and the means by which they may enact leadership in a just manner.

The curriculum plan is designed so that facilitators can conduct all activities in person over the course of a single or multiple sessions. Facilitators are encouraged, however, to segment out individual reflection activities for participants to complete on their own and/or prior to sessions.

> Activity 1—The Characteristics of Servant Leadership

This activity identifies the characteristics of servant leadership taken from Greenleaf's (1977) original work, putting them into conversation with theoretical perspectives, in addition to more deeply examining them in the context of power and authority as well as social location.

Learning Outcomes

- Understand the characteristics of servant leadership as originally defined.
- Identify influences of power, authority, and social location on servant leadership.
- Recognize how servant leadership challenges and replicates normative assumptions.

Setting Up the Activity

Group Size: Unlimited participants divided into small groups of four to five

Time: 30–45 minutes

Methods: Reading, small and large group discussion

Materials: Chapter 7 of main text for reference (Dugan, 2017)

Variations: You may wish to assign Chapter 1 from Greenleaf's (1977) *Servant Leadership* to offer participants exposure to the primary source.

Directions

1. Divide into small groups of four to five participants. If Chapter 7 of the main text (Dugan, 2017) has not been assigned, provide 5 to 10 minutes for groups to comb through it and Chapter 1 of *Servant Leadership* (Greenleaf, 1977). Ask them to identify and react to the list of characteristics of servant leadership.

2. Provide participants with 15 to 20 minutes for group dialogue examining the following questions regarding the nature of servant leadership. Prime them to apply critical perspectives to the theory and, in particular, to the list of characteristics of servant leaders.

   - *Which of these characteristics are present, explicitly or implicitly, in other leadership theories? Which are unique?*
   - *Which characteristics are fixed traits versus learnable skills?*

- *Can you think of anyone in your life you would identify as exhibiting the characteristics of servant leadership? To what extent do they align with the list of characteristics? Are there elements you would add?*
- *Do the characteristics described imply power differentials (e.g., those with power and authority choose to be "servants" for others)?*
- *To what extent can leaders of varying social locations (e.g., gender, age, ethnicity, ability) exhibit these characteristics and have them be received similarly both within their identity groups and outside of them?*

3. Conclude this activity with a large group discussion making explicit connections to trait-based assumptions in servant leadership. Trouble the roles of power and authority in the framework. One strategy to call attention to the complexity of servant leadership is to deconstruct the core components of the terms *servant* and *leader*. What stocks of knowledge are bound up in participants' understandings of these concepts and how might they reflect hegemonic norms? You might challenge participants to consider how power has manifested throughout history to frame our subconscious associations with each term.

＞ Activity 2—Historical Context: Social Movements as Undervalued Examples of Servant Leadership

This activity examines Greenleaf's (1977) inspiration and motives for writing the book *Servant Leadership* and introduces participants to social movements occurring before the traditional paradigm shift in leadership theory (see Chapter 3 in the main text for further explanation). Participants will become more aware of how social justice advocates were engaged in servant leadership practices before the approach was first published by Greenleaf.

Learning Outcomes

- Situate servant leadership in its historical context.
- Recognize social movements and draw comparisons with characteristics of servant leadership.
- Apply critical perspectives by comparing and contrasting the characteristics of leaders in social movements with servant leadership.

Setting Up the Activity

Group Size: 30–35 participants divided into five small groups

Time: 90 minutes

Methods: Group research, short informal presentations

Materials: Computer (one computer per group), Internet, projector/screen if presentations will infuse technology

Directions

1. Divide participants into five small groups and make sure each has access to a computer or tablet and the Internet. Assign each group to research a social movement that began prior to 1977 (e.g., women's suffrage, labor rights, the LGBTQ movement, the civil rights movement). Figures provided in Chapter 3 of the main text may be helpful to illustrate this. Instruct participants to spend the next 20 minutes finding as much information as they can on their particular social movement. The activity is intended to familiarize everyone at a basic level with the social justice movements that occurred prior to the traditionally recognized paradigm shift in leadership theory most often attributed to the publication of Burns's (1978) and Greenleaf's (1977) books. Participants should do their best to highlight leadership practices that characterized the movements.

2. Next, give each group 10 minutes to create a 5-minute presentation to share what they found with the large group.

Presentations should focus on characteristics of leadership in these movements.

3. Have each group present their findings.

4. Move back to small groups. Ask participants to reference the characteristics of servant leaders listed in Chapter 7 of the main text and compare and contrast this list with the characteristics generated from the social movements presentations.

5. Return to the large group and process using the following questions:

   - *Social movements around increased racial, gender, and economic equality provided Greenleaf and Burns with hope for democracy. What similarities or differences did you find between leadership exhibited within social justice movements and Greenleaf's characteristics of servant leadership?*

   - *If servant leadership characteristics mirror those from leadership in social movements that were occurring well before the "paradigm shift" in leadership theory, how great of a paradigm shift actually occurred? Why might you hypothesize that this was framed as such a monumental shift in leadership studies? Why might narratives from social movements not have served as the primary point of reference in Greenleaf's original work?*

   - *How might dominant cultural paradigms have influenced leadership theory? How might servant leadership have been defined differently if social movements had been considered part of the development of the approach?*

   - *How can we, as learners of leadership theory, become more critical about the ways in which we learn about and apply leadership theories in practice?*

Facilitator Notes

Participants more familiar with Greenleaf's work may reference his inspiration from movements like the anti-Vietnam war and/or the disillusionment associated with the Watergate scandal. It is important to note that these movements were important at the time and may have inspired his views on leadership as less hierarchical and emphasized the importance of shared power, but you will want to encourage participants to consider how these are still movements primarily situated within the dominant culture.

› Activity 3—Greenleaf and Hesse's *The Journey to the East*

Participants will critically examine the inspiration that Greenleaf ascribes to Leo, a character from *The Journey to the East* (Hesse, 1956), for his ideas of servant leadership.

Learning Outcomes

- Apply the characteristics of servant leadership through an analysis of Hesse's (1956) *The Journey to the East*.
- Critically examine Greenleaf's translation of Hesse's work to servant leadership.
- Recognize the role power and authority play in identifying servant leaders.

Setting Up the Activity

Group Size: Open to any size group divided into small groups of four to five

Time: 60–75 minutes

Methods: Critical reflection, discussion, literary analysis

Materials: Copy of Hesse's (1956) *The Journey to the East* or use of summary sheet provided

Directions

1. Organize participants into groups of three to five people. Refresh participants' minds regarding servant leadership by

instructing them to identify the characteristics of servant leadership they find most important and relevant. Provide groups with 5 minutes for this work. If needed, refer groups to Chapter 7 of the main text (Dugan, 2017).

2. Share with participants that Greenleaf named Hesse's *The Journey to the East* (1956) as the inspiration for servant leadership. If participants have not read Hesse's book, distribute the provided summary. Offer participants 5 to 10 minutes to read and reflect.

3. Give groups 20–25 minutes to engage in dialogue around the following prompts:
   - *What are your initial reactions to this story?*
   - *Identify and apply the characteristics of servant leadership to Hesse's story. Where do they seem to fit and/or misalign?*
   - *Apply critical perspectives to this story. Who gets to be a servant leader? Who wields power and authority? What are the cultural implications of servant for marginalized groups including people formerly colonized?*
   - *To what extent are there echoes of great man theory in Greenleaf's leader-centric interpretation of Hesse? How could this perspective perpetuate the marginalization of certain groups from leadership? Are there gender and social biases implied in servant leadership?*
   - *If, like Leo, the servant is the possessor of leadership, how does this promote or lessen the relational or communal aspect of leadership?*
   - *Acknowledging that Greenleaf cites this story as the primary influence for servant leadership, how does this change your perspective on it?*

4. Conduct a large group discussion. It is recommended that groups report to the large group on the question they most struggled with as this ensures deep and meaningful conversation. Offer 20 to 25 minutes for this conversation.

❯ Activity 4—Organizational Applications of Servant Leadership

This activity moves from abstract analysis to concrete applications of concepts associated with servant leadership. This is accomplished by first considering the implications of servant leadership for organizational leadership. The activity then draws on *Journey to the East* to personalize content and assist participants in reflecting on servant leadership in the context of organizations that they care about deeply.

Learning Outcomes

- Apply considerations from servant leadership to organizational leadership.
- Connect leadership efficacy, agency, and critical self-reflection to the application of servant leadership.
- Reconstruct servant leadership using critical perspectives.

Setting Up the Activity

Group Size: Open to any size group

Time: 60 minutes

Methods: Organizational assessment, large group discussion, reflection

Materials: A copy of Hesse's *The Journey to the East* (1956) or use of "Summary of Hesse's *The Journey to the East*" handout provided

Directions

1. Prior to the session, ask each participant to select a formal organization, institution, or group to which they belong and about which they care deeply. Alternatively, you could ask participants to use an organization in which they are all members for a shared frame of reference. Instruct participants to

find and review the mission statement of their selected group. Participants should reflect on what it means to be a trustee of that mission. Consider the following prompts:

- *Is the mission of the institution taken seriously? Are there other "operational goals" that undermine or comprise it?*
- *What does it mean to serve as a trustee of this organization?*
- *What does it look like when members of the organization take the mission seriously? When they do not? When they settle for mediocrity? Where would you fall along this continuum?*

2. Ask participants to review public opinions that may exist regarding their institution. Encourage them to think about the specific institution as well as its role in broader types of institutions (e.g., religious organizations, educational institutions, nonprofits). Participants should both scan media for public opinions and consider informal perceptions held by those external to it. Have participants consider these questions:

- *How does public opinion about your institution influence perceptions regarding the leaders who operate within the institution? How does it influence perceptions about what it means to serve as a trustee of the institution?*
- *If public opinions of an institution are low, to what extent might this reflect well-documented failures of a few to live up to organizational values?*

3. Provide a mini-lecture to ensure participants understand the concepts of *mediocrity* and *trusteeship* in servant leadership.

4. Put participants in small groups of four to five people. Provide 10 minutes for groups to share insights from the prompt questions that guided their reflections on institutions.

5. Next, turn the group back to the book that inspired Greenleaf's writing, *Journey to the East* (Hesse, 1956). Recount the events at Morbio Inferiore and their impact on the narrator of the

story. You may wish to read the following excerpt from Hesse's (1956) book:

With Leo's disappearance, the undertaking itself seemed in some mysterious way to lose meaning for H.H. He had moments of serious doubt and inner weakness. He not only lost faith in finding Leo again but in Leo himself. . . . For H.H. everything was unreliable and doubtful; the value and meaning of everything was threatened; and his imagination and group's now moved to persuade each other of terrible, irreplaceable loss. H.H. lost his confidence in his destiny but gained a new certainty in sad beliefs of irretrievable loss (p. 39).

Emphasize Leo's benediction that can summarize the whole of the book asserting that aspirations and despair are not a duality of opposites but an experiential combination. Ultimately, Leo's disappearance was a test as all others who had taken the journey were tested. H.H. and his group failed that test. Morbio Inferiore, it appears, is the little illness that comes with looking within ourselves and facing the doubts of whether or not we have what it takes to join a great experience, of whether such an experience is possible, and of the validity of our knowledge at different times in our lives.

6. Provide participants with a 30-minute reflection period to consider moments in which they've encountered Morbio Inferiore in their lives. Share the following prompts:

   • *When you started working with the institution that you reflected on in steps 1 and 2, did you believe, like H.H., that it was your "destiny to join a great experience?" To what extent do you still believe that?*

   • *How well do you serve as a trustee of the institution's mission? How do you express its aspirations? To what extent have you settled for mediocrity—your own and/or that of the organization?*

- *Have you experienced your own Morbio Inferiore moment and retreated from your highest aspirations? To what extent might this have been related to the "loss" of an authority figure? What are the roles of peer pressure in such retreats? What relationships exist between efficacy and these moments?*
- *Do you have any lingering regrets about a Morbio Inferiore moment? What lessons were learned?*
- *Describe a time you moved past a Morbio Inferiore moment. This often involves internal conflict about whether we can achieve our goals and if they are worth the effort. How did you handle internal conflict regarding this?*
- *What have you learned about yourself in the context of this institution that prepares you to deal with institutional mediocrity?*

7. Subdivide small groups into pairs. Invite participants to spend 10 minutes each sharing reactions to the reflection prompts in Step 6.
8. Engage participants in a final, large group conversation for 20 minutes reflecting on these questions:
   - *What lessons might you take away from exploring how we navigate Morbio Inferiore moments in organizational life? How might these lessons relate to efficacy, agency, and one's relationship with authority?*
   - *If Journey to the East served as an inspiration for servant leadership, where do the two converge and diverge in their core tenets and major takeaways?*
   - *What are the merits of servant leadership? Utilizing a critical perspective, what criticisms do you have? How might you reconstruct servant leadership?*

Facilitator Notes

This activity provides an opportunity for participants to connect themes of servant leadership to organizational realities. In facilitating this experience, you will want to push participants to reflect on moments of fallibility. It may be helpful to refer back to *Servant Leadership* and *Journey to the East* as frames of reference for this. Remind participants that in *Journey to the East*, Morbio Inferiore tested the willingness of candidates for the League to pass from one side of despair to the other and to do so without external authority, literally and metaphorically. In their journey, they came to a point where they had to trust what they had come to believe about the League and about themselves. They had to have enough faith in their beliefs to face their fear of proceeding without those who had instilled the beliefs. In doing so, they transformed themselves. They became their own authority.

The arc of the narrator in *Journey to the East* highlights two dimensions to leadership. The first and common interpretation evident in servant leadership is that a *servant leader is servant first*. This focuses attention on the characteristics of a specific person echoing back to great man and trait theories while also reinforcing leader centricity. The second and less emphasized dimension is what servant leaders do *regardless* of position. Greenleaf invites us to take on responsibilities as "trustees" of our organizations. His inspiration for servant leadership, Hesse, actually untangles service from leadership inviting us to be trustees of our own values and our belief that it is our destiny to join a great experience.

› Conclusion

Greenleaf (1977) shares the deep influence Hesse's (1956) *The Journey to the East* had on his conception of servant leadership. This curriculum offers a means to learn more about servant leadership while simultaneously interrogating its core assumptions, the historical context in which it emerged, and its application to organizational environments. Through this analysis, several critical questions are raised about the approach, including these: Who gets to be a servant leader? Who wants to be a servant leader? How do servant leaders navigate organizational dynamics? Participants' explorations of these themes offer a platform to engage with critical perspectives to advance the complexity of understanding of the theory.

Handout 7.1: Summary of Hesse's *The Journey to the East* (1956)

This novella chronicles the life of the narrator as he engages in a quest to travel to the East and fulfill his vows to the League, a group to which he committed his life in service. What lies in the East and what the League exists to promote remain mysteries throughout the novel; in fact, the narrator makes it quite clear that these objectives are mere accessories to the intent of his reflection. The narrator's primary focus is describing the lifestyle of a League servant, Leo, as he accompanies the narrator and a few other League companions on their expedition to the East. Leo serves as the group's traveling servant, carrying many of the group's articles as well as the map that guides them to the East.

In an exchange between the narrator and Leo early in their journey, the narrator asks Leo "why it was that artists sometimes appeared to by only half-alive, while their creations seemed so irrefutably alive" (Hesse, 1956, pp. 33–34). Leo's response captures the crux of the novel: "It is just the same with mothers. When they have borne their children and given them their milk and beauty and strength, they themselves become invisible, and no one asks about them any more" (p. 34). He continues explaining that this is "the law of service. He who wishes to live long must serve, but he who wishes to rule does not live long. . . . There are few who are born to be masters; they remain happy and healthy. But all the others who have only become masters through endeavor, end in nothing" (pp. 34–35).

At what becomes a pivotal moment in the story, Leo disappears while the group is at Morbio Inferiore, a deep mountain gorge. This leaves the narrator and his League companions to identify the remaining steps in their journey to the East. The group quickly falls into dissent and despair, forgetting the bond that tied them together: their vow to the League. As the narrator recounts, they forget the four life principles of the League and ultimately abandon their quest.

The narrator struggles to regain his sense of life purpose and sanity throughout the remainder of the novel. After living years of his life in a depressed and suicidal state, he makes it his objective to find Leo, discuss his memories of the League, and then record the story of the League and his journey to the East.

The narrator eventually finds Leo living a quiet life in a quaint town and is eventually taken to the League, much to the narrator's joy. Yet, in a rapid change of events, the narrator is called before the Speaker of the League and accused of being a "deserter League brother" (Hesse, 1956, p. 87). As this impromptu trial continues, the narrator examines his life with a new perspective and realizes that the life he lived following his journey to the East was not reflective of the League and its values. And in the final revelation of this tale, Leo emerges as the president of the League, completing the allegory of servant leadership.

7C: Raising the Mirror: The Social Change Model Through a Critical Lens

Lesley-Ann Brown-Henderson

Objectives/Goals of Chapter

- Understand how social identities influences the Cs of the social change model.
- Develop an action plan for creating social change based on the social change model.
- Recognize the role of critical hope in creating social change.

Critical Concepts: *critical hope, critical self-reflection, power, privilege, social identity*

› Chapter Overview

This chapter helps individuals understand how their social identities, through the lenses of critical perspectives, impact their understanding of the core values of the social change model (SCM) of leadership (Higher Education Research Institute [HERI], 1996). By spending time reflecting on social location and integrating that reflection into their understanding of the seven Cs of the SCM (i.e., consciousness of self, congruence, commitment, collaboration, common purpose, controversy with civility, and citizenship), participants will collectively consider the impact of societal challenges and personal strengths on their leadership development. Building upon this understanding, participants will develop declarations describing resilience and action. These declarations are then affirmed by their peers, showing solidarity and empowerment, which are integral to establishing and maintaining critical hope.

The SCM was developed by a group of leadership scholars in the early 1990s (HERI, 1996; Komives, Wagner, & Associates, 2009). The group created a new collaborative leadership model specifically for college students who were committed to creating social change within their communities (HERI, 1996). The seven core values of the SCM, the seven Cs, are grouped into three dimensions—individual values (i.e., consciousness of self, congruence, commitment), group values (i.e., collaboration, common purpose, controversy with civility), and societal/community values (i.e., citizenship)—all of which center around one's capacity to engage in and effect social change (HERI, 1996). The values of the SCM are "interactive," meaning "growth in one value increases the capacity for growth in the others" (Komives et al., 2009, p. 52). This model encourages social responsibility and change for the common good by developing students' self-awareness and ability to work as a group (Dugan, 2006). The SCM provides a broader definition of leadership and it embraces both developmental and process-oriented approaches to leadership rooted in "self-knowledge, service, and collaboration" (Komives et al., 2009, p. 51).

> Chapter Framework

Although the SCM continues to grow in popularity and use (Dugan, 2015, 2017), this curriculum offers a critical evaluation, asking participants to consider how systems of oppression impact one's social identities and in turn influence the enactment of the model. The impact of privilege, power, and marginalization go beyond just shaping an intellectual understanding of social change. They also influence the approach employed in justice efforts, coalition building, and navigating the complexity of emotion confronted in efforts to be an agent of change. Through this activity, participants are invited to trouble their comprehension of the SCM by unpacking issues of marginalization, power, and privilege associated with their social identities. As many recognize, creating positive social change is no small feat. Achievement of this goal is intrinsically rooted in the attention one gives to self, others, and collective actions toward a common goal.

> Curriculum Plan

This curriculum is framed using the Sue and Sue (2013) model of cultural competency, which includes four domains: awareness, knowledge, skill, and action. The first part of the curriculum increases a participant's *awareness* of social identity through the lens of leadership using facilitated critical self-reflection and group dialogue. During Part 2, participants are encouraged to position themselves in the SCM through their social identities. More specifically, they are asked to discuss with peers how social identities affect various values in the SCM. This targets gains in *knowledge*. History suggests that those who create positive social change are "willing to learn as they go; to listen to those around them and those most directly affected, and [are] open to learning where they were wrong" (Komives et al., 2009, p. 26). The *skill* domain is targeted through participants' listening intently to their peers. Listening is an important skill that will be employed throughout the curriculum. Finally, participants are asked to develop a social change declaration in collaboration with others.

These declarations will lead participants to share words of affirmation, encouragement, and shared responsibility. This will connect the curriculum to collective *action*, which is a key tenet of critical hope. This curriculum can be implemented in a single 90-minute session for groups of 14 to 28 participants. More time is needed for groups larger than 28 to discuss and share reflections with the larger group.

> Activity 1—"Raising the Mirror"

This curriculum has four parts, or subactivities, to assist participants in deconstructing the Cs of the SCM by reflecting on their experiences with social identity, power, privilege, and marginalization. Through discussions on these reflections, participants will create a social change declaration and begin to understand the importance of critical hope.

Learning Outcomes

- Understand the impact of marginalization, power, and privilege on social identities and leadership development.
- Develop an action plan for creating social change based on understanding the SCM.
- Identify the role critical hope plays in creating social change.

Setting Up the Activity

Group Size: Optimal size is 14–28 participants.

Time: 90 minutes

Methods: Discussion, reflection

Materials: Paper; writing utensils; handout of each of the Cs of the SCM and their definitions; handout of the definitions of power, privilege, marginalization, social identities, and social location; markers; self-adhesive notes; large sheets of self-adhesive paper

Directions

1. *Part I—Reflection*: Establish ground rules to help communicate expectations regarding participant engagement in the activity. You can ask the group to develop ground rules or suggest a few and have the group add to the list as necessary. Ground rules can include the following: confidentiality, assuming the best intentions, taking responsibility for your impact, challenging ideas and not people, taking risks, and/or being fully present.

2. Once ground rules are established it is important to hold the group accountable by referring to them as needed throughout the activity. For example, if a conversation is getting pointed and there is a personal attack, you could pause the conversation and say: *We agreed to assume best intentions and to challenge ideas and not people. Let's reenter the conversation with these ideals in mind.* Once the group has established and agreed upon the ground rules, move on to the next step.

3. Ask participants to select one of their salient social identities from among the following categories: ability status, age, ethnicity, faith tradition, gender, nationality, race, religion, sex, sexual identity, or socioeconomic status. Then ask them to reflect on the following:
   - *How do you understand/make meaning of the intersection of the salient identity and your leadership development?*
   - *What social disadvantages have you experienced as a result of your salient identity?*
   - *What social advantages have you experienced as a result of your salient identity?*
   - *What does your salient identity empower you to do as a leader?*
   - *In what ways have you felt disempowered as a leader because of your salient identity?*

4. Give participants a few minutes to reflect on these questions and then ask them to spend 5 minutes developing responses. When the 5 minutes are over, ask participants to share their

reflections with the larger group. Be sure to have them name the salient social identity they chose if comfortable. Make sure to affirm participants who share. It may also be useful to follow-up with participants who were particularly vulnerable in front of the group during a break or at the end of the curriculum.

5. *Part II—Living the Cs*: Break the large group into smaller groups to discuss each of the seven Cs. Have the participants count off in groups of seven with the goal being to have at least two people in a group and to have seven groups total. Ask all "like" numbers to sit together. Once the groups have formed, hand out a piece of paper that has the group's assigned C of the SCM, the definition of the C, and definitions of the terms marginalization, power, privilege, social identity, and social location. Use the following definitions:

   - *Marginalization*: The social disadvantaging of a person or persons based on social identity
   - *Power*: The ability to influence or shape other's behaviors; when abused, often connected to systematic privileging or oppression based on social location and social identities
   - *Privilege*: Unearned advantages and social power inherited by an individual because of their social location
   - *Social Identity*: A facet of an individual's sense of self connected to group membership (e.g., race, gender, ability status)
   - *Social Location*: The position a person holds in society based on their unique composition of social identities that shape how the world is experienced.

6. Ask participants to use their reflections from Part 1 to discuss their assigned C through the lens of their selected social identity bringing to light issues of marginalization, power, and privilege. As the facilitator, it is helpful for you to share a personal example of how one of the Cs manifests in your life given your social identities. For example *As a woman, consciousness of self means that I often have to think about how*

I respond to situations because I worry my male counterparts will think I'm less of a leader if I'm emotional.

7. Participants will share with their small groups. Once every member has shared, they will select a representative to report out a summary of their discussion to the larger group. After each group has shared their thoughts, move the group to the next activity.

8. *Part III—Ubuntu: Our Collective Efforts*: Explain that *Ubuntu is an African philosophy that roughly translates to "I am because we are." Ubuntu espouses the interconnectedness of humanity and embodies the spirit of kindness, openness toward others, and the success of the group over the individual.* This activity will use the concept of critical hope to frame a discussion on collective power.

9. Introduce the concept of critical hope by reading the following quote:

   Leaders learning to sustain hope in the face of struggle are purveyors of critically tempered hope. They hold no illusions about how difficult the struggle is that they face and remain unpersuaded by simplistic slogans and easy sentiments. Their hope is born of the unyielding day-to-day work that ordinary people do to make their communities better. (Preskill & Brookfield, 2009, pp. 171–172)

10. Ask participants to find a partner who was assigned a different C than they were in the previous activity. Have dyads or triads discuss how their understanding of their assigned Cs can work together to develop their ideals for social change in lieu of the issues of marginalization, abuse of power, and privilege. They will make declarations about the social change they are committed to creating by using the following stem statement:

    Through our collective power, which [insert an integrated response to the question from Part 1: what does your salient identity empower you to do as a leader?], we will [name what social change looks like for the issues you discussed] by [statement that integrates the meaning of your Cs].

The following is an example of what a declaration might look like using one participant who selected the salient social identity of being blind and one who selected the salient social identity of being Muslim and who were assigned the values of collaboration and common purpose:

Through our collective power, which allows us to be role models of resilience to marginalized people, we will create more opportunities for our communities to share their stories by bringing our organizations together to plan a collaborative program.

11. Have participants write their social change statements on large pieces of paper and display them around the room.

12. *Part IV—The Wrap-Up*: State the following: *Your social change declarations were really powerful and what we know about doing this work is that it can get exhausting and it sometimes leads to individuals wondering if their work even matters. One way to fight against this sense of hopelessness is to take care of one another. This last activity is about creating a community that affirms you as you enact your plan to create social change.*

13. Give participants a small stack of self-adhesive notes. Instruct them to write on the self-adhesive notes statements that affirm the social change declaration of the groups. Ask them to move around the room posting their affirming statements, written on the self-adhesive notes, on the posted social change declarations. Affirming statements can be words of encouragement, ways in which they would be willing to assist the group in enacting their social change declaration, or words of appreciation. For example, "*I stand in solidarity with you,*" "*Thank you for your courage,*" or "*I'd like to join you in making your declaration a reality.*"

14. To conclude, read one of the quotes below:
    - A Call to Take Care of One Another: *"One source of hope comes from working with seemingly ordinary people whose abilities often go unappreciated but who, when aroused, can accomplish great things by joining with others to make change for the better"* (Preskill & Brookfield, 2009, p. 173).
    - The Importance of Affirmation: *"Joining with others in the ongoing struggle for social justice and witnessing their commitment, self-sacrifice, and strategic intelligence is the best way to learn how to sustain hope in the face of struggle. Seeing first-hand how much is accomplished by ordinary people possessing little more than a healthy dose of critical hope remains the surest antidote against despair"* (Preskill & Brookfield, 2009, p. 183–184).
    - The Power of Our Collective Effort: *"Learning to sustain hope in the face of struggle involves nothing less than the conviction that by joining with others anything can be accomplished, any restriction can be overcome, and any limit can be eliminated"* (Preskill & Brookfield, 2009, p. 184).
15. Conclude the activity by stating: *Our differences are our collective strength and we need each other in creating social change. Thank you for participating and remember you all are powerful beyond measure.*

Facilitator Notes

As facilitators, it is important that we "model the way" (Kouzes & Posner, 2012) by doing our own work around social identities, marginalization, power, and privilege. It is imperative that you dedicate time to personal reflection as you prepare to facilitate this activity. Examples are powerful tools that assist participants in understanding what the activity is asking them to do. Therefore, if you can give concrete, personal examples, it will make the entire activity more meaningful. Lastly, discussions of the terms associated with critical perspectives included in this chapter can elicit strong emotions from participants. You must attend closely to both the verbal and nonverbal cues of participants. Using the ground rules as a facilitation tool is key to maintaining a brave space and will encourage participants to step outside of their comfort zones. It is also useful to remember that you are responsible for the flow of the discussion, so feel free to pause, redirect, or adjust the depth or scope of the dialogue to promote sharing and vulnerability as well as to prevent any foreseeable harm. After completing this curriculum, follow up with individual participants as needed.

› Conclusion

This curriculum is designed to deconstruct the social change model by considering the dynamics of an individual's social identity and the impact marginalization, power, and privilege can have on the successful enactment of leadership for social change. As individuals reflect on their social identities and come to understand how those lenses impact their leadership, they will be better positioned to articulate ways in which they can create social change within their communities by coalition building and supporting collective efforts.

8A: Relational Leadership in Organizations: Deconstructing an Aspirational Leadership Approach

Kristina C. Alcozer Garcia

◇

Objectives/Goals of Chapter

- Understand relational leadership theory and how its components can be integrated into participants' approaches to leadership.
- Recognize how authority and inclusion influence individuals' assumptions about leadership.
- Demonstrate how individual values support purpose/vision-led organizations.

Critical Concepts: *inclusion, social location, social perspective-taking, stocks of knowledge*

❯ Chapter Overview

This curriculum plan introduces participants to the relational leadership model (Komives, Lucas, & McMahon, 2013) as a tool to explore inclusion, social perspective-taking, and social identity in organizations. As participants' understandings of leadership may vary, the curriculum is designed to gradually increase knowledge from generalities to identifying specific ways they can incorporate elements of the model into their leadership approach. The curriculum also reviews components of the knowing-being-doing model (Komives et al., 2013) to frame how participants can practice individual values while also considering the diverse needs and perspectives of their team.

> Chapter Framework

The concept of relational leadership, broadly speaking, can be traced back to the initial recognition that the dynamics that occur between leaders and followers reflect a complex type of relationship. According to Burns (1978) "leaders are a particular kind of power holder. Like power, leadership is relational, collective and purposeful … leaders do not obliterate followers' motives though they may arouse certain motives and ignore others" (p. 21). This recognition that leadership is shaped by relationships differed greatly from industrial models that emphasized the vision and ideals of the leader (Dugan, 2017). Furthermore, relational leadership prompts the consideration that any given context could be heavily shaped by its relational dynamics (Wheatley, 1992). Komives et al.'s (2013) relational leadership model builds upon these fundamental ideas offering a nuanced framework for cultivating relationships (see Chapter 8 of the main text for detailed information).

The relational leadership model proves useful as a method to illustrate collective decision-making and vision-shaping for organizations. Although it does not provide prescriptions of how this process takes place, the fact that the model highlights the importance of shared vision and healthy group relationships serves as a gateway for individuals exploring less traditional approaches to leadership. This is similarly true for the model's explicit exploration of inclusiveness and emphasis on acknowledging the needs and insights of group members from diverse backgrounds. The focus on inclusiveness also assists participants in exploring how an individual's understanding of power, social identity, and authority can directly influence how they engage in the construction of a shared organizational vision. By viewing vision construction and decision making through a critical lens, this model can further complicate individuals' recognition of and relationships with power, authority, and identity. Equally as important as recognizing the role these concepts play is examining the impact of neglecting them on individuals and organizations. This curriculum deepens participants' understandings of the relational leadership model and provides a platform to examine their views of purpose/vision-led organizations and individual values.

Curriculum Plan

Given that the relational leadership model may challenge participants expecting more traditional, industrial models centered on positional authority, this curriculum is designed to gradually narrow participants' focus from a general understanding of leadership to how they can strive to incorporate components of relational leadership in their leadership practice. From there, participants can reexamine organizational and group development with their values in mind, in turn developing a better understanding of relational leadership theory as a whole. This experiencing and re-experiencing of content will aid participants in grasping the tenets of this aspirational approach. Figure 8.1 provides a visual representation of how participants will experience content throughout this section.

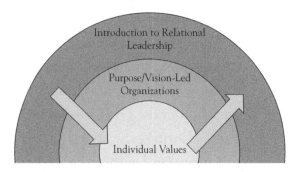

Figure 8.1   **The relational leadership curriculum**

The curriculum should be implemented over the course of two to three sessions. It can also be implemented consecutively as an extended workshop or training session.

> Activity 1—Contextualizing Relational Leadership

This section of the curriculum introduces participants to the relational leadership model (Komives et al., 2013) and the differentiation between practical and aspirational approaches to leadership. The group will then identify organizations/groups that embody components of this model and eventually challenge participants to explore their individual values and how they may impact a larger organization. This activity is designed to begin more generally, introducing participants to the broad concepts associated with this model and then gradually narrow its focus to how individual participants are guided by values and what it can mean for their organization. This path can prove useful for participants who gravitate toward practical models (i.e., where application is more concrete) and slowly build their understanding of relationships within leadership.

Learning Outcomes

- Understand the relational leadership model.
- Identify examples of purpose/vision/led organizations in every-day life.
- Identify individual values and how they influence organization involvement.

Setting Up the Activity

Group Size: Open to any size group

Time: 60–90 minutes

Methods: Dialogue, lecture, reflection

Materials: Whiteboard/chalkboard, markers/chalk, paper, writing utensils

Directions

1. Begin the activity by providing an overview of relational leadership theory in general and the relational leadership model in particular (see Chapter 8 of the main text). Begin by providing participants with a visual representation of the model. Then, explore the model component by component. Be sure to note that the model is aspirational rather than practical. This distinction may be important for those seeking more practice-related approaches to leadership. Allow time for participants to understand the model, asking questions as necessary. Consider the following prompts:
   - *Why is it that we may be drawn to more prescriptive models than those that are aspirational? What stocks of knowledge might be at play that make prescriptions more attractive?*
   - *As you consider the relational leadership model, are there component parts (e.g., inclusive, empowering) that you see manifest*

*in groups and organizations more regularly than others? Why do
you think that is?*

2. Next, create space for discussion regarding how purpose/
vision-led organizations exist in everyday society. Pose the
following questions to the larger group:

   - *What is something that you are passionate about? Family? Animals? Athletics?*
   - *Why do you believe that is important to you? Where does that passion come from? Past experience? Your social identities?*
   - *Now let's think more broadly: What are organizations that are grounded in a shared purpose or vision? What type of evidence do you look for that helps you characterize an organization as having a shared purpose or vision? Does anyone feel a personal connection to one of these organizations? Why or why not?*
   - *How does life inside an organization feel when you see alignment between its shared purpose or vision and your values? What about when there is not alignment? What specific behaviors might you engage in to build a sense of alignment between individual and organizational values?*

3. Transition the dialogue to how participants view values as
contributing to leadership. As purpose is critical to establishing
a group's drive and collective vision, participants must first
explore how an individual's values contribute to a group's relational well-being. To further explore this, instruct participants
to write a letter to their future self. In this letter, participants
should address their future selves and share what values,
commitments, and general characteristics they hope they will
maintain. Letters should address the following questions:

   - *What values would you hold as important?*
   - *What relationships would you hold as important? What would be essential to healthy and positive relationships?*
   - *How might future values be shaped by and in turn shape salient social identities?*

Although this letter is aspirational in nature, stress to participants that it is not designed to chronicle future positions they hope to hold or accomplishments they wish to achieve. Rather, it will serve as a document of reference—something to revisit when they are identifying what values they consider important.

4. After personal reflection, conclude the activity with an open-ended dialogue in which participants share what values they have urged their future selves to maintain. As a facilitator, push participants to make connections between their social identities and values.

Facilitator Notes

This activity may prove challenging for participants new to leadership study or those who seek leadership models with direct linkages to practice. When describing the relational leadership model, be clear in explaining its aspirational nature and how components of the model can be incorporated into participants' individual approaches to leadership. You might highlight this distinction while reviewing the model or briefly compare the relational leadership model to a more practice-related model the participants previously learned.

> Activity 2—Understanding Relationships Within Leadership

This activity introduces the knowing-being-doing model as a way to further explore components of the relational leadership model as well as how individuals engage in relationships within organizations. Additionally, participants will take part in a practical exercise designed to target the diverse needs of team members.

Participants will end by discussing their views of relational leadership and how they may incorporate the model in their own leadership approaches.

Learning Outcomes

- Understand the knowing-being-doing model.
- Recognize the concepts of process, ethics, and inclusion within leadership practice.

Setting Up the Activity

Group Size: Open to any size group

Time: 60–90 minutes

Methods: Dialogue, lecture, reflection

Materials: Whiteboard/chalkboard, markers/chalk, paper, writing utensils, computer, projector/screen, materials for an "active engagement" activity described in Step 5.

Directions

1. Begin by introducing the knowing-being-doing model. For more information on the concept, see Komives et al. (2013). When explaining this structure, share how each dimension touches on a vital component of leadership practice and naturally informs the next area. Begin your explanation with "knowing" (i.e., the understanding of content and concepts), "being" (i.e., demonstrating self-awareness along with awareness of self in relationship to and with others), and "doing" (i.e., the practice of living one's values consistently). Allow time for participants to understand the model, asking questions where necessary.

2. Share with participants that they are next going to connect the knowing, being, and doing dimensions to elements of the relational leadership model. Divide participants into five

groups, assigning each group a component of the relational leadership model (i.e., process, inclusive, empowering, ethical, purpose). Instruct each group that for their assigned component, they should generate three separate lists that capture what it "looks like" in terms of knowing, being, and doing. For example, the group assigned *ethical* might list knowledge of ethical decision-making models for knowledge, awareness of one's values for being, and acting in transparent ways for doing. Encourage them to create multiple items for each dimension. Give the group 10–15 minutes to complete this.

3. Once groups have generated their list, share the following prompts:

   - *Consider the items in the category of knowledge. How might these items reflect specific stocks of knowledge about what constitutes the particular dimension of the relational leadership model?* Push participants to use social perspective-taking to consider alternative perspectives that could be added to the list.

   - *How might the items you've listed in the knowledge and being categories reflect ideology? What assumptions undergird them?* Push participants to examine positive and negative ideological assumptions. For example, is there an assumption that leadership is inherently good? That inclusion is beneficial? What ideologies are embedded in what constitutes an ethic?

   - *How does social location shape the ways in which a person can exhibit the content in your doing category?* This is an opportunity to consider how social identity shapes the type of behaviors that emerge (e.g., To what extent do examples of empowering behaviors differ across communities? Can members of different social identity groups engage in a particular "doing" and have it received in the same way as others?)

4. Bring the large group back together to debrief. *How does the application of critical perspectives alter the ways we think about the*

components of the relational leadership model and dimensions of knowing, being, and doing?

5. Transition the group by indicating that the focus will now narrow to look at the inclusive component of the relational leadership model. Stress that the model is unique as it is one of the few that explicitly names the need for inclusion. The next activity will drill down into specific behaviors. Introduce participants to the "Question in Motion" exercise:

   • Begin by dividing the larger group into smaller groups of five to seven participants. You do not want these to be the same small groups as in the last exercise.

   • Present each group with a specific task to complete. The task you select can vary but should include some level of creativity and interpretation on the part of the participants. Examples include "Each group will create their own team crest," or "Each group will solve a puzzle." The more active and engaging the task, the better. The goal is to give participants an activity that should take at least 10 minutes to complete and require them to be in relationships with one another.

   • After providing participants with materials to complete their task, have the groups begin working. After they've started, provide each participant with an index card displaying a specific obstacle or preference. For instance, one might be "Cannot say any word that begins with the letter T," or "Must keep eyes closed." Each person within a group should have a different obstacle or preference ensuring that no two members share the same one. Should questions arise regarding how they should carry out their task, direct participants to their prompts and encourage them to find alternative pathways forward.

   • Teams should be given approximately 15 minutes.

6. Ask the group to reconvene and discuss their experiences within the group. Encourage participants to share their general

response first: *How did things go within your groups?* After this initial inquiry, ask follow up questions as necessary:

- *What proved challenging while trying to accomplish your task?*
- *Did your group have to adjust your process? If so, what had to change? What remained the same? How did you learn the needs of your group members?*
- *What ties do you see to the relational leadership model? To the knowing-being-doing model?*
- *Where did you see authority in this exercise? How did it play out? Considering relational leadership more broadly, how does authority influence a team? Social identity? The way power plays out in a group?*
- *Specifically, what role did inclusion play in how your group moved forward? What examples emerged of inclusive behaviors that helped the group? Are there examples of inclusive behaviors that did not help the group?*

7. To conclude this session, continue the group discussion regarding the relational leadership model. Ask participants to share their thoughts on the model: *What works? What is challenging? What proves useful in the model and what appears inaccessible or too abstract? What elements of the model will you integrate into your evolving approach to leadership?* This closing discussion will allow participants to contextualize the activity and more directly connect their view of the model to that of their peers.

› Conclusion

This chapter was constructed to lead participants through developmentally sequenced activities centered on exploring individuals' relationships, teams, and individual values in the realm of organizational leadership. Although the theory of relational leadership may be challenging to directly implement, embedded in this approach are vital skills such as social perspective-taking, self-awareness, and dialogue—skills necessary to challenge traditional understandings of leadership. By viewing vision construction and decision making through a critical lens, this model can further complicate individuals' recognition of and relationship with power, authority, and individual identity, collectively moving participants toward a more inclusive, holistic, and socially just approach to leadership.

Chapter 9: Vanguard Theories

9A: Authentic Leadership Through a Critical Lens: Resisting Dominant Narratives

Ana M. Rossetti & Mark Anthony Torrez

Objectives/Goals of Chapter

- Understand a liberatory framework of authentic leadership development through the process of self-narrative inquiry.
- Be able to deconstruct traditional definitions of *authenticity* and *authentic leadership* using critical perspectives.
- Be able to reconstruct a theory of authentic leadership rooted in lived experience that considers social identity and recognizes power as a covert mediator of behavior.

Critical Concepts: *agency, critical self-reflection, power, privilege, social location*

> Chapter Overview

Authentic leadership theory emerged as an attempt to positively reconstruct the relationship between leaders and followers after troubling world events during the late 1990s and early 2000s left many feeling uneasy about the state of society and longing for more genuine, trustworthy leadership. This chain reaction of social and political leadership blunders featured unforeseen devastation, corruption, and malpractice, which ultimately produced a climate of high follower skepticism and a public call for more "authentic" leaders (Avolio & Gardner, 2005). Moreover, the popular use of and growing scholarship on authentic leadership theory demonstrates that the idea has undeniably resonated with modern conceptualizations of and desires for leadership that commonly center trust and transparency as foundations (Avolio & Gardner, 2005; Luthans & Avolio, 2003; Komives, Lucas, & McMahon, 2013). However, as highlighted by Dugan (2017), despite the existence of significant literature and multiple approaches to authentic leadership no universal definition exists regarding the concept.

Although authentic leadership theory lacks a universal conceptualization, several common themes have emerged from authentic leadership literature—many of which are rooted in a moral construct of *goodness*. That is, *good leaders* are honest, transparent, and do the right thing for the common good. In their attempt to operationalize the theory, Gardner, Avolio, Luthans, May, and Walumba (2005) described these central tenets as "internalized moral perspective" and "relational transparency." Whereas internalized moral perspective refers to a leader's rejection of external, environmental influences to, instead, guide behavior from personal morals and values, relational transparency is more of an interpersonal construct that describes genuine and transparent presentations of the self (Gardner et al., 2005). Therefore, Gardner et al. (2005) claimed that a definition of authenticity "involves both *owning* one's personal experiences (values, thoughts, emotions and beliefs) and *acting* in accordance with one's true self (expressing what you really think and believe and behaving accordingly)" (pp. 344–345; italics in original).

Authentic leadership theory has played an important role in renewing the prominence of trust and integrity as essential mechanisms in leadership processes. However, popular theorizing and applications of authentic leadership is divorced from critical analysis of the very construct it centers: authenticity. In particular, literature commonly used to frame authentic leadership development minimally recognizes the role of culture and identity and neglects the direct influence of social location, power, and privilege altogether (Dugan, 2017). Yet, critical perspectives demonstrate how historical, intersecting systems of power and privilege continue to manifest in the lives of people with marginalized social group membership(s) and create significant barriers to "freely" thinking and believing, let alone acting, within social contexts (e.g., Crenshaw, 1991; Du Bois, 1989; Jamieson, 1995; King, 1988).

Given the centrality of this socially engineered interrelationship between goodness and authenticity, it is imperative to recognize how uncritical applications of authentic leadership perpetuate a privileging of dominant leadership narratives (i.e., those traditionally of White, able-bodied, cisgender, heterosexual, and masculine men), while invalidating leaders with marginalized identities who are less "free" to self-express and are often rejected and come under threat in certain instances of authentic self-expression. Stated simply: if we are socialized to associate leadership with images and behaviors embodied by White, able-bodied, cisgender, heterosexual, and masculine men, we are likely to invalidate leaders who fall outside of those prototype boundaries (e.g., Ayman & Korabik, 2010; Calder, 1977; Dugan, 2017; Eagly & Chin, 2010; Eagly & Karau, 2002; Ospina & Foldy, 2009). Moreover, if we feel disassociated from favored, or privileged, ways of being, we may disengage from leadership processes altogether or perhaps seek to perform and/or adopt dominant behaviors out of perceived need for survival let alone success (e.g., Goffman, 1959; Jamieson, 1995; Jones, Kim, & Skendall, 2012; Ladson-Billings, 1995).

This chapter critically examines the foundations of authentic leadership theory by exploring the nuance and possibility of authenticity within the 21ˢᵗ-century social world. Through the curriculum, participants are empowered to reflect on lived experiences, clarify values and convictions, and compare their self-authored understandings of authentic leadership to dominant narratives undergirding the theory. Ultimately, this curriculum is designed to cultivate greater critical consciousness—as well as capacities for critical self-reflection and theoretical critique—to unveil the stealth operation of power in both our practice of leadership and in the construction of the most foundational concepts we use to frame its development.

❯ Chapter Framework

Gardner et al. (2005) proposed, "The developmental process model for authentic leadership starts with how individuals interpret accumulated life experiences, and continues with their on-going interpretation of trigger events over time causing further self-development" (p. 348). Therefore, we leverage the work of Shamir and Eilam (2005), which centered the role of self-narratives in the development of authentic leadership. Self-narratives are attempts to draw meaningful connections between various life events. They can provide significant insight into an individual's sense of identity because through their construction, one creates a coherent structure around the events of their life and draws meaning through this interpretation and the process of interpreting itself. Thus, the self-narrative provides a "meaning system from which the leader acts," reflects, and derives their sense of identity (Shamir & Eilam, 2005, p. 408).

By engaging in critical self-reflection and analysis of significant events in one's life, leaders can gain clarity about their values and convictions (Shamir & Eilam, 2005). The development of self-narratives as a strategy of deriving one's values is powerful in that it is based not solely on abstract and biased notions of what is socially privileged or acceptable; rather it is grounded in lived experience and invested with emotional resonance. Shamir, Dayan-Horesh, and Adler (2005) employed this framework by using the narrative method to examine leadership development and the self-justification of leaders. A narrative method extracts the meaning that individuals attribute to their experiences through the self-analysis of their descriptions and interpretations of events (Lieblich, Tuval-Mashiach, & Zilber, 1998). Through narrative inquiry, Shamir et al. (2005) revealed an important theme in the leaders' life stories, "leadership development out of struggle," in which the leader's development arose from what Bennis and Thomas (2002) called "defining experiences."

Given that even traditional definitions of an *authentic leader* (i.e., definitions that neglect how power and bias influence the enactment and perception of authenticity) are characterized by self-knowledge, sincerity, and deeply-held convictions (Avolio & Gardner, 2005), self-narratives hold great potential to help participants become more conscious of their own complications with the socially defined construct of authenticity and discover potentially dismissed past experiences in which they may have enacted their own narrative form of authentic leadership. Therefore, this curriculum models a method of self-narrative inquiry to assist participants in dismantling power and privilege within the constructs of authenticity and authentic leadership, becoming more conscious of the ways they may have internalized dominant narratives regarding leadership development, and reconstructing more truthful definitions and narratives of their own. By leveraging self-narratives, it is our hope that participants are able to make meaning of the events of their lives more freely—within the unique contexts of their own social locations, and with lessened interference from imposing social scripts and external frameworks.

> Curriculum Plan

This curriculum is intended to serve as an experiential introduction to authentic leadership theory. To limit the influence of potential bias as a result of participants' previously held notions about leadership and its connotations of power, privilege, and oppression—as well as their relationship to and sense of agency within such power structures—there will not (and should not) be a pre-lecture, nor will there (or should there) be any mention of *authenticity* or *leadership* until the debrief at the end of Activity 1. We recognize that the possibility of this safeguarding may vary depending on the nature of the group. For example, within the context of a leadership course, participants are (hopefully) already thinking about leadership when the session begins and may even be aware, perhaps by way of the syllabus, that authenticity is the impending topic of discussion. With that said, we strongly encourage you to facilitate this activity in such a way that participants engage in the process of self-narrative inquiry with as little priming on authentic leadership theory as possible. It is our aim that participants engage in a more liberatory process of authentic leadership development: without the unnecessary labeling, framing, and, thereby delimiting, of it by extant literature.

This curriculum takes participants through an adaptation of the leadership development process described by Shamir et al. (2005). Participants will construct self-narratives based on defining experiences that have informed their understanding of leadership and then engage in a process of meaning-making that will identify the emotional resonance of their life events, clarify the values and convictions they derived from those experiences, and examine how their present behaviors and beliefs about leadership were influenced by those experiences. Participants will then confront authentic leadership literature (see Chapter 9 of the main text) to ultimately consider questions such as "What is authenticity?" and "Is authentic leadership a real possibility?" The following curriculum plan should be implemented in two sessions, ranging from 90 minutes to 2 hours each. Although two sessions are optimal for balancing continuity and focus with the chance for personal reflection and recharging, the activities can also be facilitated as an extended workshop or training with breaks between each component.

› Activity 1—Defining Experiences

This section of the curriculum introduces the process of authentic leadership development through an experiential exercise that replicates the natural conditions through which leaders make meaning of their life experiences and derive a sense of purpose (Shamir et al., 2005; Shamir & Eilam, 2005). Participants will use personal narratives, clarify values and convictions derived from a critical life event or struggle, and identify its impact on their current understandings of leadership. Participants will specifically consider the role of perception in leader behavior as a priming to challenge dominant leadership narratives in Activity 2.

Learning Outcomes

- Understand significant life events through the process of self-narrative inquiry.
- Identify values and convictions derived from life experiences.
- Recognize how significant life events influence leadership development.

Setting Up the Activity

Group Size: Open to any size group. However, given the sensitivity of content, the optimal group size ranges from 6–30 participants.

Time: A minimum of 2 hours

Methods: Dialogue, discussion, reflection, writing

Materials: Blank paper (one to two sheets per person), writing utensils, whiteboard/chalkboard, markers/chalk

Variations: Several components of the curriculum are designed for paired discussion, but small groups of two or four people are an option if working with a larger number of participants.

Directions

1. Begin the activity by working with participants to set ground rules that contribute to *brave space* (Arao & Clemens, 2013). See the Introduction of this text for details.

2. Before giving the actual prompt, make sure participants are relaxed and focused on your instruction—you might even consider having them close their eyes. Prompt participants with the following: *Think about an experience or struggle that has significantly affected you. Think about a defining experience—a pivotal moment. It could be a particular event, a recurring theme, or a general aspect of your identity that you feel has significantly affected your life. Many of you may be thinking of several things at once. For today, just pick one.* Be sure to share with them that this should be something that they will be comfortable sharing either in part or in full with a fellow participant.

3. Distribute paper and writing utensils and share the following: *Write about the defining experience you thought about and selected. I want you to write about it in narrative format, as if you are retelling the story, and include as many details as you can remember. Include contextual information, introduce the people involved, and describe related events. Write about what was challenging or difficult. Write about what was positive or rewarding. Write about what you learned.* Allow 15 to 20 minutes for this component of

the activity depending on the size and developmental maturity of the group.

4. Once all participants have finished writing their narratives, give them the following instructions: *Write down all of the emotions you feel today, right now in this very moment, when you think about your defining experience. Be as descriptive as possible and critically reflect on what you are feeling. Try to capture as much nuance as you are able.* Allow about 5 to 10 minutes for this.

5. Begin the next component of the activity by splitting participants into pairs. Explain: *You are now going to share your stories in pairs. Members of each pair will take turns being the Storyteller or the Listener. Storytellers will tell the Listener their defining experience story. As the story is told, Listeners will pay close attention and specifically try to identify the values, beliefs, or convictions the Storyteller may hold based on their story. Listeners, ask yourselves: (1) What is important or not important to the Storyteller? (2) What does the Storyteller believe or not believe? (3) What would the Storyteller agree or disagree with based on how they described their defining experience? After each story is shared, the Listener will have 5 minutes to write down what they perceived; meanwhile, the Storyteller will use the 5 minutes to reflect on how they feel from the process of sharing their story.* Allow about 20 minutes for this component of the activity.

6. Once both participants have had their turn to share and listen, instruct them as follows: *Take turns sharing the notes you took about your partner's story while you were the Listener. Discuss what each of you observed and contribute any additional values, beliefs, or convictions that you wish to add about your own story to what your Listener identified. Also be sure to acknowledge any differences between what Listeners wrote down and what you actually think, believe, and value.* As the facilitator, you should walk around to check in with pairs during this exercise to help them identify values, beliefs, and convictions. Allow 10 minutes for this component of the activity.

7. Next, ask participants to individually reflect on this question: *How do you think, believe, or behave differently today as a result of the defining experience you wrote about? Write down at least two changes you can identify.* Allow 5 minutes for this.

8. When participants are ready to move on, give them this prompt: *Continuing to work on your own, reflect on the connections you might see between the emotions elicited by your story, the values and convictions coidentified with your partner, and the changes in your values, beliefs, and behaviors you feel are informed by your defining experience. Also, think about any current goals or causes you may feel connected to—how, if at all, do you feel they are connected to the emotions, values, and behaviors inspired by your defining experience?* Allow 5 minutes for this.

9. Once participants have finished, facilitate a large group discussion in which participants are invited to share pieces of their stories and the connections they made. The goal is to help participants understand how life experiences can shape us—who we know ourselves to be, what we believe, and how we behave in the future. Over time, we build a collection of experiences within us that are tied together by the self-narratives we construct or the meaning we attach to their connection. Example prompts to guide conversation include these:

   - *What connections did you make between your defining moments, the emotions you experienced related to those moments, and the values, beliefs, and behaviors you and your Listener coidentified?*

   - *What connections did you make between your defining moment and who and where you are now as it relates to the causes and goals you are either considering or actively pursuing?*

   - *How accurate/inaccurate was your Listener in identifying your values, beliefs, and behaviors from simply hearing your story? How did that make you feel?*

   - *Have you ever experienced a situation in which something happened (something serious or important like in your defining*

moment) and someone didn't understand it or misjudged you or what was happening? If yes, how so? How did you feel about being misunderstood or otherwise inaccurately labeled?
- *How do you believe life experiences shape who we are and how we evolve as people and as leaders?*
- *Thinking specifically about our reflections on the Storyteller-Listener dynamic, how important is perception in our everyday interactions? How do we manage perception?*
- *What role does perception play in how we live and lead?*

Facilitator Notes

As you introduce the activity it is essential to create a space conducive to dialogue. Creating a brave space invites participants to share to the extent that is beneficial for their learning. Additionally, your language and facilitation approach should be calibrated according to the participants' degrees of experience with critical self-reflection, their level of prior knowledge of leadership theory, and their past experiences with leadership. For example, if participants are struggling to see the connections between their defining experiences and their values or convictions, emphasize that leadership development is understood as a life-long process involving intentional critical self-reflection. This is a skill that is developed and honed with practice over time. If participants have not previously confronted aspects of their social identity, this exercise may raise challenging questions or they may have difficulty completing it. Such instances will need to be handled with sensitivity and encouragement.

> Activity 2—Troubling Authenticity

The second half of this curriculum builds upon the critical self-reflection and social perspective-taking processes from Activity 1. Participants are introduced to the primary themes and core tenets of authentic leadership theory and are challenged to juxtapose their lived experiences with literature to deconstruct and reconstruct the base concept of authenticity.

Learning Outcomes

- Understand the foundational definitions and core tenets of authentic leadership theory.
- Apply critical perspectives to the constructs of *authenticity* and *authentic leadership*.
- Integrate knowledge gained from critical perspectives to personally and collectively reconstruct a theory of authentic leadership.

Setting Up the Activity

Group Size: Open to any size group. Given the sensitivity of content, optimal group size ranges from 6–30 participants.

Time: A minimum of 2 hours

Methods: Dialogue, discussion

Materials: Blank paper (one to two sheets per person), writing utensils, whiteboard/chalkboard, markers/chalk

Variations: Several components of the curriculum are designed for paired discussion, but small groups of three or four people are an option if working with a larger number of participants.

Directions

1. Introduce key tenets and themes of authentic leadership theory (see Chapter 9 of the main text). For the purposes of this activity, spend focused time on the ideas of *authenticity, goodness, morality,* and *leadership for the common good* as discussed in this chapter's introduction and "Chapter Framework" sections. Ask participants to share their ideas and use a whiteboard/chalkboard to capture themes. You might

also consider visually showcasing the following definition of authenticity and using these questions to frame conversation:

- *Authenticity*: "Involves both *owning* one's personal experiences (values, thoughts, emotions and beliefs) and *acting* in accordance with one's true self (expressing what you really think and believe and behaving accordingly)" (Gardner et al., 2005, pp. 344–345; italics in original).

  Based on what we've read and discussed, what is the basic premise of authentic leadership theory? What are its core tenets? How does it define leadership? What assumptions does the theory make regarding leadership? Allow participants ample time for discussion and encourage them to dissect the theory using the framework and concepts presented in Chapters 1 and 2 of the main text (Dugan, 2017). Allow 10 to 20 minutes for this conversation.

2. Ask participants to think about their reflections from Activity 1 and draw connections between that process and what they read about authentic leadership theory. Document what participants share to create a visual comparison of Activity 1 and Activity 2. Allow 5 to 10 minutes for this. Guiding questions might include the following:

   - *Think back to when we reflected on defining moments. How does that process align or not align with what we know as authentic leadership theory?*
   - *In what ways do self-narratives relate to the development of authentic leadership?*

3. Ask participants to remember their conversation at the end of Activity 1 regarding perception. Allow 5 minutes for group reflection using the following guiding questions:

   - *Think back to our conversation on perception—how did it influence your defining moments? What did we discuss, related to the role of perception, in how we think, behave, and feel in leadership? How did we discuss our management of perception?*

- *Given our understanding of perception, how does it relate to the theory of authentic leadership? How is perception considered in the theory? How does perception support the core tenets of the theory? How does perception conflict with the theory?*

4. Transition the group to apply a critical perspective by naming social location, power, and privilege in the discussion. If possible, visually present the terms *authenticity, social identity, perception, power, goodness,* and *leadership* in a nonsensical or scattered way (i.e., present them in seemingly disconnected locations on the board or screen). Then, provide the group with 10 to 15 minutes for critical dialogue. Transition the conversation by saying this:

   - *Now, I want us to engage in some critical thinking to consider how all of these concepts might be connected. More specifically, how do social identity and the dynamics of power and privilege relate to how we perceive and are perceived? How might identity motivate the ways we manage perception? Is it necessarily "good" or "bad" to manage perception?*

5. Once the group has begun to critically question the concept of authenticity, share this short excerpt from Jones et al. (2012). You can either read the prompt aloud (or ask a volunteer to do so) or distribute copies to read. Depending on the nature and context of the group, you can also ask participants to read the article in its entirety. However, the following excerpt is an excellent primer for reflexive dialogue:

   We found that our discussion of the lived experience of intersecting identities led us to the question of what it meant to live authentically and whether or not authenticity was a meaningful construct. Our narratives and ensuing discussions found us engaged in a persistent pattern of decision making about what and who we show to the world and what we keep to ourselves. The need to manage both privileged and oppressed identities, as well as the tensions and interactions between the two, brought an awareness of both the internal and external influences on the possibility of authenticity. We wondered: Is authenticity also contextual? If one is constantly negotiating identities and managing the perceptions of others, is that an authentic way to live?" (Jones et al., 2012, p. 715)

6. Instruct participants to find a partner to discuss the following for 15 to 20 minutes:

   - *What are your reactions to the excerpt? How does what the authors shared resonate with you? How might it differ from your own lived experience?*

   - *Have you ever experienced a need to manage your privileged and/or oppressed identities? Have you ever felt misperceived? Have you ever felt pressure to act in a certain way that felt unnatural to who you know and believe yourself to be? Or, have you ever felt uncomfortable, anxious, or even afraid to be transparent?*

   - *If so, what was that situation like? Why did you feel pressured? How did you actually manage yourself? Was it what you shared? How you spoke? How you physically presented yourself? What course of action you decided to take? Also, how did the experience make you feel both during and after? If you could go back in time, would you change your decision?*

7. The final component of this curriculum challenges participants to juxtapose multiple definitions and ideas regarding authenticity and authentic leadership to reconstruct a framework of their own. Invite participants to come back to the large group and share what they discussed in their pairs. Allow 10 minutes for this discussion. *What were your reactions to the excerpt? Do you agree or disagree with the authors? What do you think about authenticity after reading it? Is authenticity possible?*

8. Return to the initial conversation on authentic leadership theory. It is helpful to visually present the Gardner et al. (2005) definition and/or model of authentic leadership as a visual cue for reflection. Engage participants in a 20-minute

dialogue that ties together the multiple ideas and reflections presented throughout this curriculum. The following is an intentional sequence of questions that should facilitate an evolution in the dialogue:

- *Think about the defining moments you discussed with your partners. Do your lived experiences relate more to the Jones et al. discussion of authenticity and perception or its presentation in authentic leadership theory?*

- *How do your lived experiences and the excerpt from Jones et al. specifically complicate the tenets of authentic leadership theory such as* internalized moral perspective *and* relational transparency? *Can you manage perceptions and be authentic at the same time? Is doing so necessarily a good or bad thing? What are the potential benefits and detriments of constructing a relationship between morality and authenticity?*

9. Finally, ask participants to engage in 5 to 10 minutes of written reflection using the following prompt. Note that this can also be assigned as a formal reflection essay.

   - *How does applying a critical perspective complicate the overall process, development, and enactment of authentic leadership? How would you change or reconstruct the theory given our conversations on social location, power, and perception? How would you change or reconstruct the theory given your lived experiences? Ultimately,* what do authenticity *and* authentic leadership *mean to you?*

10. Invite people to share how they would reconstruct the theory to be more inclusive and cognizant of critical perspectives. As participants share their suggested models and personal definitions of authenticity and authentic leadership, track themes across their ideas to identify a collective reconstruction. A minimum of 10 to 15 minutes should be allotted. The prompts for this final dialogue are simple and focus on rebuilding and redefining the theory: *What is authenticity? When, how, and for whom is it possible? What is authentic leadership? When, how, and for whom is it possible?*

> Conclusion

Authentic leadership theory lacks full conceptualization and little research exists on strategies for developing or enhancing authentic leadership behaviors. However, we believe that engaging in a process of self-narrative inquiry—before learning about the theory itself—may increase participants' agency and self-efficacy for defining and enacting a model of authentic leadership that is rooted in their lived experiences. By centering social location, this curriculum unveils the stealth strands of power, privilege, and oppression that are laced throughout authentic leadership theory and knotted in its traditional, biased definition of authenticity. We intend this process of deconstruction and reconstruction to liberate people who may have adopted and internalized these delimiting definitions and, subsequently, may not see themselves as being authentic or authentic leaders. We hope participants will find an avenue in authentic leadership that resonates with them and through which they can enact their leadership in a way that feels genuine—and perhaps cultivate greater agency (as both learners and leaders) along the way.

9B: Adaptive Leadership: Helping the Work of the Group Move Forward

Scott J. Allen & Marc Lynn

Objectives/Goals of Chapter

- Understand the difference between adaptive and technical challenges.
- Understand the major components of adaptive leadership.
- Practice, identify, and diagnose failures in leading groups through the resolution of adaptive challenges.

Critical Concepts: *agency, authority, power, social capital, social location, stocks of knowledge*

> Chapter Overview

This curriculum is designed to challenge participants on two levels. First, participants will be challenged to better understand the difference between adaptive and technical challenges. Likewise, participants will be exposed to the primary components of Heifetz and Linsky's (2002) adaptive leadership: their process for leading groups through adaptive challenges. Specifically, we will explore the need to *get on the balcony*, *think politically*, *orchestrate the conflict*, *give the work back*, and *hold steady*. Beyond a basic understanding of adaptive challenges and adaptive leadership, the curriculum is designed to help participants better understand the difficulty in leading groups through adaptive challenges by providing intriguing case studies and experiential opportunities for exploration.

Chapter Framework

Adaptive leadership is a theory that helps people understand and navigate adaptive challenges (Heifetz & Linsky, 2002). Adaptive work can be challenging as it requires the leader to push, but in doing so, not lose the various factions in the room. Likewise, the leader must acknowledge and honor what various factions are being asked to give up in the process. Adaptive challenges are different from technical challenges where the use of an expert or authority figure is more the norm (e.g., "I have a flat tire and need a mechanic"). Adaptive challenges are not as straightforward. First, adaptive challenges are often difficult to define (Heifetz & Linsky, 2002). Because of this ambiguity, the second hallmark asserts that new learning needs to occur. A third hallmark of adaptive challenges is that they often challenge people in the group to give something up, alter their value system, or reframe their views (Heifetz & Linsky, 2002). Moving past each of the hallmarks is difficult and rare and helps one understand why many adaptive challenges persist. For example, everyone knows heart disease kills, but it persists. People know that if they eat processed/unhealthy food and do not exercise that their risk of death increases—yet these behaviors continue.

The application of critical perspectives to adaptive leadership reveals realistic and significant barriers particularly for individuals who hold marginalized social identities (e.g., women, People of Color). More specifically, there is substantial evidence of the ways leaders from minoritized social groups are systematically impeded from assuming power and authority and are often challenged, invalidated, or altogether rejected by follower bias and/or mismatch with implicit leader prototypes (e.g., Dugan, 2017; Chin & Trimble, Eagly & Chin, 2010; Eagly & Karau, 2007; Ospina & Foldy, 2009). Although Heifetz and Linsky's (2002) framing of adaptive leadership called attention to the ways leaders may struggle with followers who fear or resist the instigated disequilibrium essential to adaptive work, their discussion must be extended to recognize the influence of social location and power dynamics in the validation of leaders as well as the sensitive process of orchestrating conflict for change. The application of critical perspectives perhaps best informs adaptive leadership by extending Heifetz and Linsky's (2002) idea of *getting on the balcony* to include closer examination of the influences of stocks of knowledge, ideology/hegemony, and social location. We must ask the following questions: *How does power operate both within and outside of formal structures of authority? How might the risks associated with attempting to instigate conflict and change vary depending on one's social location? Who is able to assume (and enact) authority and also be perceived (and received) as legitimate?*

> Curriculum Plan

Conger (1992) identified four types of leadership learning activities: conceptual understanding, personal growth, feedback, and skill building. This curriculum covers all four of these. First, we hope that a participant's conceptual understanding of adaptive leadership will increase. Likewise, we hope that the activities will begin to build skills in identifying and navigating adaptive challenges. Personal growth will occur via reflection questions as participants think about their own experience with adaptive challenges. Finally, we have embedded opportunities for feedback and reflection following each activity. The curriculum should be implemented over two sessions each ranging from 85 to 90 minutes. Although segmented sessions are optimal for the curriculum to allow ample processing and recentering time, the sessions can also be facilitated consecutively as an extended workshop or training.

❯ Activity 1—The Conundrum in Carpentersville

Participants will read a brief summary of adaptive leadership and then watch a video of a town hall meeting. Participants will identify the adaptive challenge and have an opportunity to determine how well the leader does at implementing the primary components of adaptive leadership.

Learning Outcomes

- Distinguish between adaptive and technical challenges.
- Understand the components of adaptive leadership.
- Recognize the messy nature of adaptive work by applying the concepts to a case study.

Setting Up the Activity

Group Size: 10–30 people

Time: 90 minutes

Methods: Case methodology

Materials: "Summary of Adaptive Leadership" and "Adaptive Leadership Checklist" handouts

Multimedia: Computer, projector/screen, access to the Internet, audio

- Video clip: *Bill Sarto Says Carpentersville Is "A Bad Soap Opera"* (www.youtube.com/watch?v=OOiIjGQZs5g)

- Video clip: *Most Outrageous Local Government Board Meeting EVER!!!* (www.youtube.com/watch?v=rFeA-pM0o8Y)

Directions

1. Begin the session by asking participants to read the three-page synopsis handout of adaptive leadership along with its summary in Chapter 9 of the main text. Request that they underline or circle key words that stand out for them. Then spend 5 minutes facilitating a dialogue about their shared understanding of the theory. Conclude by articulating Heifetz's definition of an adaptive challenge and asking participants to generate contemporary examples facing either an organization or local community with which they are familiar (e.g., poverty and quality/access to education; health disparities in communities).

2. Explain that participants are about to watch the Village of Carpentersville President Bill Sarto attempt to remove a fellow board member from office because he was convicted of domestic violence. Show the video clip (9 minutes) *Bill Sarto Says Carpentersville Is "A Bad Soap Opera."* After viewing the clip, place participants in small groups for 10 minutes and pose the following questions:

   - *Based on the clip, is this a technical or adaptive challenge for the community of Carpentersville? Identify which you think and why.*
   - *Who has power in this situation? How is power being used? Why?*
   - *In what ways do you think social location plays a role in the situation? Consider how the situation might be framed differently, or even change, if certain characters had alternate social identities.*

3. Take 10 minutes to debrief the small group conversations. First, see if the larger group can come to consensus on whether

the situation within the video depicts a technical or adaptive challenge. Then, ask participants to characterize the situation through the lens of power and social location.

4. Explain that Bill Sarto is now working to remove the convicted board member, but cannot get anyone to second his motion for removal. The rest of the board wants the convicted board member to remain in office. Ask participants to review the "Adaptive Leadership Checklist" as they watch the clip. Show the video clip (10 minutes): *Most Outrageous Local Government Board Meeting EVER!!!*

5. Next, instruct the small groups to answer the following questions (10 minutes):

   - *How did Bill Sarto perform in leading the group through the adaptive challenge?*

   - *How did concepts of power and authority present themselves in this second clip?*

   - *How did social location influence the process and outcome of the meeting?*

6. Debrief the small group conversations (10 to 15 minutes) and see if there are common themes across the groups.

7. Conclude the session with a large group discussion on the following questions:

   - *What does this activity tell us about leadership? Why was it difficult to determine if Carpentersville was facing an adaptive or technical challenge?*

   - *Has considering concepts like power and social location generated any new thoughts on what you believe the challenges (technical or adaptive) may be in that community? If so, how? How might your social location influence your perspectives on the situation?*

   - *Based on what you have seen and our discussion, why is leading a group through an adaptive challenge so difficult?*

   - *How does a critical perspective complicate adaptive leadership?*

Facilitator Notes

Be sure to watch each clip and review each case prior to the start of the activity. Essentially, Village of Carpentersville President Bill Sarto is trying to remove a member from office who has been convicted of domestic violence. Only one other board member supports Sarto and the rest of the board is protecting the convicted board member. Interestingly, it is revealed that Sarto may not have a squeaky-clean past himself. If you use your favorite search engine, you can find additional background on how the drama in Carpentersville, Illinois, unfolded.

Be prepared for participants to struggle with the discussion on whether or not this is a technical or adaptive challenge. Some may feel that it is a technical problem, because they may believe that he just needs to be removed from office. The problem is that the individuals protecting him are also the figures with the authority to remove him. There is no policy stating that he must resign if convicted. The adaptive challenge may be something like: "What is acceptable for us as a community?" or "How do we remove individuals who do not live the values we feel the organization should espouse?"

> Activity 2—Gilmore Fasteners: A Case Study in Adaptive Leadership

Participants will read a brief summary of adaptive leadership and then review a case study. Participants will have an opportunity to act out the case and come to a resolution as a group. Likewise, participants will be prompted to identify the adaptive challenge and discuss how volunteers did at implementing the primary components of adaptive leadership.

Learning Outcomes

- Distinguish between adaptive and technical challenges.
- Utilize the components of adaptive leadership to solve an adaptive challenge.
- Understand and experience the challenge of adaptive leadership.

Setting Up the Activity

Group Size: 15–30 people

Time: 85 minutes

Methods: Case methodology

Materials: "Summary of Adaptive Leadership," "Adaptive Leadership Checklist," and "Gilmore Fasteners: A Case Study in Adaptive Leadership" handouts

Directions

1. Refer participants to the three-page "Summary of Adaptive Leadership" handout used in the last session along with its summary in Chapter 9 of the main text.

2. Next, provide participants with about 15 minutes to read the "Gilmore Fasteners" case study and then choose five participants to play the parts of Chief Executive Officer Alan Gilmore, Chief Financial Officer Matt Peters, Chief Marketing Officer Jon Smith, Chief Technology Officer Steve Whiteman, Director of Operations Paul Western, and Director of Human Resources Robert Sims. Likewise, pick a faction of five other participants to play the parts of the individuals about to lose their jobs (Shea Jackson, front desk/phones; Cynthia Ramirez, mailroom clerk; Jackson Black, secretary; Juanita Mayers, secretary to CEO; and Anu Patel, secretary to Jon Smith). Provide each group with 5 minutes to re-review the case and get their

thoughts together. While the two groups are preparing, suggest that the third group use the "Adaptive Leadership Checklist" handout to take notes on how Alan and the others perform in this difficult meeting.

3. Remind the group that Alan is the CEO and the leader of the meeting and that he genuinely wants to come to a best resolution but frankly does not see any other options. Likewise, remind group members that during the dialogue their actions should, as closely as possible, reflect their given character and that person's relationship with others in the case. For example, if they are assigned to be the front-desk receptionist, make sure those duties and that role within the organization guides the person's presentation of the role. Next, open discussion and let them know they have 25 minutes for this role-play dialogue. Announce that the entire 25 minutes must be used.

4. Provide each small group (i.e., executive team, employees, observers) with approximately 5 minutes to debrief their experiences and request that each participant identify one statement that links the exercise to concepts of stocks of knowledge, social perspective-taking, social location, and flow of power. Likewise, as the facilitator, bring the dialogue back to the challenges of adaptive work by providing the observation group with an opportunity to share what they witnessed.

5. Close the session by challenging participants to leverage their critical reflections and consider how they might reconstruct Heifetz and Linsky's (2002) core concepts. Example prompts include these:

   - *What should you attend to when getting on the balcony? How can you specifically attend to the presence and influence of power? What stocks of knowledge may shape what a person sees and attends to versus does not see and attend to? How can a person actively work to challenge and expand their stocks of knowledge when engaging in adaptive work?*

- *How might you redefine what is means to think politically? How are politics mediated by social location? Are there differing levels of risk and loss that should be addressed when creating holding environments? How should those be acknowledged and navigated?*

- *What should you consider before and during an attempt to orchestrate the conflict? How should a clear understanding of power, authority, and agency inform the process?*

- *What are realistic challenges to adaptive leadership? What are the potential risks for attempting to lead a process of change? What might be some strategies to increase your resilience to these challenges? Ultimately, what do you believe is essential for successful adaptive work?*

Facilitator Notes

Be sure you are familiar with the case study and have thought through potential questions participants may have regarding the role play. You may want to provide the actors with name/role placards so observers and actors can easily identify the characters in the conversation.

It is helpful to revisit group expectations prior to engaging in this exercise but also discuss with the group how those expectations should play out in a simulation attempting to address real-world dynamics. Be prepared for this dialogue to become heated if participants truly take on their roles. You may need to remind the participant playing Alan that he is leading the meeting. Be sure you are ready to provide some summarizing statements about the intersection of social identities and critical perspectives (e.g., power, capital, authority) within adaptive leadership. For example, adaptive leadership necessarily involves challenging others through a process of transformation. Therefore, initiating adaptive work often requires a certain level of power and/or authority. The pervasive and systematic nature of oppression can inhibit leaders with marginalized social identities from assuming power and authority, or in dominant environments, the sources of power and social capital that person possesses may be more fragile, in turn influencing the process of how adaptive leadership may need to unfold.

> Conclusion

Adaptive leadership is at the heart of what leaders *do*: helping groups work their way through complex problems without easy answers. By helping participants better identify the type of challenges facing the group (e.g., technical versus adaptive) and by providing a general framework for navigating adaptive challenges, individuals can better understand the inherent complexity in helping groups navigate change. Whether they are global challenges that have persisted for years, or localized issues of a personal nature, all issues require skilled individuals who can help the work of the group move forward. For these initiatives to be successful, however, adaptive leadership cannot operate with a presumption that leadership occurs within a vacuum failing to recognize the complexity of social stratification and its implications. This curriculum serves as an entry point into naming, considering, and redressing how critical perspectives derived from stocks of knowledge as well as social location may shape the way that adaptive work unfolds.

Handout 9.1: Summary of Adaptive Leadership

At times, leadership is dangerous—very dangerous. It only takes a moment or two to think of struggles (great and small) that make up our collective narrative as a human race. Leaders and the concept of leadership are at the heart of all these struggles. Whether it's a Palestinian mother who wants her children to live in a free state, a Buddhist monk working to save his country, or a young woman fighting for her right to attend school in Afghanistan, all involve leadership and an understanding of the vast complexity inherent in each of the challenges they face.

However, not all leadership challenges exist on a global scale. At times, the challenges facing a group of people exist at a national level as well. For instance, in the United States, these struggles may address topics such as gun violence, abortion rights, the death penalty, immigration, systemic racism, and environmentalism. At the local level, how a community reforms its struggling school system, attracts business, and manages public health issues such as obesity are also examples of complex leadership challenges. On a college campus, some of the challenges confronting the community may be adaptive, such as, How do we truly eliminate hazing in social organizations, the band, or athletic teams? How do we ensure that individuals of various backgrounds (e.g., faith, sexual orientation, political orientation, race) have a voice? and How do we curb the challenges associated with underage drinking?

This handout is designed to highlight the concept of adaptive challenges and, more specifically, components of Heifetz and Linsky's (2002) theory of adaptive leadership. The types of challenges previously mentioned have various names, such as ill-structured problems, wicked problems, ill-defined problems, and adaptive challenges. A leader or group of concerned individuals on either side of the previously mentioned issues will need to determine how to win the day for their followers, peers, and/or constituents. However, there is no solution book for *any* of the examples previously mentioned. There is no authority figure we can turn to fix the problem with a ready-made solution.

Adaptive challenges have a few different hallmarks that differentiate them from technical challenges where the use of an expert or authority figure is more the norm (e.g., "I have a flat tire and need a mechanic"). One hallmark is that adaptive challenges are often difficult to define (Heifetz & Linsky, 2002). A second hallmark is that new learning needs to occur. The expertise to solve the issue does not exist in the system/organization/culture, so the individuals working to solve the adaptive challenge need to run experiments and learn in real time (Heifetz & Linsky, 2002). A third hallmark of adaptive challenges is that they often challenge people in the group to give something up, alter their value system, or reframe their views (Heifetz & Linsky, 2002). Moving past each of the hallmarks is difficult and rare and helps one understand why many adaptive challenges persist. For example, everyone knows hazing is wrong, but it persists. People know if they eat processed/unhealthy food and do not exercise their risk of obesity increases—yet these behaviors continue.

Adaptive leadership is a theory Heifetz and his colleagues have been exploring as a way to help people understand and navigate adaptive challenges (Heifetz & Linsky, 2002). Adaptive work can be challenging because it requires the leader to push, but in doing so, not lose the various factions in the room. Likewise, the leader must acknowledge and honor what various factions are being asked to give up in the process. To navigate adaptive challenges, Heifetz and Linsky (2002) suggested that a leader needs to focus on the following:

- *Get on the Balcony*: This is a metaphor for what the Jesuits would call *contemplation in action*. The leader must distinguish between adaptive and technical challenges, understand the many sides of the issue, accurately diagnose the situation, and look to formal and informal leaders for clues about the current realities (Heifetz & Linsky, 2002).

- *Think Politically*: This requires the leader to find partners in the work who have similar ends in mind. Likewise, there is a need to keep those in disagreement close and acknowledge your piece of the mess. Further, thinking politically necessitates acknowledgment of the other side's loss and requires the leader or group to model effective behavior. In the end, the leader and/or group needs to accept that there may be "casualties," which can result in anger and dissent (Heifetz & Linsky, 2002).

- *Orchestrate the Conflict*: Adaptive leadership requires a *holding environment*, which is described by Heifetz and Linsky (2002) as "a space formed by a network of relationships within which people can tackle tough, sometimes divisive questions without flying apart. Creating a holding environment enables you to direct creative energy toward working the conflicts and containing passions that could easily boil over" (p. 102). Within this container, there is a need to control the heat in the room. By nature, change raises the heat in many situations. After all, one faction of people will be faced with giving something up (e.g., time, resources, their privilege). This is a difficult process to manage. There needs to be just enough heat, but not so much that things boil over. Likewise, Heifetz and Linsky (2002) suggested the need for pacing the work. Finally, they expressed the need to highlight a bright future and keep people grounded in *why* the work is important, needed, and worth the struggle.

- *Give the Work Back*: Heifetz and Linsky (2002) highlighted the need to keep the work focused on the people who need to engage and take responsibility for solutions. There is a natural desire for the authority figure to have the answers and make it better. With adaptive challenges, there is a need to place the work on the factions who need to identify a path forward. This is risky, but if clear ground rules have been established (e.g., the leader's role is not to provide solutions/answers), this may be minimized. Because of the fluid nature of this work, it is difficult to provide a formula for giving the work back. If the leader does choose to intervene, it should be short and simple. These micro interventions can occur in the form of questions, short statements, observations, interpretations, and actions.

- *Hold Steady*: According to Heifetz and Linsky (2002), "Holding steady in the heat of action is an essential skill for staying alive and keeping people focused on the work. The pressure on you may be almost unbearable, causing you to doubt" (p. 141). Although some in the room may want to make the leader the issue, the leader must maintain focus on the issue. Likewise, some participants (perhaps unknowingly) will distract the group from the work. These distractions (e.g., moving topics, personal attacks, unrelated observations), gone unnoticed, can erode the work of the group and take their eye off the true issue.

Heifetz, R. A., & Linsky, M. (2002). *Leadership on the line: Staying alive through the dangers of leading*. Boston: Harvard Business School Press.

Handout 9.2: Adaptive Leadership Checklist

Get on the Balcony

- Distinguish technical from adaptive challenges.
- Find out where people are.
- Listen to the song beneath the words.
- Read the behavior of authority figures for clues.

Think Politically

- Find partners.
- Keep the opposition close.
- Accept responsibility for your piece of the mess.
- Acknowledge their loss.
- Model the behavior.
- Accept casualties.

Orchestrate the Conflict

- Create the holding environment.
- Control the heat.
- Pace the work.
- Show them the future.

Give the Work Back

- Take the work off your shoulders.
- Place the work where it belongs.
- Make your intervention short and simple.

Hold Steady

- Take the heat.
- Let the issues ripen.
- Focus attention on the issue.

The dangers of exercising leadership derive from the nature of the problems for which leadership is necessary. Adaptive change stimulates resistance because it challenges people's habits, beliefs, and values. It asks them to take a loss, experience uncertainty, and even express disloyalty to people and cultures. Because adaptive change forces people to question and perhaps redefine aspects of their identity, it also challenges their sense of competence. Loss, disloyalty, and feeling incompetent: That's a lot to ask. No wonder people resist.

—Heifetz and Linsky, 2002, p. 30

Heifetz, R. A., & Linsky, M. (2002). *Leadership on the line: Staying alive through the dangers of leading.* Boston: Harvard Business School Press.

Handout 9.3: Gilmore Fasteners: A Case Study in Adaptive Leadership

Gilmore Fasteners started out in 1932 with just seven employees and a garage-like factory on the lower west side of Cleveland. Today, the company has close to 300 employees who are involved in the manufacturing and sales of fasteners used mainly in the aviation industry. Since the Great Recession of 2008, business has been rough and the company is losing money at a frightening pace. Debt is so high, and sales are so slow, that creditors are no longer willing to consider the solid record Gilmore has had in the past. Alan Gilmore, CEO and son of the late Leo Gilmore (who started the company), has been relying on bank loans to cover payroll for the last four months and has just received a phone call informing him that the practice will no longer be supported until the bankers see evidence of "significant change and a commitment to debt reduction or serious promise of increased revenues in the very, very near future."

Gilmore Fasteners has always been loyal to their employees, and their employees have evidently been appreciative of this as demonstrated by the fact that the average length of employment at Gilmore is greater than 12 years. More than 20 employees have one or more family members who have also worked for the company, pay has been above average even when compared to union shops, and benefits have been outstanding. But now Alan Gilmore and the management team have to make some difficult decisions and do so quickly.

Also important to understanding the context is the fact that in May 2008 Gilmore Fasteners made a commitment to diversify its work force, which had historically been comprised of White males in the plant, sales, and management positions, and White females in the secretarial and lower staff positions. Although this was not done by design, Alan Gilmore realized that it wasn't right and had ordered his management team to be proactive in recruiting women and people from under-represented groups. Over the next two months, this policy resulted in the hiring of 23 new employees, including 19 African Americans and 4 Latinos. Eleven of the new employees were women, and one of them, Cindy Gonzales, was hired as the Assistant Director of Human Resources (the position she holds now). No new employees have been hired since that time.

Because of the current financial situation and the pressure being applied by creditors, the management has determined that 30 employees must be removed from the payroll immediately if "the company is to have any hope of surviving the crisis at hand." In the past, layoffs were only considered after management had taken cuts, and employees were retained solely on the basis of seniority. No layoffs had been made since the mid-1980s when Gilmore was almost forced into bankruptcy because of a major product liability lawsuit. They won the case, but only after four years of financial losses and astronomical legal fees.

A few hours after receiving the disturbing phone call from the bank, Alan Gilmore calls a meeting of his management team. After a lengthy and frank discussion, he orders the management team to immediately take a 10% pay cut across the board with the most highly paid senior managers taking an additional 10% cut voluntarily. All agree to the request. The management team (Chief Executive Officer Alan Gilmore, Chief Financial Officer Matt Peters, Chief Marketing Officer Jon Smith, Chief Technology Officer Steve Whiteman, Director of Operations Paul Western, and Director of Human Resources Robert Sims) then collectively decide to lay off 30 employees based upon seniority, as they have been selected in the past. They know this is the only option.

In her position as Assistant Director of Human Resources, Cindy Gonzales has taken part in the discussions involving what actions are to be taken regarding pay cuts and layoffs. As soon as the final decision is made, she goes directly to her boss, Director of Human Resources Robert Sims, and threatens to "take whatever action is necessary to prevent the unfair and clearly discriminatory layoffs of 30 loyal employees, 23 of whom are African Americans or Latinos, while only 7 White employees must pay the price of poor management and planning by corporate executives." She specifically threatened to go to the media and consult with legal counsel if the decision is not reversed, or unless "White male employees comprised the majority of the layoffs." She tells Robert to "remind them of how they publicized their commitment to diversifying their work force just a few years ago," and "how they will look like hypocrites at best and may be seen by many as racists and criminals," if they do not reconsider their decision.

In no time, the executive committee's plans leak and a faction of five employees demand a meeting with Alan and his executive team prior to any final decision being made. The meeting begins and it's well established that the leadership team is set on cutting jobs to save money. However, it is clear the leadership team wishes there was a better option. The five employees are mad, angry, and disheartened by such callous decision-making—Cindy is their champion and she believes there has to be a better way....

Marc P. Lynn

9C: Complexity Leadership Through a Critical Lens: Context and Complexity for Adaptive Change

Kevin M. Hemer & Laura Osteen

Objectives/Goals of Chapter

- Understand complexity leadership theory (CLT) and its integration of leaders' use of position and authority along with emergent and interactive dynamics within organizations to create adaptive change.
- Identify and accurately characterize both dominant and counter-dominant ideologies.
- Recognize CLT foundational concepts to distinguish complex from complicated and to introduce the critical contextual component of complex adaptive systems.

Critical Concepts: *agency, equity, identity, inclusion, power, systematic oppression*

Chapter Overview

Complexity leadership theories are bridge-building models connecting position and process; authority and emergence; and top-down and grass-root leadership strategies. From a critical perspective, this bridge-building framework provides a practical yet neutral position on positional power versus relational process.

Through a comprehensive focus, complexity leadership sidesteps making value judgments between hierarchical administrative uses of power and collective adaptive work. This curriculum plan reviews the core concepts and leadership strategies of complexity leadership theories, specifically using the work of Uhl-Bien, Marion, and McKelvey's (2007) complexity leadership theory (CLT). In addition to CLT, the chapter is informed by the work of Hazy, Goldstein, and Lichtenstein (2007) and their colleagues who explored leadership through the complex relationships within and between organizations.

Following a review of CLT, a curriculum plan comprised of four hands-on workshop activities is described. These activities are designed to introduce and familiarize participants with the grounding concepts of CLT: (1) distinguish concepts of complicated versus complex; (2) recognize that leadership stems not only from position and authority but also from emergent and interactive dynamics; (3) identify and describe complex adaptive systems (CAS); and (4) differentiate the three types of leadership behavior as administrative, enabling, and adaptive. The chapter concludes with resources for further reading on the topic.

> Chapter Framework

CLT positions leadership as a process that results in changes within complex systems. Building on Heifetz's adaptive models of leadership, Uhl-Bien et al. (2007) described CLT as "a complex interplay from which a collective impetus for action and change emerges when heterogeneous agents interact in networks in ways that produce new patterns of behavior or new modes of operating" (p. 299). The three core assumptions of this dynamic are (1) the context of complex adaptive systems matters; (2) within systems, three types of leadership exist: adaptive, administrative, and enabling; and (3) leadership in the knowledge era should focus on adaptive versus technical challenges. Across these three core assumptions two critical challenges are intertwined: equity of agency and deconstructing the use of power.

CAS are dynamic networks of interacting, interdependent agents united by common purpose. CAS have multiple levels of hierarchy that are linked through networks. CLT outlines a framework and three leadership strategies to foster creativity and learning within CAS (Uhl-Bien et al., 2007). CLT incorporates three leadership functions: administrative, adaptive, and enabling. *Administrative leadership* is actions by people in formal roles of authority within organizations. *Adaptive leadership* is "emergent change behaviors under conditions of interaction, interdependence, asymmetrical information, complex network dynamics, and tensions" (Uhl-Bien et al., 2007, p. 309) and occurs in CAS and in the interactions among agents rather than by the actions of individuals. Central to this process is the concept of emergence. *Emergence* consists of reformulation of a system to produce something that is fundamentally different and self-organizing. *Enabling leadership* creates conditions in which adaptive leadership can occur and thrive, managing the entanglement between bureaucratic and emergent functions of the organization. Enabling leadership fosters adaptive leadership in places where it is needed and facilitates the flow of knowledge and creativity to administrative structures. Enabling leadership occurs at all levels of the organization but takes different forms depending on hierarchical level.

The foundational belief that CAS emerge naturally from social systems and are capable of problem solving through adaptation and learning is the first and most significant critical issue in complexity leadership theory. Power is socially defined and constructed. Our individual and collective resources to gain, use, and be seen as powerful are directly linked to social identities, organizational history and structure, and feelings of psychological safety in the group (Dugan, 2017). How these relationships emerge is significantly more complex than CLT addresses. When evaluating CAS and their emergent properties, individuals in these relationships must be aware of who does and does not emerge with agency. Without this awareness and conscious work to include diverse voices, individuals will emerge who only confirm the power structures.

The bureaucratic functions of organizations cannot be separated from the dynamic CAS. The inability to separate bureaucracy associated with administrative leadership and the dynamic emergent forces of adaptive leadership is known as *entanglement*. In CLT, enabling leadership is employed to balance the structures and systems of bureaucracy with emergent forces. Enabling leadership manages entanglement. CLT describes enabling leaders who help prevent administrative leaders from suppressing beneficial creativity and foster adaptive dynamics appropriate for the organization's purpose. Enabling leadership articulates the mission of a project or task ensuring it is consistent with the strategy and mission of the organization. It is exactly this behavior that could be critically tailored to ensure equity of voice and not only alignment of mission. CLT focuses on ensuring a project or task is not defined too narrowly to risk the creative and emergent process of adaptive leadership. However, CLT should worry just as much, if not more, on whether the organizational structure, feel, and behavior are too narrowly constructed to risk the engagement and emergence of diverse voices. Emergent processes associated with adaptive leadership can be both con-trary to the mission of the organization and the inclusion of all individuals. In addition to realigning projects and tasks, enabling leaders must realign power structures through evaluating both mission-based and equity-based adaptive outputs for any given stage of development.

CLT responds to the challenge that leadership theory has overwhelmingly focused on the actions of the individual people or units instead of the complex dynamic of systems within an organization. This comprehensive focus is necessary and fills a void of models that focus too narrowly on a single aspect of organizational change. However, the lack of incorporation of how identity and power impact emergence and entanglement is significant. The knowledge era calls for a new paradigm—a paradigm of adaptive instead of technical bureaucratic changes. These adaptations emerge from interaction and emergence and not simply from control of or incentives to individuals. Grounded in these interacting systems are systems of power and oppression. Who is invited, allowed, and acknowledged in this process of interaction is critical to the understanding and just use of CLT. When applying the concepts of CLT, leaders must consciously engage in the interaction of these systems with an understanding of the forces that encourage some to emerge and others to be silenced. Going beyond individual action to the power of interaction, CLT offers a more comprehensive focus to creating change. Engaging in this work through a critical lens, we can extend beyond individual interaction to create inclusive interaction resulting in the emergence of more just organizations.

› Curriculum Plan

This curriculum is designed to teach and critically examine four components of CLT: distinguish concepts of complicated versus complex systems, recognize that leadership stems not only from position and authority but also from emergent and interactive dynamics, position CAS as emergent contexts, and describe three types of leadership behavior. Teaching a model intentionally designed to be complex can be a pedagogical challenge. CLT is designed as a whole-systems view of the leadership process. Therefore, the activities that follow are created in line with the model's recognition that leadership cannot be described as simply individual action; instead it is the dynamic interaction of many.

With a critical lens, these activities are also designed to examine how equity and power show up across concepts. The following activities are offered as building blocks to understand and deconstruct the components of complexity.

The curriculum is designed for two 75 minute sessions covering two CLT concepts. These sessions could not be offered as a combined session unless you had a chance to assign and explain the homework observation project before the session. In its current form, a reflection homework assignment occurs after the first session to prepare for the second. These sessions could be combined with a planned break in the middle to provide time for the assigned observation task. The resulting curriculum would be an approximately 4-hour, half-day session.

› Session 1: Distinguishing Complexity Activity 1—Complex versus Complicated

This is an experiential, hands-on activity that introduces and demonstrates complex versus complicated dynamics.

Learning Outcomes

- Distinguish definitions and examples of complex and complicated realities.
- Understand the appropriate use and application of the terms *complex* and *complicated* when discussing problems.
- Ability to recognize and critique personal biases in observations and understandings of reality.

Setting Up the Activity

Group Size: Up to 30 total participants
Time: 45 minutes

Methods: Experiential workshop

Materials: Complex and complicated definitions, complex and complicated examples (on slides, hard copies, and/or samples), crayons, water color paint, paper clips, paper

Directions

1. Begin by clarifying the definitions of complex and complicated from Uhl-Bien et al. (2007) and Chapter 9 of the main text:
   - *Complicated*: Can be described in terms of its individual constituents (even if there are a huge number of constituents)
   - *Complex*: The interactions among the constituents of the system and the interaction between the system and its environment are of such a nature that the system as a whole cannot be fully understood simply by analyzing its components.
2. Offer the following initial examples: Stackable blocks or a linked charmed bracelet? Salad or soup? Mixing crayons or paint colors? These examples are all written in the format of complicated versus complex. You can project this information on slides or have real-life objects with you. Ask participants to identify which are complicated and which are complex along with why.
3. Build upon the examples through an activity that involves creating crayon and paint drawings. Any of these examples can be used although the crayon and paint example may be easiest. For example, *Which is more complex: crayon or paint pictures?*
   - Direct participants to design the most creative, imaginative picture possible using crayons to layer colors and a paper clip to scratch out a picture. First participants brightly color one sheet of paper with the crayons provided, drawing blocks of colors in any size desired. Then, participants color over the blocks of colors with a black crayon.

- Using a paper clip, participants lightly scrape away the top layer of black crayon to create multicolored, imaginative images. Encourage creativity. When complete, have participants set their pictures aside.

4. For a second picture, distribute watercolor or paints to participants. Direct participants to paint what they imagine is a simple picture by mixing two colors together. Be sure to give participants significantly more time on the crayon picture than for the watercolor picture.

5. Participants should then compare the two pictures. Frame the discussion as follows:
   - *How would you describe the two pictures? How would you describe the difference between them?*
   - *How does the crayon picture reflect complicated versus complex? How does the painting reflect complex versus complicated?*
   - *What assumptions would you have made about which was complex? How does this connect to your definitions and assumptions of simple or simplicity?*
   - *What connections to real-life examples can you make?*
   - *How do the pictures you drew connect to who you are?*
   - *What similarities and differences do you observe in the pictures of your peers?*
   - *How do you distinguish complicated and complex in someone else's pictures?*
   - *How does your knowledge of someone else affect how you define whether their picture is complicated or complex?*

6. For the closing (5 minutes), facilitate a large group dialogue of discussed examples and their impact on participants' lives. Specific prompts include these: (a) *What happens when we assume a complex problem to be simply complicated?* (b) *How does this impact our response?* (c) *Can we create sustainable solutions if we misdiagnose complexity for simply complicated?*

7. Review the key tenets of CLT and summarize the definitions of complicated and complex, noting how they are often

confused in our daily lives and leadership strategies. A key to leadership in the knowledge era is understanding the difference and responding appropriately.

Facilitator Notes

An optional activity structure is to conduct small group discussions if art projects are not feasible. Follow the first two steps as outlined, but instead of Steps 3–5, have participants break into pairs for a reflection exercise. They should brainstorm examples of realities in their lives that are complex versus complicated. These realities may be experiences, challenges, and/or problems they are facing.

Next, they should discuss the difference between how these realities affect their lives and how they react to them. It will be important to remind participants that what one person experiences as complicated might be complex for another person and vice versa. Finally, replace "pictures" with the language of their stories for the reflection prompts.

Debriefing Notes

CLT can be a challenging concept to grasp. In the final debriefing section, it may be helpful to review these three core points of the curriculum to ensure that all participants feel confident in their understanding.

- A key distinction of CLT is the concept of complexity. Often complexity is confused with the seemingly intricate yet simply layered concept of complicated. Tangled fishing lines are extremely challenging but only complicated; whereas, the intricate interweaving of twine into rope is a complex interaction that creates something new.
- Complexity does not have to be hard or time consuming to create; it happens faster and more often than we imagine. Instead

of colors, simply mix two people (i.e., have two people interact with each other) and the dynamics of complexity can emerge in moments. By interacting with each other we create new realities.

- It takes complexity to lead within complex systems. Leadership responses must be as nuanced and as complex as the challenges we seek to solve. CLT is grounded in optimizing a system's capacity for learning, creativity, and adaptability.

- How we define complex and complicated is directly connected to our own experiences. When distinguishing between the two, it is important to note how individual similarities and differences show up in our understanding of others.

> Session 1: Distinguishing Complexity Activity 2—Emergence

This segment builds on the idea of human complexity by introducing leadership as an emergent dynamic of a collective versus the static action of an individual.

Learning Outcomes

- Understand leadership as a dynamic interaction with emergent realities.
- Apply the concept of emergence to an organization.
- Recognize the similarities and differences among those who emerge.

Setting Up the Activity

Group Size: Up to 30 total participants
Time: 30 minutes, including assigned homework activity
Methods: Hands-on application, presentation

Materials: "Homework—1 & 1 = 2: Observing Emergence" hand-out describing homework or in-person assignment; computer, projector/screen

Variations: May be modified to fit a longer session versus assigned as homework

Multimedia: Video clip: *Emergence* (http://video.pbs.org/video/ 1511364559/).

Directions

1. Begin by reviewing *complex* versus *complicated* as an introduction to the session. Example language can include this: *Moving on from our analogy of crayons and painting, human interaction is where complexity emerges in organizations. How we interact with each other is the heart of the complex dynamic within CLT. We are now going to dive deeper into this grounding using an activity to recognize, observe, and consider supporting this emergence.*

2. Introduce the idea of *emergence*: a combination that brings forth something that was not there before (Lichtenstein et al., 2006). Seek initial examples of emergence from participants. Examples you could share to prompt thinking include these: *Someone who recently ran for a position in your organization that you did not expect; a roommate who showed up unexpectedly and changed the direction of your day; and/or how your siblings have recently made a specific unexpected impact in your life.*

3. Show the *Emergence* video clip.
   - Process reactions to the video. Prompts can include these: *What did you see? How does this connect to your understanding of CLT? What did you learn about emergence?*
   - Bridge examples in the video with observations they can make in their organizations and daily life: *How did the video connect to emergence as you observe it in your day-to-day life?*

How do you see these concepts in your organizations, communities, and/or families?

- Push the participants to consider their roles as agents in these processes, not just as objects that are influenced by such processes, but as leaders who can recognize and respond to them. Sample language may include the following: *Not only do these events occur, as leaders, it is our responsibility to recognize them in our daily lives. It is our work to pay attention and to be present in these dynamics. How do we begin to practice seeing emergence and interactions in our lives? How do we ensure that we pay attention to what is happening around us? How do we come to understand what it is that we are seeing?*

- The answers and discussion that result from this dialogue should lead to the next activity. Bridge the conversation with the quote from Hazy et al. (2007): *"Emergence in organizations requires constant attention and support; its success depends on the quality of attention individuals bring to the process"* (p. 4). Then, share this: *This next activity is designed to assist you in your practice of paying attention to emergence and interactions that create complexity.*

4. Assign "Homework—1&1 = 2: Observing Emergence." Introduce the concept that the 1's matter individually yet it is the *&* that makes all the difference—it is the combination from which 2 emerges.

    - Remind participants of the grounding philosophy of CLT: *Leadership is not vested "in" or done "by" a single person but emerges between people.* Possible questions you may use to prompt "and" thinking include these:
      - *When has an event mattered more than the actual people involved?*

        ○   *When have you seen context change the dynamics of a group or of yourself?*

        •   The assignment is designed to observe this phenomenon of emergence. More specifically, the objective is to observe the "ands" between people that create new realities: *How can you see "and" at work in your life, organizations, and communities?*

Facilitator Notes

It is important that you set aside time to preview the *Emergence* video so that you can edit it for time and the specific images you deem most appropriate. Use your discretion in encouraging participants to turn in homework in a manner you deem appropriate for the learning setting. Or, if completed during the session, regather and see Activity 3 for a debriefing outline.

› Session 2: Understanding Complexity Activity 3—Context Matters: Complex Adaptive Systems

This activity will debrief the "Homework—1 & 1 = 2: Observing Emergence" assignment to explore the impact of complex adaptive systems as influential context.

Learning Outcomes

• Recognize the powerful influence of context as a holding environment for change.

• Identify and analyze the existence of CAS in participants' lives.

• Critique how issues of inclusion and exclusion emerge in organizations.

Setting Up the Activity

Group Size: Up to 30 total participants

Time: 45 minutes

Methods: Homework/assignment, reflection exercise

Materials: Completed "Homework—1&1 = 2: Observing Emergence" handout

Directions

1. Check in with participants to ensure everyone has their completed homework. Start by sharing learnings with each other and then review the core components of CAS.

2. Ask for immediate reactions to and/or observations from the "Homework—1&1 = 2: Observing Emergence" assignment and ask the group to casually share some immediate connections they saw that connected their conversations on *complicated* versus *complex* and *emergence* in the last session.

3. Have participants get into pairs in which they should share lessons they learned and observations they made from the two-page narrative they created as part of the homework. Ask participants to identify similarities and differences in the lessons they learned that apply to the concepts of complicated versus complex, emergence, contexts of CAS, and inclusion/exclusion.

4. Return to the large group and have participants again share similarities and differences.

5. Briefly review and summarize complicated/complex and emergence: *It is important to remember that our influence upon each other—these emergent interactions—are like air for us or water for fish: often invisible. Yet, it is our responsibility as leaders to observe and pay attention to these dynamics to understand our contexts of CAS.*

6. Provide a brief lecture using the following four bullet points to connect the core concepts of CAS (Plowman & Duchon,

2007; Uhl-Bien et al., 2007) to participants' observations and day-to-day organization/group realities:

- *CAS are dynamic networks of interacting, interdependent agents united by common purpose. An example of CAS is Olympic sports teams within larger national team structures— think of networks of interdependent teams at the Olympics.*
- *CAS emerge naturally from social systems and are living systems of people and resources that are capable of problem-solving through adaptation and learning.*
- *A critique of CLT's approach to CAS is that these naturally occurring networks are influenced by social norms and structures of who has access to power, creating contexts of inclusion and exclusion.*
- *Adaption and learning is possible because CAS are characterized as/by*
  - Nonlinear: *A direct relation of cause and effect does not exist.*
  - Disequilibrium: *Organizations do not reside in a place of static calm; tensions create conflict and possibility for change.*
  - Emergence: *There is an organic capacity for interactions to create influence and newness.*

7. Take a moment to open for discussion. Explore these three concepts by having participants apply them to their homework assignment and lived experiences:
   - *How did you see these descriptors in your 1 & 1 = 2 observations? How do you see them in your organizations, families, or groups?*
   - *Specifically thinking about this from a critical lens, what similarities and differences did you observe on who emerged in interactions and who did not?*
   - *Who had access to power and how was it used in the CAS dynamic?*

8. Close with four strategies to enhance leadership and emergence within complex systems:
   - Distribute intelligence: *Ensure everyone has access to information; create self and system awareness.*
   - Foster conversation: *Encourage talking to each other; conversations multiply energy, information, and connections.*
   - Sustain tensions: *Recognize conflict, discomfort, and paradox as sources of energy, learning, and growth.*
   - Seek to see patterns: *Step back and identify patterns of behavior; patterns contain meaning for what people need and value; attempt to see the wholeness of the system.*

9. Pause for open conversation and application of these strategies to participants' experience:
   - *How did you witness these strategies in your 1 & 1 = 2 observations? How do you see them in your organizations, families, or groups?*
   - *From a critical perspective, what similarities and differences did you observe regarding who had access to the intelligence and conversations? Who created and/or responded to the tensions? What patterns did you see emerge? How might patterns reflect useful or restrictive stocks of knowledge?*

10. Summarize lessons learned and connections between complexity, emergence, and CLT in the context of CAS.

Debriefing Notes

If this point does not come out in your discussion, it may be helpful to close by stating this: *Our leader development work is to enhance and practice our capacity to be aware—to see—the dynamics of CAS in our lives. Emergence occurs naturally, and yet our capacity to be present to and support it enhances its development and influence. Our recognition of this influence increases opportunities for learning and leadership throughout the system.*

❯ Session 2 : Understanding Complexity
Activity 4—CLT Leadership Strategies

This activity closes out CLT conversations with small group discussion and application of the three leadership strategies identified by Uhl-Bien et al. (2007).

Learning Outcomes

- Understand the appropriate application of administrative, adaptive, and enabling leadership strategies.
- Connect the foundational CLT concepts of complexity, emergence, and CAS to the three leadership strategies.
- Critique and address how CLT strategies can be inclusive of diverse voices and create inclusive organizational structures.

Setting Up the Activity

Group Size: Up to 30 total participants

Time: 30 minute.

Methods: Small group exercise

Materials: Participants should have already read Chapter 9 from the main text (Dugan, 2016).

Directions

1. Begin by transitioning from the previous activity: *Building on our conversations of complexity, emergence, and CAS, we are going to close by applying each to the three leadership strategies identified by Uhl-Bien et al. (2007). These three behaviors work differently and are based on the concept that CAS exist and are linked through an organization's multiple levels of hierarchy. As you examine the three strategies, explore specifically the responsibility*

complexity, emergence, and CAS have when considering the influence of the inclusion and exclusion dynamics of power.

2. Divide the participants into three small groups and provide them with approximately 20 minutes. Each group gets one of the three leadership strategies: administrative, enabling, or adaptive. Ask participants to discuss the strategy using content from Chapter 9 of the main text:

   - *Describe how this particular strategy relates to/depends upon the concepts of complexity, emergence, and CAS.*
   - *Identify examples you have observed of this leadership strategy.*
   - *Critique your particular strategy, specifically identifying how it might contribute to the inclusion or exclusion of diverse voices. How might it be leveraged to create inclusive collective structures?*

3. Instruct each of the three small groups to share: (a) examples of their strategy; (b) its connection to complexity, emergence, and CAS; and (c) their critique of how to ensure inclusive structures. Clarify and distinguish responses to highlight each of the three leadership behaviors.

4. After small groups have finished sharing, begin a wrap-up conversation with the entire group: *Although many of our post-industrial paradigms provide pathways to nonpositional, process-based leadership, CLT builds a bridge to understand and design leadership behavior grounded in organizations that exist in the dual realities of hierarchal and emergent structures. And yet this bridge does not explicitly instruct us on how to be aware, observe, and change the potentially exclusionary dynamics of power and social location. To justly and critically apply CLT, one must be cognizant of how structures include or exclude diverse voices in emergent processes.*

5. Summarize conversations and lessons learned over the past two sessions. You may want to close with an example of CLT in your personal life and/or professional communities.

> Conclusion

CLT and its companion CAS are bridging the theoretical and practical realities of conventional and complex organizational life. These theories connect position and process; authority and emergence; and top-down and grass-root leadership strategies. Although connected, the model does not provide a critique of how top-down and emergent models often silence diverse voices within a group. This chapter reviewed CLT, provided four activities within a comprehensive CLT curriculum plan, and provided a critical lens from which to view and enact CLT.

Handout 9.4: Homework—1 & 1 = 2: Observing Emergence

- Choose a place to observe people in action. This could be a large gathering space like a mall or a campus green or it could be something more enclosed like an organization's meeting room or a restaurant.

- Spend at least 30 minutes, and up to an hour or more, observing behavior that emerges between people.

- In a two-page narrative, describe the patterns of emergence you observe. Your description should consider and respond to the following prompts:
  - *What behaviors emerged? Consider behaviors such as communication, movement, influence, decisions, dominance, submission, newness, or change.*
  - *What patterns can you identify in the behaviors?*
  - *What patterns of inclusion and exclusion did you observe? Did the group address them? How?*
  - *How did you observe people learning or adapting from their interactions? What social forces did you see at work?*
  - *How did the context of your surroundings influence the interactions?*
  - *What did you see emerge that surprised you?*

Chapter 10: Toward a Justice-Based Leadership Model

⌄

10A: Cultivating Critical Hope Through Communities of Praxis

Willie Gore & Satugarn P. Limthongviratn

◇

Objectives/Goals of Chapter

- Understand the importance of resiliency and critical hope in leadership for justice.
- Adopt tactics to recognize resources and capital within communities.
- Recognize how to leverage communities as resources that can enhance critical hope and resiliency in leadership for justice.

Critical Concepts: *critical hope, community cultural wealth, praxis, resilience, social capital*

⟩ Chapter Overview

Leadership for social change can be difficult, challenging, and taxing due to the seemingly insurmountable barriers that come with addressing systems of oppression (Freire, 2008; Boggs & Kurashige, 2012). This work runs the risk of resulting in hopelessness, discouragement, and perceived powerlessness.

Therefore, it is crucial to draw upon the infinite power contained within communities because that is the only way to shine through the darkness of despair, maintain critical hope, and illuminate the path to justice.

Once we ground ourselves within community and gather strength, we need to strategize on how to use our power effectively through our spheres of influence. Otherwise, we may fail to accomplish any changes. Therefore, to effectively push for social change, we must foster resilience by cultivating critical connections within our communities, building collective capacity by identifying sources of community capital, and strategically utilize that enormous power to transform the world (Boggs & Kurashige, 2012; Ospina et al., 2012; Yosso, 2005). Within this chapter, we integrate Ospina et al.'s (2012) strategic social change leadership framework, Freire's (2008) notions of praxis, Boggs and Kurashige's (2012) lens on grassroots community organizing, and Yosso's (2005) critical analysis of community cultural wealth to highlight methods of overcoming the challenges inherent to leadership for social change. In addition, we provide activities to help participants identify the resources, capital, and power within their communities to cultivate the agency, resilience, and critical hope necessary for social change.

> Chapter Framework

Due to the pervasiveness of embedded societal inequities, enacting leadership for justice can be draining and result in hopelessness. Therefore, it is necessary to create a means for both establishing and sustaining critical hope. Critical hope is a strong and fierce form of hope that recognizes how destructive the absence of hope can be, but it also understands that the fight for justice is both complex and multifaceted (Preskill & Brookfield, 2009). An individual's mere engagement in the fight for social justice and equity is an expression of critical hope. This fight is the antithesis of complacency; it claims change as both a possibility and a necessity. However, it is also important to know you are not fighting alone.

According to Boggs, "The real engine of change is never 'critical mass'; dramatic and systemic change always begins with 'critical connections'" (Boggs & Kurashige, 2012, p. 50). These critical connections can be tremendous sources of hope, resilience, social capital, and power that allow us to continue making dents in the walls of injustice (Boggs & Kurashige, 2012; Preskill & Brookfield, 2009; Yosso, 2005). However, it may initially be difficult to recognize and identify the different types of resources present within communities. We have been socially conditioned to value specific types of capital such as economic, educational, and social through a dominant lens (Bourdieu, 1986; Dugan, 2017; Yosso, 2005). By doing this, we lose sight of the hidden and immense power contained within the community cultural wealth of marginalized communities. Community cultural wealth is defined as the collection of resources, wisdom, information, skills, and relationships that are used by marginalized communities to survive within systems of oppression (Yosso, 2005). This framework identifies six forms of capital including aspirational, navigational, social, linguistic, familial, and resistant capital (Yosso, 2005). Together, these alternative forms of capital empower individuals to sustain hope, navigate hostile social institutions, foster healthy connections to community, and provide leadership tools that are grounded within legacies of resistance (Yosso, 2005).

Although we may have access to resources and capital, it is important to strategically implement them, which can be done through *praxis*. Freire (2008) suggested that the pursuit of social justice "cannot be purely intellectual but must involve action; nor can it be limited to mere activism but must include serious reflection: only then will it be a praxis" (p. 65). Freire also placed great emphasis on the importance of communing with others while seeking hope, healing, and justice. This reference to solidarity and the power of community expresses the importance of creating a community willing to both reflect and take strategic action when leading for justice and the common good: a community of praxis.

Effective communities of praxis must find agency in recognizing that social change is both possible and necessary. Ospina et al. (2012) introduced a framework for social change that focuses on strategic action highlighting two key concepts: Images of the Present and Visions of the Future. *Images of the Present* speak to the process of acknowledging and naming a current, pressing, systemic inequity. The act of naming an issue provides communities with a shared direction and consciousness, which are key motivating factors of leadership for the common good. Creating a community of praxis must involve reflection that ultimately acknowledges the existence of injustice. Being unaware of the causes of injustice can cause a fatalistic acceptance of degradation and inequity (Freire, 2008). Awareness can be expressed by collectively naming an issue, concern, or social injustice to create a shared purpose. *Visions of the Future* refers to envisioning a world without the inequity that was named. Envisioning a more just future is an exemplification of critical hope beginning with an effective critique of the present and sustained by a collective vision for the future (Preskill & Brookfield, 2009).

Community can be a source of both critical hope and resilience for critical leadership. According to Heifetz and Linsky (2002), "The enduring basis for all civilization ... lies in the formation of attachments to one another, and these loyalties are based upon the ability to love, care, or take interest in other people" (p. 210). The interdependency of humans has created opportunities to experience love, care, and hope. Engaging in leadership for justice is a journey, not a destination. The Ospina et al. (2012) conceptualization of Images of the Present and

Visions of the Future speaks to the strategic action necessary to exhibit leadership for justice. The power of communities of praxis lies in their ability to name a present injustice, envision a brighter future, and take strategic, collective action to enact change.

Curriculum Plan

This curriculum explores the concepts of community, hope, connectedness, and praxis as essential to leadership for the common good. Through the use of critical self-reflection and dialogue, participants will be challenged to consider their spheres of influence and abilities to effectively engage in communities of praxis. This curriculum will help participants to examine the pervasiveness of injustice while also garnering hope and resilience to envision and create a more just future. The following curriculum plan should be implemented over two sessions each ranging from 60 to 90 minutes. Although segmented sessions are optimal for the curriculum to allow ample processing and reflection time, the sessions can also be facilitated consecutively.

Activity 1—Mapping Out Spheres of Influence and Building Community

To pursue justice and social change, weaving relationships with others to build community is necessary (Ospina et al., 2012). This activity will challenge participants to identify the resources, skills, knowledge, and power within their communities through the use of Yosso's (2005) framework of community cultural wealth. Furthermore, it will encourage participants to conceptualize potential pathways in their lives to enact social change.

Learning Outcomes

- Understand different types of capital using the community cultural wealth framework.
- Develop a greater understanding of one's ability to enact social change through the use of community cultural wealth.
- Recognize the importance of community and collective capital for enacting social change.

Setting Up the Activity

Group Size: The optimal group size is from 15 to 30 participants.

Time: 90 minutes

Methods: Critical self-reflection, dialogue, lecture

Materials: Blank sheets of paper (one to two sheets per person), whiteboard/chalkboard, markers/chalk, writing utensils

Directions

1. Begin by explaining Yosso's (2005) concept of community cultural wealth, which discusses how there are numerous sources of power, resources, knowledge, and skills that are contained within the community. It may be helpful to define and discuss the framework's six forms of capital. Allow sufficient time for processing and questions.
   - *Aspirational*: The capacity to maintain hope and dreams for the future
   - *Navigational*: The ability to navigate or maneuver complex situations and systems
   - *Social*: A relational support network of peers and community members
   - *Linguistic*: The capacity to engage socially and intellectually through communication
   - *Familial*: A core unit of support, community, and kin
   - *Resistant*: The capacity to oppose domination

2. Ask participants to individually think about Yosso's (2005) six types of capital and what kind of skills, knowledge, and resources they have access to within their communities. Note that it may be difficult for some participants to initially understand the term *community*. It may be helpful to collectively define the word, or provide a definition, as a frame of reference. Instruct participants to write down answers and organize them according to Yosso's (2005) model. It may be helpful to provide a visual of the model to guide participants as they "map" the sources of capital in their community.

3. Form groups of five. Have participants process their thoughts and feelings in small groups. Encourage the participants to share their written responses but do not force them because participants may not want to disclose personal information. Additional reflection and/or dialogue questions can include these:
   - *What thoughts and feelings guided you when you were doing this activity?*
   - *Why did you choose to include the people you listed on your community cultural wealth model/map?*
   - *What capital would you use to enact social change and how would you do it? How might this reflect social location?*
   - *What do you think you can do to achieve a greater impact?*
   - *How would you collectively use your group's total capital to enact change?*

4. Come back as a large group and have each small group briefly share key points discussed with their dialogues.

5. End the activity with a closing reflection. This can either be an individual or group reflection. Consider the following: *How did you feel when mapping your community's cultural wealth? When you think about how capital is obtained, what thoughts come to mind to continue fostering your community's capital?*

Debriefing Notes

Upon completion of this activity, encourage the participants to continue reflecting on their spheres of influence and the key points that they learned. In addition, encourage participants to implement these concepts into their daily lives by strengthening the relationships within their spheres of influence.

Facilitator Notes

When facilitating this activity, it is important to be cognizant of the sensitivity and comfort levels of the participants because it delves deeply into people's lives, relationships, narratives, and connections. Thus, it becomes important to develop and maintain ground rules for dialogue and engagement. In addition, it may be difficult for participants to identify and map out their spheres of influence. It may be useful for you to do your own reflection prior to facilitating this activity to provide a solid example of a map of influence.

> Activity 2—Creating Communities of Praxis

The work of social justice leadership is often motivated by images of both the present and the future (Ospina et al., 2012). This activity introduces the Ospina et al. (2012) present and future ideology as a framework for creating collective power and exhibiting leadership for the common good. It will encourage participants to name injustices while also engaging in the practice of envisioning a future where that issue or injustice is eliminated.

Learning Outcomes

- Recognize the importance of collective power through the formation of communities of praxis.

- Create a shared consciousness around a social injustice.
- Understand the concept of hope regarding social justice leadership.

Setting Up the Activity

Group Size: Groups ranging from 9 to 35 participants

Time: 90 minutes

Methods: Dialogue, lecture, reflection

Materials: Projector/screen, blank paper (one per participant), writing utensils

Directions

1. Begin the activity by explaining Freire's (2008) concept of praxis reading the following quote: *"Human activity consists of action and reflection: it is praxis; it is transformation of the world. And as praxis, it requires theory to illuminate it. Human activity is theory and practice; it is reflection and action"* (Freire, 2008, p. 125). You can also use a PowerPoint or other form of multimedia to visually present this quote.

2. Ask participants to share how this quote speaks to them. More specifically, how is it related to their personal lives, jobs, learning experiences, or purpose regarding social justice leadership?

3. Introduce the concepts of Images of the Present and Visions of the Future from the work of Ospina et al. (2012): "The work of social justice leadership is driven by images of both the present and the future. Individuals identify a current, pressing systemic inequity and name it. They also envision a world without that inequity; they create a picture of a just and fair future" (p. 269). Again, multimedia can be used to visually present these concepts. Allow time and space for questions, comments, and reactions.

4. Begin with Images of the Present. Ask participants to individually reflect on what issues or injustices they can collectively address or challenge through praxis (participants have the option of utilizing the provided blank paper).

5. Instruct each participant to pick one of the issues/injustices they reflected on to individually share with the group. Encourage them to be both clear and concise with what it is and why they chose it. Provide no more than 30 seconds per participant to share.

6. Instruct participants to form no more than five groups. This can be done randomly, by either combining participants who share similar ideas, or by having individuals gather with participants whose ideas they find intriguing.

7. Explain to participants that their groups can now be considered communities of praxis. For the first five minutes, instruct participants to come up with a list of issues/injustices they are interested in addressing, giving each individual an opportunity to share an issue. This list will allow space for each participant's voice to be heard and can be revisited in future group gatherings. Then give participants 20 minutes to dialogue about one of the issues/injustices considering the following:
   - *How has this issue/injustice affected you personally, socially, and/or systemically?*
   - *Envision a future without this issue or injustice. What does it look like?*
   - *How do we get there? What are some realistic goals and outcomes that can be set? What capital or resources are needed? What capital or resources do you currently have access to?*

8. Gather the large group back together and ask each community of praxis to share a short summary of what they discussed. Each group should take no longer than three minutes.

9. Engage in a dialogue in which participants respond to the following questions:
   - *What did you learn from this activity?*
   - *What are some examples of communities of praxis?*

- *What are the benefits of creating a community of praxis?*
- *What do you foresee as challenges to creating communities of praxis?*
- *How can your current community of praxis be sustainable?*

Debriefing Notes

As you wrap up the activity, encourage participants to recognize that what has been created and learned in this space should not end or be forgotten at the conclusion of the activity. These communities of praxis can be revisited and utilized after this session either by further examining the issue that was discussed or by referring back to the lists that were originally created within the groups. It may be an effective strategy to allow these groups to gather and meet periodically on a long-term basis to fully exemplify praxis.

Conclusion

The rocky path of social justice will always be filled with obstacles, challenges, and struggles. However, the journey should not be traveled alone. This curriculum was designed to help participants understand how to become effective leaders for social change. The critical frameworks and theories from Ospina et al. (2012), Freire (2008), Boggs and Kurashige (2012), and Yosso (2005) provide participants with fundamental theoretical concepts that are necessary for social justice. By learning how to maintain resilience and critical hope, identify community cultural wealth, create communities of praxis, and engage in strategic action, participants begin cultivating the tools necessary to transform the world.

10B: Ethics and Leadership

Kathryn Kay Coquemont

Objectives/Goals of Chapter

- Ability to deconstruct traditional definitions of ethical leadership using critical perspectives.
- Recognize influences on the development of an ethical framework.
- Challenge incongruencies in the intention and impact of decision making to facilitate a broader awareness of socially unjust ethical frameworks.

Critical Concepts: *bias, critical consciousness, marginalization, power, privilege, social capital*

Chapter Overview

General stipulations that leadership must be ethical are not enough to create leaders who prioritize "human flourishing" (Levine & Boaks, 2014, p. 230). Because many equate ethical leadership with values-driven influence, ethical meaning-making is left to personal interpretations of social definitions, which often hold deeply imbedded prejudices and inequities (Larson & Murtadha, 2002). This curriculum elevates participants' views of ethical leadership to a definition that accounts for the relationships among leadership, power, and privilege (Levine & Boaks, 2014). The activities are not meant to solely identify the intricacies in the relationship between ethics and leadership, but also to engage participants in cultivating a critical consciousness for enhancing the lives of others through ethical leadership (Larson & Murtadha, 2002). The purpose is to give participants a framework for expanding the leadership theories already presented and their relationship with ethics and ethical decision making. The following activities include intentional reflection on the impact of a leader's influence and its connection to increased equity and justice for others.

Chapter Framework

Levine and Boaks (2014) posited, "Not all values are ethical or moral values; [and] not all ethical or moral values are ones we would all agree with or endorse" (p. 233). This thought problematizes the idea that the intersection of a leader and socially understood ethics results in good leadership. Because ethics have traditionally been structured on individual behavior and social values, they are frequently built on systemic biases and cultural prejudices that often unknowingly run deep in individuals' thinking and actions. To combat inequitable frameworks, Larson and Murtadha (2002) documented the importance of rebuilding structures of leadership to include new viewpoints for social justice.

By redefining ethical leadership from personal intention to the impact of enhancing others' lives, its understanding moves from the theory of "right" to the theory of value (Levine & Boaks, 2014). This means leaders must cultivate critical consciousness to recognize and legitimize the experiences of populations not previously included in their frameworks. Thus, the new definition of leadership is focused on social benefit and collective well-being recognizing relationships between privilege, influence, and leadership (Kaufman, 2008; Levine & Boaks, 2014).

❯ Curriculum Plan

By engaging in the curriculum, participants will broaden their understanding of ethical leadership as they transition from an intention-focused to an impact-focused framework. Through the use of multimedia, reflection, discussion, and application, participants will be challenged to address how privilege, power, and bias affect the development of personal ethics. Through engaging in the following sessions, participants will challenge the traditional belief that "what is moral is good," expand the definition of ethics to include an awareness of the "other," and highlight the complexity of true ethical decision making as a leader. The curriculum plan should be implemented over two sessions, each ranging from 90 minutes to 2 hours. Although segmented sections are optimal to allow time for processing and recentering, the sessions can also be facilitated consecutively as an extended workshop or training.

❯ Activity 1—Defining Ethics and Exploring Impact

In this activity, participants create a definition of ethics that includes concepts of impact and power. The intention is to increase participant awareness of the experiences, influences, and identities that led to the development of their ethical frameworks. Participants will be challenged to consider areas of privilege that may have created blind spots related to what and who is included in the idea of "the common good."

Learning Outcomes

- Identify incongruencies between the intention and impact of ethical decision making.

- Understand influences that affect ethical decision making.
- Develop a socially just definition of the word *ethics* and reflect on elements that inform participants' personal ethical frameworks.

Setting Up the Activity

Group Size: Open to any size group

Time: 2 hours

Methods: Dialogue, lecture, multimedia, reflection.

Materials: Blank paper, writing utensils, computer, projector/ screen, audio, Internet access

Multimedia: TED2009 talk video by Dan Ariely: *Our buggy moral code* (www.ted.com/talks/dan_ariely_on_our_buggy_moral_code?language=en#t-946871)

Directions

1. Begin the activity by explaining that leadership is a values-based process because personal and social ethical guidelines influence how leaders make decisions. Explain that the focus of this activity is to critically examine traditional beliefs about ethical frameworks and influences on ethical decision making.
2. Show *Our buggy moral code* video (approximately 16 minutes).
3. Engage the group in a discussion using the following prompts:
   - *In what ways do societal norms and personal relationships influence ethical decision making?*
   - *How do we assess if our ethical intuition is having the desired impact on others?*
   - *As leaders, how do we create reminders of morality for ourselves to help guide our ethical decision making?*
   - *How, if at all, do you believe the video and its concepts relate to leadership?*

4. Introduce the idea that a critical perspective on ethics dismantles the traditional belief that "what is moral is right" due to the focus on self and the social majority. When based on critical perspectives, the definition broadens to include the idea that ethical behavior socially benefits the collective and considers not only impact on self but impact on others. Critical perspectives demand that leaders intentionally note the impact of decision making on those from historically marginalized and privileged identities, recognizing social location.

5. Ask participants to reflect for 5 minutes on their personal ethical framework and how it was developed, utilizing the following questions:
   - *How do you define ethics? How has this definition influenced the development of your ethical framework?*
   - *In one sentence, how would you describe your personal ethical framework?*

6. Have the group split into evenly distributed smaller groups to complete the next portion of the activity. Ask each group to share how their experiences, influences, and identities contributed to the development of their individual ethical frameworks.

7. Ask groups to reflect on their personal identities and discuss how they may have created blind spots in noticing how their decision making influenced others. This is an opportunity to explore how stocks of knowledge may shape assumptions regarding ethics. Give an example from your life to acknowledge we all have limitations in our perspectives. A literary/theatrical example would be from *Les Misérables* (Hugo, 2013/1862) in how Javert is from the middle class and does not understand how anyone might ever make the choice to steal food since his understanding is that stealing is always wrong.

8. Have groups brainstorm ways to minimize blind spots when making leadership decisions. Ask each group to share their insights with the larger group.

9. Have participants engage in individual written reflection (one to two pages) to identify at least one blind spot in their ethical framework and examine how they can expand it to be more conscious of negative impacts on others.

Debriefing Notes

The conclusion of this section is designed to increase participants' self-awareness regarding how their personal ethical frameworks may have marginalized or negatively influenced others. Debriefing activities that discuss sensitive topics like identity should be tailored to the developmental readiness of the group.

> Activity 2—Understanding Societal Factors in Ethical Frameworks

This activity builds upon the knowledge and awareness gained in Activity 1 by engaging in sociocultural dialogue to problematize what society teaches its members to value. It will challenge participants to think of ethical leadership as more than the institutional definition that focuses on cultural morality.

Learning Outcomes

- Deepen understanding of influences on the development of ethical frameworks.
- Recognize temporal, privileged, and cultured understanding of ethical decision making.
- Be able to apply socially just frameworks to ethical decision making.

Setting Up the Activity

Group Size: Open to any size group
Time: 90 minutes–2 hours

Methods: Dialogue, multimedia, reflection

Materials: "Sojourner Truth's 'Ain't I a Woman?' Speech" and "Ethics and Leadership: Activity 2 Case Study" handouts, computer, projector/screen, audio, Internet access

Multimedia: If possible, find a multimedia performance of the "Ain't I a Woman?" speech.

Directions

1. Begin the activity by explaining that the focus is to build upon the content and themes of the first activity and to apply the concepts to current and historical situations. Ask participants to share any additional insights or questions from the previous session.

2. Facilitate a reading or viewing of Sojourner Truth's (1851) "Ain't I a Woman?" speech. Engage the group in a discussion using the following prompts:

   - *In what ways did privileged and marginalized identities affect the differing ethical frameworks depicted here?*

   - *How can we, as leaders, enact change when we witness the negative impact of "moral" decisions on those with less social capital or those who have less access to resources due to differences in social location?*

   - *As leaders, how do we move ourselves and others beyond morality that is constrained by specific time periods, cultures, or societal beliefs to a more socially just understanding of ethical dilemmas?*

3. Have the group split into evenly distributed smaller groups. Introduce the impact of global and cultural differences on the development of ethical frameworks. Ask each group to share among themselves experiences where they have noticed differences in ethical frameworks due to global or cultural diversity. Remind groups that the purpose of the activity is

to identify differences and their root causes, but not to apply judgment to other cultures' ethical frameworks.

4. Have each group share their insights with the larger group. Lead the whole group in a discussion with the following prompts:

   - *Can anyone describe a time when they witnessed someone's belief in an ethical model where there were prescriptions of ethical behaviors that consider differences in situation, environment, and identity?*

   - *In what ways, if at all, did this belief influence another person or group who defined ethical behavior differently?*

   - *How do bias, power, and privilege affect the way society values different ethical frameworks? How do social systems of power and privilege shape how we define ethical leadership? How can we challenge these preconceptions?*

5. Have participants rejoin their small groups. Give each person a copy of the "Ethics and Leadership: Activity 2 Case Study" handout. Ask each group to discuss and brainstorm a strategy for the case study.

6. Ask each group to share their process and resulting ideas with the larger group. Facilitate discussion in the larger group to analyze the strengths and concerns of each idea, asking participants the following questions:

   - *What strengths and concerns do you recognize in each of the responses?*

   - *Did any ideas from others challenge the initial way you reacted to the case study? How?*

   - *Can you recognize any biases, power, or privilege that affected the way you originally formulated your idea?*

   - *How might the situation look different for someone with a different perspective, experience, or identity?*

   - *As an ethical leader, are there pieces of this situation that you would take higher priority in addressing first? Which are they and why?*

7. Have participants engage in individual written reflection (one to two pages in length) to compare and contrast their previous definition of ethical leadership and their current understanding of the relationship between ethics and leadership. Ask the following questions: *Before these activities, how did you define ethical leadership? Are there any differences in your current definition? If so, what do you think changed your feelings about ethical leadership?*

> Conclusion

This curriculum was designed to broaden participants' understandings of ethical leadership by moving their framework from intention-focused to impact-focused. Through reflection, discussion, and application, participants are challenged to address how privilege, power, and bias affect the relationship between leadership and ethics. By stimulating participants to consider a leader's ethical responsibility to enhance the lives of others, the definition of leadership is expanded to include an awareness of influence and the impact of socially imbedded norms that lead to a personal development of ethics. Participants should be able to connect their broadened understanding of ethical leadership to other concepts in the main text that encourage the prioritization of increased equity and justice for others through leadership.

Handout 10.1: Sojourner Truth's "Ain't I a Woman?" Speech (1851)

Well, children, where there is so much racket there must be something out of kilter. I think that 'twixt the negroes of the South and the women of the North, all talking about rights, the White men will be in a fix pretty soon. But what's all this here talking about? That man over there says that women need to be helped into carriages and lifted over ditches, and to have the best place everywhere. Nobody ever helps me into carriages, or over mud-puddles, or gives me any best place! And ain't I a woman? Look at me! Look at my arm! I could have ploughed and planted, and gathered into barns, and no man could head me! And ain't I a woman? I could work as much and eat as much as a man—when I could get it—and bear the lash as well! And ain't I a woman? I have borne thirteen children, and seen them most all sold off to slavery, and when I cried out with my mother's grief, none but Jesus heard me! And ain't I a woman? Then they talk about this thing in the head; what's this they call it? ["Intellect," somebody whispers] That's it, honey. What's that got to do with women's rights or negro's rights? If my cup won't hold but a pint, and yours holds a quart, wouldn't you be mean not to let me have my little half measure-full? Then that little man in black there, he says women can't have as much rights as men, 'cause Christ wasn't a woman! Where did your Christ come from? Where did your Christ come from? From God and a woman! Man had nothing to do with Him. If the first woman God ever made was strong enough to turn the world upside down all alone, these women together ought to be able to turn it back, and get it right side up again! And now they is asking to do it, the men better let them. Obliged to you for hearing me, and now old Sojourner ain't got nothing more to say.

Truth, S. (1851, May). "Ain't I a Woman?" Speech, presented at the Women's Convention, Akron, OH.

Handout 10.2: Ethics and Leadership: Activity 2 Case Study

The economy has recently shifted, leaving many citizens out of work. This has resulted in more people who are homeless than local shelters can take in. It has also led to more people living in hunger than food pantries and soup kitchens can support. Your friend owns a local, high-end grocery store that has been struggling in the recent economic downfall. To prepare for the potential situation of having to close her store, she has begun to make inquiries to see if she can move in with a wealthy sibling if she cannot turn her business around. Two main reasons her company and other local businesses are losing money is due to the decrease of sales and the increase in shoplifting. Your friend and other community leaders have introduced a new city ordinance that would carry much harsher penalties for those caught shoplifting, including jail time if the fine cannot be paid. While walking into the store to visit your friend, you notice a family of one adult and three children who appear to be shoplifting. Although you are not an elected representative, you are highly respected in the community. *How would you approach this immediate circumstance and the wider situation at hand through the lens of one leadership theory of your choosing and a socially just model of ethics?*

10C: Justice and Leadership

Valeria Cortés

Objectives/Goals of Chapter

- Be able to deconstruct ideas of leadership and draw connections to understanding social justice, ethics, and social change.
- Engage with transformational theatre techniques to identify inherent power imbalances and inequities in different situations.
- Recognize how to challenge and change oppressive behaviors and structures.

Critical Concepts: *consientization, critical pedagogy, ideology, leadership, social justice*

> Chapter Overview

Attaining social justice, where a society's distribution of power and resources is equitable and all members are physically and psychologically safe and secure, is not an easy task (Bell, 2013). The forces that, consciously or unconsciously, reinforce inequality and maintain the status quo are systemic and embedded in society (Dugan, 2017). Therefore, a process of leadership in which social change is at the core requires active and intentional analysis and exploration of how these forces shape individuals, institutions, and culture to reach a level of critical consciousness that enables action. Most importantly, in postsecondary settings where leadership development is an increasing priority, it requires examining our own privilege, power, and responsibilities; inquiring about the notion of the common good, which is pervasive in recent leadership theory (Komives & Dugan, 2010); and enacting change grounded in ethics and justice.

Transformation through education can occur by inviting all involved in the learning process to stretch beyond their comfort zones and to recognize political, social, and economic contradictions (Brown, 2004; Freire, 1982), and thus take action. Through transformational theatre techniques inspired by the work of Freire (1982), participants can engage in a journey of deconstruction, inquiry, and dialogue by engaging their whole body. As a result, the exploration and understanding of issues of justice, ethics, and the common good in critical leadership emerge from the experiences of participants and your calculated guidance as a facilitator.

The curriculum within this chapter starts with the deconstruction of participants' understanding of leadership bringing to awareness their social location, or place in history and society (Dugan, 2017; Kirk & Okazawa-Rey, 2013) as well as embedded beliefs about social categories (e.g., ability status, class, gender, race, religion, sex, sexual orientation). It continues with an examination of their experiences as the focal point to understand the complexities of power, privilege, and systemic oppression, not as abstract and remote problems, but as issues that are prevalent in participants' lives. It ends with the development of a social justice perspective that might increase leadership efficacy and can be used to analyze multiple dimensions of oppression at the individual, institutional, and societal/cultural level (Hardiman, Jackson, & Griffin, 2013) as well as practical tools to create inclusivity and enact change in their everyday lives. Through this journey of arts-based and critical pedagogy, the curriculum explores essential concepts related to the study of leadership, ethics, and justice—and to the transformation of participants into active agents of change in society. Accordingly, the social change model of leadership development (Higher Education Research Institute

[HERI], 1996)—and its interconnected domains of individual, group, and societal change values—serves as the backbone of the curriculum.

> Chapter Framework

Freire (1982) described *conscientization*, or consciousness-raising, as the way for learners to take active roles in the process of discovery and inquiry and to develop critical thinking with the hopes of becoming recreators, rather than spectators, of reality. This critical pedagogy situates educational activity in the lived experience of participants: the teacher cannot do the thinking for the learners; the learners themselves unveil their own realities and become "critical co-investigators in dialogue with the teacher" (Freire, 1982, p. 68). The alternative pedagogy described in this chapter is rooted in transformative processes and critical perspectives (Brown, 2004). The techniques are based on the work of Brazilian director and activist Boal (1979), who developed the *Theatre of the Oppressed* based on Freire's theories of popular education. This curriculum is based on two techniques: Image Theatre and Forum Theatre.

Image Theatre is a descriptive method of representation, which means that an image—one particularly embodied by one or more people—can offer different meanings to the observers. Participants are encouraged to use their bodies, rather than language, to portray and communicate realities and make thought visible (Butterwick & Selman, 2003; Cahnmann-Taylor & Souto-Manning, 2010). Generally, a number of people looking at the same image offer their reactions to it; this multiple reflection usually reveals to the image-maker its hidden aspects (Boal, 2002). *Forum Theatre* transforms audience members into the protagonists of the theatrical action, which depicts an unresolved situation, conflict, or injustice. At the core of Forum Theatre lies the notion of bringing the passive spectators to the active role of "spect-actors" and inviting them to enact solutions to the problem presented. Participants' leadership efficacy, or their internal belief that they can successfully effect change or engage in a leadership process, determines whether or not they will use their skills or enact leadership capacity (Dugan & Komives, 2010). Therefore, creating a brave space where participants can rehearse how to address problems, challenge oppressive behaviors, or envision how to engage in a leadership process, might positively impact both leadership efficacy and capacity.

Theatre techniques are powerful and transformative because the use of the body allows participants to make invisible thoughts visible and to express what they otherwise would not if they were relying solely on verbal or written expression. The pedagogical framework of this curriculum focuses on the complexities and struggles of all the different characters, protagonists and antagonists alike. The purpose is to move away from oppressor/oppressed dichotomies, otherness, or simplistic solutions to explore the true complexity of social systems. This perspective is influenced by understanding community as an integrated living organism (Diamond, 2007) and by placing the focus on relationships. Leadership is a relationship—a collaborative process where people intend to effect changes for the common good (Komives, Wagner, & Associates, 2009). The ultimate goal of this curriculum is to empower participants to take action, to engage in leadership for social change, to explore the root causes of their ethical and social justice problems, and to collaborate with others, as a group, to resolve them.

❯ Curriculum Plan

The curriculum aims to promote learning and change through the implementation of a systems-oriented framework, transformational theatre techniques, and critical pedagogy.

Furthermore, the curriculum attends to both process and outcome: it is an invitation to explore other ways of learning due to its arts-based orientation and community-based nature, and it is, itself, a leadership practice to enact positive social change. Everything explored during the activities comes from the participants, as they are seen as experts of their lives. Therefore, your role, as the facilitator, is to set the space for inclusive exploration of issues that are intricately related to leadership, ethics, and justice. This curriculum explores power dynamics and values embedded in participants' conceptualizations of leadership and analyzes oppression from a multileveled perspective. It also sets the basis for exploring social mobilization through change rehearsals.

If you are an proficient facilitator with some experience or awareness of transformational theatre techniques, you might find the curriculum easier to implement than if you identify as less proficient. Cofacilitation models, curriculum variations, or support from applied theatre practitioners can ease the facilitation process and bolster impact. Nevertheless, you must take care to establish an open-ended context that brings participants into deeper engagement and transforms the notions of shame, blame, and guilt into those of responsibility, change, and awareness—and this curriculum is intended to support you in the process. The curriculum is designed for one activity per session (a total of three sessions) to allow participants time to process complex ideas.

> Activity 1—Deconstructing Leadership

In this section participants deconstruct the general concept of leadership through critical perspectives. Participants will use their bodies to create images of leadership. The image exploration and debrief are key in exposing power dynamics and possible structural oppression present in their images.

Learning Outcomes

- Cultivate greater efficacy and capacity for deconstructing leadership using critical perspectives.
- Identify power dynamics embedded in day-to-day life.

Setting Up the Activity

Group Size: Optimal group size for this activity ranges from 12 to 25.

Time: 3 hours, decrease/increase the time depending on the group size.

Methods: Image Theatre, participatory-based dialogue

Materials: Flipchart and markers

Directions

Note that it is highly recommended that participants engage in active collaborative games or physical warm-ups before they start working with Image Theatre. If necessary, search the Internet or consult an applied theatre professional for more information and examples.

1. Cultivate a judgment-free and inclusive climate by setting group agreements or having a conversation with the group to create a high-trust, low-fear space. For more information on creating *brave spaces*, see the Introduction of this guide.
2. Begin by inviting participants to learn in a different way, engaging their whole body and emotions. Be firm about this invitation. Explain that it will be challenging to engage in a different way of learning and invite them to be aware of that discomfort.
3. Invite participants to work in small groups of four or five for the next 7 to 10 minutes to create a frozen image that represents leadership. Everyone should be part of the image.
4. Once the images are created, invite participants to come back to the large group. Share with participants that images carry a

great deal of meaning. Place yourself in the center of the circle with a frozen image (e.g., as if you were about to hit a baseball with a bat). Do not move and continue with the explanation: *For example, take a look at this image. What do you see? Shout it out!* Participants will say different things, like "hitting a baseball," "carrying a flag," "an umbrella," and so on. Unfreeze and say: *All of those things that you said are right. When we deconstruct an image, we invite and consider all potential meanings. So there is no right or wrong in this work. In a moment, we will deconstruct the images that you created using a critical perspective.*

5. Explain that the group will explore one image at a time. Then introduce the following tools that will be used for deconstruction and dialogue:

- *Reactions*: In this phase of exploration ask participants what they see (descriptive) and what is the meaning of what they see (symbolic). Ask about emotional reactions and invite participants to think if the image or the characters represent them in any way.

- *Systems view*: This is an inquiry about the institutional, macro, and global levels. Encourage participants to identify actors that are not represented in the image, especially if the image represents a naïve or idealistic view of reality, such as one representing a circular, nonhierarchical structure.

  - *If this image were a representation of the world, who are the characters?*

  - *How does this image relate to issues of social justice? Who is not represented?*

  - *Is this typical or the reality of how the world operates? What needs to change for our systems to look more like that?*

- *Drill down*: Whenever there is something of interest in one of the characters or a relationship between characters, drill down by asking questions such as these: *Who is the character? Who is the character in relation to the others? What does*

*the character want? What does the character need? What are
the character's values? What is the character's social location?
Are there dynamics based on social identity (e.g., gender) in
the image?*

6. Deconstruct each of the images and make an effort to point
   out representations of power dynamics, particularly those
   related to social identity, that are present in the images. For
   instance, a White, male, cisgender participant may be the one
   representing the leader in a hierarchical image. Or a White,
   male, cisgender participant may be represented at a higher
   level (e.g., standing while the rest of the participants are
   sitting or kneeling). Take notes on flip chart paper about all
   these nuances.

7. Debrief the activity. Start by asking participants for their
   reactions to using their bodies to create meaning. Then
   acknowledge that leadership is a socially constructed term
   and that there are different paradigms of leadership. Point
   out the values that emerged in each image. Ask participants
   what the images say about social dynamics, privilege, and
   power, and ask them what they think the intersection between
   leadership and social justice is. Expand the conversation to
   structural power and how we are socialized to accept systems of
   oppression as normal. The following questions can help guide
   the conversation:

   - *Do you think behavior affects systems/structures or the other
     way around?*
   - *What is the challenge that revolutionaries face when overthrow-
     ing an oppressive regime?*
   - *What are some examples of social systems of oppression? Why
     do we accept oppression as normal?* Then, describe the role
     history and specific political, social, and economic contexts
     have on what we understand as *norms* or values. Chapter 2
     of the main text offers useful content and reflection ques-
     tions to support this. This reflection will set the foundation
     for the following session.

8. Wrap up by inviting participants to share in a circle what the highlight of the activity was.

Debriefing Notes

This section of the curriculum is designed to increase awareness of hidden perceptions. Images make thought visible uncovering hidden meanings and assumptions. Participants experience contradiction: *I can't believe I did not notice the gender dynamics when creating the image.* These contradictions will be important moments and the tone of the debrief will be key to engage participants in developing agency and to empower them to intentionally assess situations by identifying who benefits and who does not. Focus on developing responsibility and awareness, rather than guilt and shame.

Facilitator Notes

This activity will be challenging for everyone involved. Most likely participants will start with a superficial exploration of the image; they might be defensive or dismissive of the image, or have difficulty making connections. Invite participants to think about their experiences, acknowledge their good intentions, and model behavior by offering your analysis. If the image exploration takes too long, invite breaks so the characters in the image can relax their pose.

Image Theatre processes invite participants to share their views and to shout them out. However, not all participants feel comfortable speaking out loud. It is essential that the facilitator is always aware of the way the space for voicing ideas is being managed. Note that this activity can be adapted in several ways to explore different concepts through Image Theatre. For instance, you can ask half of the participants to create an image of privilege, and the other half to create an image of oppression. These images can then be contrasted to illustrate two facets of the same issue. Finally, and of great importance, this curriculum relies heavily on the use of bodily senses and movement. Although theatre of the oppressed pedagogy is a powerful medium for learning and enacting justice, it can simultaneously marginalize individuals with differing abilities. As a facilitator, it is important that you consider your audience and adapt these activities to accommodate the needs of your participants, specifically considering different mobility levels.

❯ Activity 2—Stories of Power and Privilege

In this activity participants engage in storytelling as a vehicle to share their experiences.

Learning Outcomes

- Recognize and validate stories of oppression.
- Identify personal power and privilege.
- Model a nonhierarchical, collaborative group process.

Setting Up the Activity

Group Size: Optimal group sizes range from 12 to 25.
Time: 90 minutes–2 hours
Methods: Storytelling
Materials: Flip chart paper and markers

Directions

1. Start by revisiting the group agreements from the previous activity and adjusting them as necessary. Describe the process that participants are about to engage in: from storytelling to staging. Tell participants that what they do in the storytelling activity will set the groundwork for the change rehearsals.

2. Begin by inviting participants to think about their social location and about a moment when they felt silenced or treated unfairly—a moment when they felt powerless and did not act. Encourage participants to think about issues that arose based on social identity and to consider how these issues relate to leadership and the common good. Remind participants to take care of themselves during the storytelling activity and to think about their emotional well-being before they decide to share.

3. Pair participants and write the storytelling guidelines on the board or flip chart paper. Share with participants that stories need to show an unresolved problem, a moment of injustice. Stories must be real and include the storyteller and at least one additional person.

   - For storytellers:
     - *Start by stating: "My story is about …"*
     - *Keep stories short (3 to 4 minutes maximum).*
     - *End with: "and this is my story."*
   - For listeners:
     - *Engage in deep listening.*
     - *Do not interrupt the speaker or make comments afterward.*
     - *When the story is over you will only say: "Thank you."*

4. Invite participants to work in small groups of four and share their stories. Stress the importance of maintaining confidentiality. It is okay if participants decide not to share their stories with the group.

5. After participants share their stories, ask them to choose one story that resonates the most; that is the story they will stage. You may say something like this: *Select the story that most resonates with you; don't choose your friend's story, or the most entertaining one. Think also about the story that offers opportunities for exploration about change interventions.* Once the story is chosen, the group must ask permission from the storyteller to work with the story and to own it. From that moment on, the story will be the group's story and it can be slightly

modified if the group wants. Asking permission to work with someone's story is essential and must be taken seriously. This is often an opportunity to acknowledge that social justice issues affect us all and that there is no such thing as "That is not my issue."

6. Give small groups 15 minutes to stage the story. Ask the group to give a title to the story. Make sure you have a chance to see the staging and support the groups. Remember that scenes need to show unsolved issues. Be aware of stereotypes, language, power dynamics, and hidden assumptions, as they will be sources of exploration and deep learning during the change rehearsals. This activity is an opportunity for participants to practice a group process where all ideas and perspectives are considered. Invite them to intentionally engage in an inclusive and collaborative process of cocreation.

7. Elicit the titles of each play and the issue to be addressed and write them on the flip chart paper. Keep this information and use it during the change rehearsals to expand on the complexities of issues. Explain that during the following session participants will *rehearse the change* by trying different strategies to address the issue presented. Invite them to come prepared with their plays for the next session.

8. Check in as a large group to assess how everyone is doing. Invite them to share their experiences or to write down their thoughts, feelings, and learning. Intentionally reflect on the group process. Thank participants for sharing their stories, acknowledge the difficult moments, and remind them that the work together is meant to address stories of struggle.

Debriefing Notes

This section of the curriculum can be emotional and challenging for participants. Prepare a list of resources and support contacts for the participants and follow up with anyone who might need to talk. Conversely, there is a possibility of scenes staying superficial. Assess whether the scene lacks depth as a result of group dynamics or lack of trust. Invite groups to think about the root causes of the scene and be prepared to drill down during the rehearsals. Use the following questions to help groups have a scene ready for Forum Theatre during the change rehearsals: *Does the scene show an unresolved conflict? Does the scene have at least two characters? Does the scene have opportunities for change interventions?*

Facilitator Notes

It is important to note that this activity can be challenging for participants from privileged backgrounds who might have difficulties thinking about stories of powerlessness. If this situation occurs, acknowledge the participant and facilitate an exploration of power imbalance, even if it does not fall on the social justice domain. For example, you might ask the following:

- *Think about a time when you were affected by discrimination.*
- *What about a time when you felt like an outsider? In sports? Perhaps with a particular subject matter? In a peer group?*
- *Have you witnessed an injustice and done nothing about it?*

Unpacking the role and power of the bystander is key for this work. Invite participants to reflect on their privilege and the power they hold to effect change.

If there is no safety or trust in the group, or if the group is homogeneous, the activity can be adapted after the paired storytelling. Rather than choosing one story, the group creates a fictional story of an unresolved social justice issue that they care deeply about. Or perhaps the issue can be something that is happening in a local context at that moment.

> Activity 3—Change Rehearsals

This section of the curriculum is a continuation of the previous activity. Through theatrical scenes, participants *rehearse the change*—they deconstruct situations of injustice and rehearse different approaches to challenge and to change behaviors, attitudes, institutions, and cultural beliefs. As a result, participants can start a leadership development plan based on social justice action.

Learning Outcomes

- Identify ways in which oppression operates on multiple dimensions: individual, institutional, and societal levels.
- Develop strategies and action plans to engage in leadership for social justice.

Setting Up the Activity

Group Size: Optimal group sizes for this activity range from 12 to 25.

Time: 3 hours

Methods: Dialogue, Forum Theatre

Materials: Flip chart paper and markers

Directions

1. Review group agreements to create a brave space. Facilitate a game or group activity that builds trust and increases energy. Then provide a brief introduction to the work of Boal (1979) in *Theatre of the Oppressed*:
   - *Forum Theatre brings the passive spectator into the active spect-actor who will provide solutions to the problem presented. Forum Theatre will let us practice leadership by rehearsing change. We will use the social change model of leadership development as a framework for our exploration and we will gain insights that will help us be more effective agents of change.*
2. Explain the process: *Each scene will be shown once so that everyone knows who the characters are and can identify the problem. Once the problem is understood, audience members will become spect-actors and they will have an opportunity to intervene and*
   - *Replace a character.*
   - *Add a character.*

- *Create another scene.*
- *Pose questions to the characters.*
- *Create a leadership process with stakeholders where the issue can be addressed and action can spiral.*

  The goal of the intervention is to address the problem and to provide different perspectives on the situation.

3. Once the scene is presented, ask participants to raise their hands if they identify a problem. Invite them to come to the stage and address the issue or rehearse the change—they deconstruct situations of injustice and rehearse different approaches to challenge and to change behaviors, attitudes, institutions, and cultural beliefs. Emphasize the importance of trying: there is no right or wrong in this process. Another way to encourage participation is to ask participants to pair up and discuss possible solutions before acting them out. After a change intervention, thank the participant. Avoid using language that judges the intervention as good or bad. Focus on the impact of the action. Use the following guiding questions to invite deeper analysis of the rehearsal of change and to make connections to the larger themes of ethics, justice, and the common good.

   - Individual Level: *How would the scene look if characters had a social justice perspective? What are the oppressive behaviors and attitudes present in the scene? Where do these behaviors come from? Might specific stocks of knowledge be informing them?*
   - Institutional Level: *What are the social institutions or systems represented (embedded) in this scene—for example, family, government, education, industry, religious organizations? How might the issue reflect ideology and/or hegemony? What actions can be taken to influence/challenge/change the system/institutions? What policies/procedures/rules need to be in place to address the issue?*
   - Societal Level: *What are the cultural assumptions present in the scene? What needs to happen for characters in the*

scene to question their beliefs? What actions can be taken to influence/challenge/change cultural norms? How is this scene related to the common good? Who determines the common good?

- Leadership Perspective: *Can a process of leadership be effective to address the issue? How can you effect change in your local context (e.g., organization, company, community)? What resources can you access?*

Not all answers to these questions will be put on stage; however, some of these systemic-level interventions will be worth rehearsing. For example, if the intervention is to organize an educational campaign at a university, invite an intervention in which the characters ask for support from the university administration.

4. Write on the flip chart paper the strategies that are successful and elicit others that they can also implement. These strategies will be useful for participants when they are creating their leadership development plan. Use graphic recording if you have the skill; move away from bullet points and look for patterns and interconnections.

5. When all scenes are shown, summarize everyone's ideas on the flipchart paper and praise participants for their work. Invite participants to think about how their combined efforts relate to leadership for social change. Refer to the main text and to other sources and resources to encourage participants to continue their exploration.

6. To end, invite participants to write about what they experienced and start their leadership development plan by deciding on one tangible action that they will implement in the next two months to develop their leadership competency. Explain how to write a goal that they can define, measure, and accomplish within a reasonable time frame.

Debriefing Notes

Facilitating Forum Theatre requires preparation and understanding of the tool. According to Boal (2002), facilitators must be *maieutic* (i.e., engage in a Socratic approach to engaging with participants) and, like a midwife, facilitate the birth of ideas. Asking the right questions and inviting reflection is essential after each intervention. Most likely, participants will focus on the individual level: trying to change attitudes or behaviors of individual characters. Therefore, using the guiding questions in this activity will be useful in helping participants explore the systematic complexity of social problems.

Facilitator Notes

This section of the curriculum is action-based. It is not meant to be a lecture, so it is important that participants rehearse as many interventions as possible and that they feel empowered to speak up and effect change. Invite everyone to participate, especially those who recognize that speaking up or challenging other people's behaviors is difficult for them. Emphasize that the session is a rehearsal and a space in which participants can experiment with and test new approaches and solutions. Some participants will be inclined to replace a character behaving unjustly with one who is inclusive. If this happens, acknowledge the good intentions and question how realistic it would be for that to happen. Challenge them to instead consider this: *What is needed for that character to behave differently?* Stay away from dichotomies and from using labels like *oppressor* and *oppressed*. Move away from "us" and "them" dynamics, and unpack stereotypes and discrimination. Try to take a systems perspective as much as possible, connecting individual behaviors to institutional assumptions and societal values.

› Conclusion

The concepts of leadership, justice, ethics, and the common good can all be explored by the activities presented in this curriculum. Through Image Theatre, participants can understand the impact of a value-based process of leadership. Storytelling, a means of eliciting participants' experiences, is in itself a transformative tool (Bell, 2010). Capra (1989) stated that "what is important in a story, what is true in it, is not the plot, the things, or the people in the story, but the relationships between them" (p. 78). The storytelling activity will enable participants to learn from each other, to acknowledge different narratives, and to listen to understand, not respond. Finally, Forum Theatre can serve both as process and outcome. It can be a consciousness-raising process, a skill development tool, and a form of activism. The activities described are meant to critically explore issues of social justice and to set the ground for collaborative leadership, social mobilization, and community organizing.

Transformational theatre work is deep and layered; it is embodied and emotional. A fair amount of information lies underneath the images and scenes. Your role is to bring the hidden ideas, emotions, relationships, and values to the surface and to provide the participants with space to engage critically in the analysis. The curriculum presented in this chapter is an alternative pedagogy; it is a call to engage in learning differently; and it is aimed at preparing participants to engage in a process of leadership for social justice and equity.

Chapter 11: Integration and the Path Forward

11A: Charting One's Own Theory of Leadership

M. Sonja Ardoin

Objectives/Goals of Chapter

- Exercise social perspective-taking to compare and contrast societal/systematic viewpoints on leadership with participants' personal views of leadership.
- Understand the concept of self-authorship and facilitate participants' engagement in authoring their personal narrative and theory of leadership.
- Critically reflect upon leadership perspectives and theory.

Critical Concepts: *critical self-reflection, power, social location, social perspective-taking*

Chapter Overview

Similar to social identity (e.g., gender, race, sex), leadership is a socially constructed phenomenon (Dugan, 2017; Komives, Lucas, & McMahon, 2013). As such, social location plays an important role in shaping assumed beliefs, expectations, traits, and skills related to leadership that constrain who is welcomed into the leadership process (Dugan, 2017). Many leadership theories were created from a limited perspective and, knowingly or unknowingly, perpetuate societal systems of power and oppression based on social identities. To affirm the proposition that leadership is attainable by all people, these theoretical shortcomings need to be addressed and individuals must be empowered to create a personal narrative and theory to guide their practice.

The first step to re-creating leadership theory is to examine the congruencies and incongruencies between the societal/systematic perspectives of leadership and one's personal perspectives. The practices of social perspective-taking and critical self-reflection allow for the analysis of traditional and developing theories and invite people to both challenge the "experts" who created existing theories and embrace the call to create a personal narrative while re-creating existing theories of leadership.

> Chapter Framework

This curriculum advances critical perspectives on leadership theory through arts-based education research (ABER). ABER is a method of exploration that encourages individuals to discover new perspectives and provokes unique queries (Barone & Eisner, 2006). ABER allows for a coalescence of the "often underutilized and yet powerful interface between the mind, emotions, and imagination" (Welkener & Baxter Magolda, 2014, p. 580). It also accommodates various learning styles and inspires use of multiple senses.

ABER invites the process of *dissonance*, which is the disturbing of both unconscious and recognized belief systems that can create the ambiguity and inquisitiveness necessary for social perspective-taking and critical self-reflection (Griffin & Ouellett, 2013). Both privileged and marginalized identities can experience dissonance, engendering emotional responses and fostering more depth in discussion. Dissonance typically results in a more socially just perspective and tends to increase people's capacities for congruence and resilience over time because it challenges people to consider multiple perspectives, values, and behavioral actions and, thus, reassess their own (Griffin & Ouellett, 2013).

Once dissonance has encouraged a broadened perspective, the concept of self-authorship (Baxter Magolda, 2008; Pizzolato, Nguyen, Johnston, & Wang, 2012) will be exercised to allow for a reconstruction of the phenomenon of leadership based on emotional intelligence (Goleman, 1996; Shankman, Allen, & Haber-Curran, 2015), particularly one's consciousness of self (Komives, Wagner, & Associates, 2009; Shankman et al., 2015) and how that self is situated within the process of leadership. Ultimately, the curriculum is designed to facilitate the process of mattering that supports people "feeling … significant to others and to the process" of leadership (Komives et al., 2013, p. 123). If individuals believe and feel like their identities matter, then they are more likely to feel empowered to seek out and practice leadership in multiple contexts. ABER gives people the opportunity to explore mattering from personal and societal leadership lenses and to develop representations of leadership that broaden the scope of who matters.

> Curriculum Plan

ABER is used to introduce participants to the three dimensions/questions of self-authorship as a tool for reconstructing leadership narratives and theories. Doing so reveals the potential congruencies and incongruencies between varying perspectives and invites participants to embrace the challenge of rewriting a leadership theory that represents themselves *and* is inclusive of others.

The following curriculum design should be implemented over two to three sessions. The first session should cover Activity 1 and provide a 2-hour time frame. The second session could be completed as either a single, 2-hour session or as two 60-minute sessions in which Activities 2 and 3 are used. Although segmented sessions allow ample time for processing and personal examination, the sessions can also be facilitated consecutively as an extended workshop or training.

› Activity 1—Creating a Societal Leadership Portrait and a Personal Leadership Portrait

This activity uses the ABER practice of portraiture to compare and contrast the societal or systematic perspective of leadership to the participants' personal perspective of leadership. ABER allows participants to engage in the "often underutilized and yet powerful interface between the mind, emotions, and imagination" (Welkener & Baxter Magolda, 2014, p. 580) to answer the key questions of self-authorship (Baxter Magolda, 2008; Pizzolato et al., 2012) and to explore emotional intelligence (Goleman, 1996; Shankman et al., 2015) and consciousness of self (Komives et al., 2009; Shankman et al., 2015).

Learning Outcomes

- Discover how critical concepts of patriarchy, power, privilege, oppression, and marginalization manifest throughout society and effect leadership enactment.
- Enhance personal knowledge and actualization of self-authorship.
- Develop skills to explore and nurture consciousness of self.

Setting Up the Activity

Group Size: Optimal group size is 5–20 given the intimate nature of the conversation.

Time: 120 minutes

Methods: Activity, dialogue, lecture, reflection

Materials: Blank paper (two sheets per person), whiteboard/chalkboard, computer, projector/screen, magazines and newspapers (choose ones that represent national and global news and/or public figures and can be cut up), scissors (one each or enough to share), tape or glue, writing utensils

Variations: Rather than using hard-copy magazines and newspapers, participants could utilize computers to locate and arrange images and then print their portraits.

Directions

1. Begin the activity by explaining how both the emotionally intelligent leadership model (Goleman, 1996; Shankman et al., 2008) discussed in Chapter 4 of the main text and the social change model of leadership development (Higher Education Research Institute [HERI], 1996) discussed in Chapter 7 of the main text incorporate consciousness of self as a central tenet. In addition, both models call attention to the consciousness and needs of others in the community or society. Show participants the graphics of each model that appear in the main text.

2. Explain that one way we learn about societal and systematic viewpoints is by paying attention to what is printed in magazines and newspapers. These publications represent varying perspectives on who is valuable in society and who can serve in certain roles—in other words, who matters.

3. Introduce the activity of portraiture. Explain that ABER allows participants to engage in the "often underutilized and yet powerful interface between the mind, emotions, and imagination" (Welkener & Baxter Magolda, 2014, p. 580).

4. Create groups of two to five participants. Explain that each group will construct a portrait of how society views leadership using magazine and newspaper clippings. They are to temporarily set aside personal viewpoints and focus on the systemic, societal viewpoint.

5. Distribute materials. Share that the activity is not about artistic expertise but self-exploration and expression. Give groups 20–30 minutes to construct their societal portrait.

6. Ask small groups to revisit their societal portrait and explore if, or how, the portrait illuminates ideology, hegemony, patriarchy, power, privilege, oppression, or marginalization. Note that participants may need to be provided with definitions and examples of social justice terminology. Do not assume these are common knowledge and refer them to content from Chapter 2 of the main text. Encourage dialogue around the following questions:
   - *What identity groups are represented in your portrait? What identity groups are not represented?*
   - *How, if at all, does your portrait represent the people, or identity groups, society has taught you to view as capable of leadership? What stocks of knowledge does this reflect?*
   - *How do you relate to this portrait, if at all? How does this portrait make you feel?*

7. Invite a few small groups to share any insights from their dialogue with the large group.

8. Ask participants to return to their individual seating arrangements. Transition the conversation from a societal perspective to a personal perspective by offering that leadership is a socially constructed phenomenon (Dugan,

2017; Komives et al., 2013) and, thus, can be reconstructed. Introduce the concept of self-authorship (Baxter Magolda, 2008) and its three dimensions/questions:

- Cognitive: *How do I know that I matter? How do I know that I am a leader?*

- Intrapersonal: *Who am I as a leader? How do my identities and values shape what leadership means to me?*

- Interpersonal: *Who are we (identity groups) as demographic groups? What relationships do I want to foster with others similar to and different from myself through leadership?*

9. Instruct participants to explore the three dimensions/ questions of self-authorship through an individual portrait exercise. Invite participants to create a personal portrait of leadership using the same materials as the group activity or to draw their images. Remind them the activity is not about artistic expertise but about self-exploration and expression. Give individuals 20–30 minutes to construct their personal portrait.

10. Ask each participant to write a short reflection on if/how their individual portrait answers the following questions:

- *Which, if any, of your emotions about leadership are showcased in your portrait?*

- *How are your values and principles represented?*

- *Which, if any, of your strengths, talents, skills, and/or knowledge are represented in your portrait?*

- *How does the portrait incorporate your aspirations or dreams?*

- *How does your portrait include balance, authenticity, openness, achievement, optimism, and/or intuition?*

11. Facilitate a large group dialogue on the creation of the personal portraits and the reflection of participants' consciousness of self. Consider the following prompts:

- *How are you feeling after creating your personal portrait of leadership?*

- *What aspects, if any, of consciousness of self were addressed in your portrait?*
- *To what extent do you believe that your personal portrait is represented in society?*

Debriefing Notes

The conclusion of this activity is designed to serve as a catalyst for potential dissonance between the societal portrait of leadership and participants' personal portraits of leadership. As a reminder, debriefing activities involving sensitive topics, such as identity and social justice, should always be tailored to the developmental readiness of the group. Use your professional judgment in the solicitation of sharing insights on critical perspectives and revealing consciousness of self during the dialogue portions.

Facilitator Notes

It is important to note that the societal portraiture activity may be challenging for participants who do not see examples of their identities in media representation. Likewise, it may be challenging for participants with dominant identities when the group discusses patriarchy, power, privilege, oppression, or marginalization in the media/societal perspective. Additionally, the self-portraiture activity may be challenging for participants who have not explored their identities, values, and beliefs in depth. As the facilitator, attempt to support participants in their developmental capacity while also challenging them to practice both social perspective-taking and critical self-reflection. Finally, you will want to ensure that if you use magazines for this exercise, you draw on a wide range that offer extensive representation of social identity groups. Avoid replicating the marginalization evident in societal portraits in the actual activity itself by failing to offer a diverse representation of content and images.

> ## Activity 2—Composing Your Leadership Narrative

This activity builds on the first inviting participants to revisit their portraits to explore the congruencies and incongruencies between their group's societal portrait and their self portrait. The following activity will encourage critical self-reflection through a free writing activity in which participants create a personal narrative/story of leadership.

Learning Outcomes

- Identify congruencies and incongruencies in societal and personal portraits of leadership.
- Deepen understanding of personal leadership values through leadership narratives.
- Recognize challenges that arise between societal and personal understandings of leadership.

Setting Up the Activity

Group Size: Optimal group size is 5–20 given the intimate nature of the conversation.

Time: 60 minutes

Methods: Activity, dialogue, lecture, reflection

Materials: Blank paper, whiteboard/chalkboard, computer, projector/screen, writing utensils

Variations: Rather than using paper and writing utensils, participants could utilize computers to draft narratives/stories.

Directions

1. Begin by informing participants that this activity will build upon the content and themes that emerged during the first

session and will further explore the possible variations between the societal perspective of leadership and participants' personal perspectives.

2. Invite participants to share any insights or reflections that may have emerged after having time to process the first session.

3. Have participants review their societal portrait and personal portrait of leadership from Activity 1. Invite participants to explore congruencies and incongruencies between the two portraits. The following prompts may be helpful:
   - *What identity groups are represented in each portrait?*
   - *Do you feel represented in each portrait? Why or why not?*
   - *How, if any, are the concepts of consciousness of self and consciousness of others illuminated in each portrait?*

4. Ask participants to craft a personal narrative of leadership through a free writing or storytelling exercise. This activity allows participants to practice another ABER method—"narrative construction and storytelling" (Welkener & Baxter Magolda, 2014). There is no specific structure to the narrative/story; participants should free-write or brainstorm about what leadership means from their perspective or about their personal story of leadership. There is no right or wrong "answer." Allow 20 to 30 minutes for this.

5. Invite participants to partner with someone with whom they feel comfortable sharing their narrative/story. Participants should take turns speaking and actively listening. The listener should take notes and be prepared to share critical feedback with the speaker about how their narrative/story could be challenged by others/society. For example, the participant may believe that women should be able to be bold and aggressive, although society may believe that women should be demure and deferential. The idea is not to accept these challenges, but to name and disrupt them. Allow 10 to 20 minutes.

Debriefing Notes

The conclusion of this activity is designed to serve as a medium of additional, potential dissonance between the societal and participants' perspectives of leadership. It is also an opportunity for participants to begin to define their narrative/story around leadership. As a reminder, debriefing activities involving sensitive topics—such as congruence, incongruence, and personal stories—should always be tailored to the developmental readiness of the group. Use your professional judgment in the solicitation of sharing insights and narratives/stories.

Facilitator Notes

The free-writing exercise may come more naturally to some participants than others with some finishing the exercise more quickly. It may be helpful to have additional prompts on hand to encourage participants to think more critically about their narrative/story. Additionally, it will be important to allow participants to choose their partners to achieve the optimum level of comfort in sharing their narrative/story and providing feedback to their partner. The facilitator can add an additional, deeper layer to the debriefing conversation by asking participants to assess why they chose their sharing partner (e.g., proximity, perceived identity similarities, perceived identity differences, prior experiences with the individual) and how others may have discerned their choice. Then, allow the group to share their reflections and discernment with one another.

> Activity 3—Rewriting Your Leadership Theory

This activity expands upon participants' personal narratives by inviting them to revisit the theories included in the main text and rewrite a more inclusive theory. This invites participants to critically reflect upon and craft a theory that they can use to guide their practice of leadership while also welcoming others into the process. Sharing these personal theories of leadership will allow participants to contemplate how their theories align or diverge from others.

Learning Outcomes

- Enhance critique skills by deconstructing and reconstructing select leadership theories.
- Re-create each participant's version of leadership theory from a critical perspective.
- Gain greater awareness of theory alignment by examining personal representation, social justice, and inclusivity within leadership theory.

Setting Up the Activity

Group Size: Optimal group size is 5–20 given the intimate nature of the conversation.

Time: 60 minutes

Methods: Activity, dialogue, lecture, reflection

Materials: Whiteboard/chalkboard, computer, projector/screen, blank paper (one piece per person), writing utensils; laptops/computers (optional)

Directions

1. Begin by informing participants that this activity will further expand the free-write of their personal leadership narratives. Invite participants to share any insights or reflections that may have emerged after having time to process the second activity.

2. Ask participants to review their personal narratives/stories of leadership from Activity 2. Invite participants to reflect on the various theories presented in the main text and deconstruct

how the theories align and are divergent with their personal narrative/story.

3. Inform participants that they now have the opportunity to rewrite the theories into one theory that both encompass their personal narrative of leadership and is inclusive of others in the leadership process. Allow 30 minutes for this exercise.

4. Invite several participants to share their rewritten theories of leadership with the overall group. Ask the rest of the group to provide constructive and affirming feedback regarding the theory. Allow 20 minutes for this exercise.

5. Ask participants to individually reflect on this process of crafting a leadership theory and on the alignment or divergence between different participants' theories. The following prompts may be incorporated:

    *   *How do you feel about the process of rewriting a leadership theory? Does the process feel empowering and/or constraining?*
    *   *Within your theory, is power named? Who has power? What risks exist for marginalizing others? In short, who does it communicate explicitly and/or implicitly matters in society?*
    *   *How do you move forward in furthering your narrative and theory of leadership?*

6. Have participants share any final thoughts. Conclude the session by encouraging participants to continue thinking about how to embrace their identities in the leadership process while also allowing the voices and skills of others to be present.

Debriefing Notes

Participants may find it challenging to rewrite theories that were composed by experts in the field of leadership, particularly if they choose to re-create a theory that already applies a critical lens. Offer that there is always room for enhancement of theory and research, particularly with the evolution of time and societal viewpoints.

Facilitator Notes

Participants may feel a bit unfinished at the end of this session, especially if they shared their theory and received some critical feedback or if their personal theory contrasted with others' theories. Welcome participants to continue the conversation among themselves and invite them to present revised versions of the theories with you.

> Conclusion

This chapter was deliberate in its sequential curriculum of ABER activities. Utilizing ABER as the framework serves as a catalyst for dissonance and encourages participants to exercise social perspective-taking and critical self-reflection around the socially constructed phenomenon of leadership. Although the curriculum is presented as a capstone activity, it is at the facilitator's discretion to utilize it in that matter or to incorporate the first two activities in the beginning of a learning experience and the third activity at the end of that experience.

Examining the congruencies and incongruencies between the societal/systematic perspective of leadership and participants' personal perspectives allows participants to reconsider how the leadership process has been captured in narrative and theoretical forms. The introduction of self-authorship and consciousness of self empowers participants to see themselves in the leadership process and create their own narrative/story of leadership. Further expansion of this concept into the critical rewriting of theory invites participants to both challenge the expert opinion on leadership and experience the challenge of attempting to bring voice to oneself while also being inclusive of others' voices. The questions become these: *How can theory be reconstructed to allow all people to feel welcomed and represented in the process of leadership? How can leadership theory invite all of us to feel like we matter?*

REFERENCES

Adams, M., Bell, L. A., & Griffin, P. (Eds.). (2007). *Teaching for diversity and social justice*. New York, NY: Routledge.

Adichie, C. N. (2009, July). The danger of a single story [Video file]. Retrieved from www.ted.com/talks/chimamanda_adichie_the_danger_of_a_single_story?language=en.

Althusser, L. (1971). Ideology and the ideological state apparatuses. In *Lenin and philosophy and other essays* (pp. 127–186). New York, NY: Monthly Review Press.

Alvarez, J. L., & Svejenova, S. (2005). *Sharing executive power: Roles and relationships at the top*. Cambridge, UK: Cambridge University Press.

American Psychological Association. (2011). The guidelines for psychological practice with lesbian, gay, and bisexual clients. Retrieved from www.apa.org/pi/lgbt/resources/sexuality-definitions.pdf.

Arao, B., & Clemens, K. (2013). From safe spaces to brave spaces. In L. M. Landerman (Ed.), *The art of effective facilitation: Reflections from social justice educators* (pp. 135–150). Sterling, VA: Stylus.

Avolio, B. J., & Bass, B. M. (2004). *Multifactor leadership questionnaire (MLQ)*. Menlo Park, CA: Mind Garden.

Avolio, B. J., & Gardner, W. L. (2005). Authentic leadership development: Getting to the root of positive forms of leadership. *The Leadership Quarterly, 16*, 315–338.

Ayman, R., & Korabik, K. (2010). Why gender and culture matter. *American Psychologist, 65*, 157–170.

Bandura, A. (1997). *Self-efficacy: The exercise of control*. New York, NY: W. H. Freeman and Company.

Bar-On, R. (2006). The Bar-On model of emotional-social intelligence (ESI). *Psicothema, 18*, 13–25.

Barone, T., & Eisner, E. (2006). Arts-based educational research. In J. L. Green, G. Camilli, & P. B. Elmore (Eds.), *Handbook of complementary methods in educational research* (pp. 95–109). Washington, DC: American Educational Research Association/Lawrence Erlbaum.

Bartolomé, L. (2010). Daring to infuse ideology into language-teacher education. In S. May, & C. Sleeter (Eds.), *Critical multiculturalism: Theory and praxis* (pp. 47–60). New York, NY: Routledge.

Bass, B. M. (1985). *Leadership and performance beyond expectations.* New York, NY: The Free Press.

Bass, B. M., & Riggio, R.E. (2005). *Transformational leadership.* New York, NY: Taylor & Francis.

Baxter Magolda, M. (2008). Three elements of self-authorship. *Journal of College Student Development, 39,* 269–284.

Bell, L. (2010). *Storytelling for social justice: Connecting narrative and the arts in antiracist teaching.* New York, NY: Routledge.

Bell, L. (2013). Theoretical foundations. In M. Adams, W. Blumenfeld, C. Castañeda, H. Hackman, & X. Zúñiga (Eds.), *Readings for diversity and social justice* (3rd ed.; pp. 21–26). New York, NY: Routledge.

Bem, S. L. (1981). Gender schema theory: A cognitive account of sex typing. *Psychological Review, 88,* 354–64.

Bennis, W. (2009). *On becoming a leader.* Cambridge, MA: Perseus.

Bennis, W. G., & Thomas, R. J. (2002). *Geeks and geezers: How era, values, and defining moments shape leaders.* Cambridge, MA: Harvard Business School Press.

Berger, P. L., & Luckmann, T. (1966). *The social construction of reality: A treatise in the sociology of knowledge.* New York, NY: Random House.

Blake, R. R., & McCanse, A. A. (1991). *Leadership dilemmas: Grid solutions.* Houston, TX: Gulf Publishing Company.

Bloom, B. S., & Krathwohl, D. R. (1956). *Taxonomy of educational objectives: The classification of educational goals.* New York, NY: Longmans.

Boal, A. (1979). *Theatre of the oppressed.* New York, NY: Urizen Books.

Boal, A. (2002). *Games for actors and non-actors* (2nd ed.). New York, NY: Routledge.

Boggs, G. L., & Kurashige, S. (2012). *The next American revolution: Sustainable activism for the twenty-first century* (2nd ed.). Berkeley: University of California Press.

Bourdieu, P. (1986). The forms of capital. In J. G. Richardson (Ed.), *Handbook of theory and research for the sociology of education* (pp. 241–258). New York, NY: Greenwood.

Brookfield, S. D. (1990). Using critical incidents to explore learners' assumptions. In J. Mezirow (Ed.), *Fostering critical reflection in adulthood: A guide to transformative and emancipatory learning* (pp. 177–193). San Francisco, CA: Jossey-Bass.

Brookfield, S. D. (2005). *The power of critical theory: Liberating adult learning and teaching.* San Francisco, CA: Jossey-Bass.

Brown, B. (2012). *Daring greatly: How the courage to be vulnerable transforms the way we live, love, parent, and lead.* New York, NY: Avery.

Brown, K. (2004). Leadership for social justice and equity: Weaving a transformative framework and pedagogy. *Educational Administration Quarterly, 40,* 77–104.

Burns, J. M. (1978). *Leadership.* New York, NY: Harper Row.

Butterwick, S., & Selman, J. (2003). Deep listening in a feminist popular theatre project: Upsetting the position of audience in participatory education. *Adult Education Quarterly, 54,* 7–22.

Cahnmann-Taylor, M., & Souto-Manning, M. (2010). *Teachers act up! Creating multicultural learning communities through theatre.* New York, NY: Teachers College Press.

Calder, B. J. (1977). An attribution theory of leadership. In B. Staw & G. Salancik (Eds.), *New directions in attribution research.* Chicago, IL: St. Clair Press.

Cammarota, J., & Fine, M. (2008). Youth participatory action research: A pedagogy for transformational resistance. In J. Cammarota & M. Fine (Eds.), *Revolutionizing education: Youth participatory action research in motion* (pp. 1–12). New York, NY: Routledge.

Capra, F. (1989). *Uncommon wisdom: Conversations with remarkable people.* London, UK: Flamingo.

Carr, W., & Kemmis, S. (1986). *Becoming critical: Education, knowledge, and action research.* Philadelphia, PA: The Falmer Press.

Chang, M. J., Denson, N., Saenz, V., & Misa, K. (2006). The educational benefits of sustaining cross-racial interaction among undergraduates. *The Journal of Higher Education, 77,* 430–455.

Chin, J. L., & Trimble, J. E. (2015). *Diversity and leadership*. Thousand Oaks, CA: Sage.

Cho, S., Crenshaw, K., & McCall, L. (2013). Intersectionality: Theorizing power, empowering theory. *Signs, 38*, 785–810.

Clifton, D. O., Anderson, E., & Schreiner, L. A. (2001). *StrengthsQuest: Discover and develop your strengths in academics, career, and beyond*. New York, NY: Gallup Press.

Collinson, D. (2011). Critical leadership studies. In A. Bryman, D. Collinson, K. Grint, B. Jackson, & M. Uhl-Bien (Eds.), *The SAGE handbook of leadership* (pp. 181–194). Thousand Oaks, CA: Sage.

Conger, J. (1992). *Learning to lead: The art of transforming managers into leaders*. San Francisco, CA: Jossey-Bass.

Cooks, L. (2010). The (critical) pedagogy of communication and the (critical) communication of pedagogy. In D. L. Fassett & J. T. Warren (Eds.), *The SAGE handbook of communication and instruction* (pp. 293–314). Thousand Oaks, CA: Sage.

Crenshaw, K. (1991). Mapping the margins: Intersectionality, identity politics, and violence against women of color. *Stanford Law Review, 43*, 1241–1299.

Crumpacker, L., & Vander Haegen, E. (1987). Pedagogy and prejudice: Strategies for confronting homophobia in the classroom. *Women's Studies Quarterly, 15*(3/4), 65–73.

Dant, T. (2004). *Critical social theory: Culture, society, and critique*. London, UK: Sage.

Day, D. V., & Harrison, M. M. (2007). A multilevel, identity-based approach to leadership development. *Human Resource Management Review, 17*, 360–373.

Davis, T. L., & Harrison, L. M. (2012). *Advancing social justice: Tools, pedagogies, and strategies to transform your campus*. San Francisco, CA: Jossey-Bass.

Day, D. V., Harrison, M. M., & Halpin, S. M. (2009). *An integrative approach to leader development: Connecting adult development, identity, and expertise*. New York, NY: Routledge.

Delgado, R., & Stefancic, J. (2001). *Critical race theory: An introduction*. New York, NY: New York University Press.

Diamond, D. (2007). *Theatre for living: The art and science of community-based dialogue*. Victoria, BC: Trafford.

Downton, J. V. (1973). *Rebel leadership: Commitment and charisma in the revolutionary process*. New York, NY: The Free Press.

Du Bois, W. E. B. (1989). *The souls of Black folk*. New York, NY: Random House.

Dugan, J. P. (2006). Involvement and leadership: A description analysis of socially responsible leadership. *Journal of College Student Development, 47*, 335–343.

Dugan, J. P. (2011). Research on college student leadership development. In S. R. Komives, J. P. Dugan, J. E. Owen, C. Slack, W. Wagner, & Associates (Eds.), *The handbook for student leadership development* (pp. 59–84). San Francisco, CA: Jossey-Bass.

Dugan, J. P. (2015). The measurement of socially responsible leadership: Considerations in establishing psychometric rigor [La misurazione della leadership socialmente responsabile: Considerazioni sulla definizione del rigore psicometrico]. *Journal of Educational, Cultural, and Psychological Studies, 12*, 23–42.

Dugan, J. P. (2017). *Leadership theory: Cultivating critical perspectives*. San Francisco, CA: Jossey-Bass.

Dugan, J. P., Kodama, C., Correia, B., & Associates (2013). *Multi-Institutional Study of Leadership 2012. MSL insight report: Leadership program delivery*. College Park, MD: NCLP.

Dugan, J., & Komives, S. (2010). Influences on college students' capacity for socially responsible leadership. *Journal of College Student Development, 51*, 525–549.

Duncan-Andrade, J. M. R. (2009). Note to educators: Hope required when growing roses in concrete. *Harvard Educational Review, 79*, 181–194.

Dweck, C. S. (2007). *Mindset: The new psychology of success*. New York, NY: Ballantine.

Eagly, A. H., & Chin, J. L. (2010). Diversity and leadership in a changing world. *American Psychologist, 65*, 216–224.

Eagly, A. H., & Johannesen-Schmidt, M. C. (2001). The leadership styles of women and men. *Journal of Social Issues, 57*, 781–797.

Eagly, A. H., Johannesen-Schmidt, M. C., & van Engen, M. L. (2003). Transformational, transactional, and laissez-faire leadership styles: A meta-analysis comparing women and men. *Psychological Bulletin, 129,* 569–591.

Eagly, A. H., & Karau, S. J. (2002). Role congruity theory of prejudice toward female leaders. *Psychological Review, 109,* 573–598.

Edmondson, A. C. (2012). *Teaming: How organizations learn, innovate, and compete in the knowledge economy.* San Francisco, CA: Jossey-Bass.

Evans, N. J., Forney, D. S., Guido, F. M., Patton, L. D., & Renn, K. A. (2009). *Student development in college: Theory, research, and practice.* San Francisco, CA: Jossey-Bass.

Freire, P. (1970, 1982, 2000, 2008). *Pedagogy of the oppressed.* New York, NY: Continuum.

Gardner, W. L., Avolio, B. J., Luthans, F., May, D. R., & Walumba, F. O. (2005). Can you see the real me? A self-based model of authentic leader and follower development. *The Leadership Quarterly, 16,* 343–372.

Gehlbach, H. (2004). A new perspective on perspective taking: A multidimensional approach to conceptualizing an aptitude. *Educational Psychology Review, 16,* 207–234.

Gilligan, C. (1982). *In a different voice.* Cambridge, MA: Harvard University Press.

Giroux, H. A. (1983). Theories of reproduction and resistance in the new sociology of education: A critical analysis. *Harvard Educational Review, 53,* 257–293.

Gist, M. E., & Mitchell, T. R. (1992). Self-efficacy: A theoretical analysis of its determinants and malleability. *The Academy of Management Review, 17,* 183–211.

Goffman, E. (1959). *The presentation of self in everyday life.* New York, NY: Anchor.

Goleman, D. (1995). *Emotional intelligence.* New York, NY: Bantam.

Goleman, D. (1996). *What makes a leader? HBR's 10 must reads on leadership* (pp. 1–21). Boston, MA: Harvard Business Review Press.

Goleman, D., Boyatzis, R., & McKee, A. (2013). *Primal leadership: Learning to lead with emotional intelligence* (2nd ed.). Boston, MA: Harvard Business School.

Goodman, A., Wolff, A., Bockenfeld, D., Tiedeman, B., & Kim, M. (2010). Leadership portal (Version 1.0). Evanston, IL: Northwestern University Center for Leadership and McCormick School of Engineering and Applied Science. Retrieved from http://lead.northwestern.edu/pages/portal/.

Graen, G. B., & Uhl-Bien, M. (1991). The transformation of professionals into self-managing and partially self-designing contributions: Toward a theory of leader-making. *Journal of Management Systems, 3*(3), 25–39.

Graen, G. B., & Uhl-Bien, M. (1995). Relationship-based approach to leadership: Development of leader-member exchange (LMX) theory of leadership over 25 years. *The Leadership Quarterly, 6,* 219–247.

Greenleaf, R. K. (1977). *Servant leadership: A journey into the nature of legitimate power and greatness.* New York, NY: Paulist Press.

Greenwald, A. G., McGhee, D. E., & Schwartz, J. K. L. (1998). Measuring individual differences in implicit cognition: The Implicit Association Test. *Journal of Personality and Social Psychology, 74,* 1464–1480.

Griffin, P., & Ouellett, M. L. (2007). Facilitating social justice education courses. In M. Adams, L. A. Bell, & P. Griffin (Eds.), *Teaching for diversity and social justice* (pp. 89–113). New York, NY: Routledge.

Guba, E. G., & Lincoln, Y. S. (1994). Competing paradigms in qualitative research. In N. K. Denzin & Y. S. Lincoln (Eds.), *Handbook of qualitative research* (pp. 105–117). London, UK: Sage.

Hannah, S. T., & Avolio, B. J. (2010). Ready or not: How do we accelerate the developmental readiness of leaders? *Journal of Organizational Behavior, 31,* 1181–1187.

Hardiman, R., Jackson, B., & Griffin, P. (2013). Conceptual foundations. In M. Adams, W. Blumenfeld, C. R. Castañeda, H. W. Hackman, M. L. Peters, & X. Zúñiga (Eds.), *Readings for diversity and social justice* (3rd ed.; pp. 26–34). New York, NY: Routledge.

Hazy, J. K., Goldstein, J. A., & Lichtenstein, B. B. (2007). Complex systems leadership theory: An introduction. In J. K. Hazy, J. A. Goldstein, & B. B. Lichtenstein (Eds.), *Complex systems leadership theory* (pp. 1–13). Mansfield, MA: ISCE Publishing.

Heider, J. (1985). *The Tao of leadership: Leadership strategies for a new age.* New York, NY: Bantam.

Heifetz, R. A., & Linsky, M. (2002). *Leadership on the line: Staying alive through the dangers of leading.* Boston, MA: Harvard Business School Press.

Hersey, P., & Blanchard, K. H. (1969). Life cycle theory of leadership. *Training & Development Journal, 23*(5), 26–34.

Hersey, P., & Blanchard, K.H. (1981). So you want to know your leadership style? *Training & Development Journal, 35*(6), 34–54.

Hesse, H. (1956). *The journey to the east*. New York, NY: Picador.

Higher Education Research Institute (HERI). (1996). *A social change model of leadership development: Guidebook version III*. College Park, MD: NCLP.

Hoffman, M. L. (2000). *Empathy and moral development: Implications for caring and justice*. New York, NY: Cambridge University Press.

Hofstede, G. (1980). Motivation, leadership, and organization: Do American theories apply abroad? *Organizational Dynamics, 9*, 42–63.

Hofstede, G. (1983). National cultures in four dimensions: A research-based theory of cultural differences among nations. *International Studies of Management & Organization, 13*, 46–74.

Hofstede, G., Hofstede, G. J., & Minkov, M. (2010). *Cultures and organizations: Software of the mind*. New York, NY: McGraw-Hill.

Hofstede, G. J, Pedersen, P. B., & Hofstede, G. (2002). *Exploring culture: Exercises, stories, and synthetic cultures*. Boston, MA: Intercultural Press.

Hogg, M. A. (2001). A social identity theory of leadership. *Personality and Social Psychology Review, 5*, 184–200.

hooks, b. (1994).*Teaching to transgress: Education as the practice of freedom*. New York, NY: Routledge.

House, R. J. (1971). A path goal theory of leader effectiveness. *Administrative Science Quarterly, 16*, 321–339.

House, R. J., Hanges, P. J., Javidan, M., Dorfman, P. W., & Gupta, V. (Eds.). (2004). *Culture, leadership, and organizations: The GLOBE study of 62 societies*. Thousand Oaks, CA: Sage.

Hugo, V. (2013). *Les miserables*. New York, NY: Signet Classic.

Jamieson, K. H. (1995). *Beyond the double bind: Women and leadership*. New York, NY: Oxford University Press.

Jenkins, D. M., & Cutchens, A. B. (2011). Leading critically: A grounded theory of applied critical thinking in leadership studies. *Journal of Leadership Education, 10*(2), 1–21.

Johnson, A. (2006). *Privilege, power, and difference* (2nd ed.). New York, NY: McGraw-Hill.

Jones, S. R., Kim, J. C., & Skendall, K. C. (2012). Reframing authenticity: Considering multiple social identities using autoethnographic and intersectional approaches. *The Journal of Higher Education, 85*, 698–724.

Kaufman, R. (2008). A practical definition of ethics for truly strategic planning in higher education. *New Directions for Higher Education, 142*, 9–15.

Kegan, R. (1994). *In over our heads: The mental demands of modern life.* Cambridge, MA: Harvard University Press.

Kegan, R. (2009). What "form" transforms? A constructive-developmental approach to transformative learning. In K. Illerris (Ed.), *Contemporary theories of learning: Learning theorists … in their own words* (pp. 33–52). New York, NY: Routledge.

Kincheloe, J. L., & McLaren, P. (2005). Rethinking critical theory and qualitative research. In N. K. Denzin & Y. S. Lincoln (Eds.), *The SAGE handbook of qualitative research* (3rd ed.; pp. 303–342). Thousand Oaks, CA: Sage.

King, D. K. (1988). Multiple jeopardy, multiple consciousness: The context of Black feminist ideology. *Signs, 14*, 42–72.

Kirk, G., & Okazawa-Rey, M. (2013). Identities and social locations: Who am I? Who are my people? In M. Adams, W. Blumenfeld, C. Castañeda, H. Hackman, & X. Zúñiga (Eds.), *Readings for diversity and social justice* (3rd ed.; pp. 9–14) New York, NY: Routledge.

Kohlberg, L. (1976). Moral stages and moralization: The cognitive-developmental approach. In T. Lickona (Ed.), *Moral development and behavior: Theory, research, and social issues* (pp. 170–205). New York, NY: Holt, Rinehart, and Winston.

Kolb, D. A. (1984). *Experiential learning: Experience as the source of learning and development.* Englewood Cliffs, NJ: Prentice-Hall.

Komives, S. R., & Dugan, J. P. (2010). Contemporary leadership theories. In R. A. Couto (Ed.), *Political and civic leadership: A reference handbook* (pp. 109–125). Thousand Oaks, CA: Sage.

Komives, S. R., Lucas, N., & McMahon, T. R. (2013). *Exploring leadership: For college students who want to make a difference.* San Francisco, CA: Jossey-Bass.

Komives, S. R., Owen, J., Longerbeam, S., Mainella, F., & Osteen, L. (2005). Developing a leadership identity: A grounded theory. *Journal of College Student Development, 46*, 593–611.

Komives, S. R., Wagner, W., & Associates (2009). *Leadership for a better world: Understanding the social change model of leadership development.* San Francisco, CA: Jossey Bass.

Kouzes, J. M., & Posner, B. Z. (2012). *The leadership challenge* (5th ed.). San Francisco, CA: Wiley.

Ladson-Billings, G. (1995). But that's just good teaching! The case for culturally relevant pedagogy. *Theory Into Practice, 34,* 159–165.

Ladson-Billings, G. (1998). Just what is critical race theory and what's it doing in a nice field like education? *International Journal of Qualitative Studies in Education, 11,* 7–24.

Laird, T. F. N. (2005). College students' experiences with diversity and their effects on academic self-confidence, social agency, and disposition toward critical thinking. *Research in Higher Education, 46,* 365–387.

Larson, C. L., & Murtadha, K. (2002). Leadership for social justice. *Yearbook of the National Society for the Study of Education, 101,* 134–161.

Leithwood, K., & Jantzi, D. (2008). Linking leadership to student learning: The contributions of leader efficacy. *Educational Administration Quarterly, 44,* 496–528.

Lencioni, P. (2002). *The five dysfunctions of a team: A leadership fable.* San Francisco, CA: Jossey-Bass.

Leonard, P. J. (1996). Consciousness-raising groups as a multicultural awareness approach: An experience with counselor trainees. *Cultural Diversity and Mental Health, 2*(2), 89–98.

Levine, M. P., & Boaks, J. (2014). What does ethics have to do with leadership? *Journal of Business Ethics, 124,* 225–242.

Lichtenstein, B. B., Uhl-Bien, M., Marion, R., Seers, A., Orton, J. D., & Schreiber, C. (2006). Complexity leadership theory: An interactive perspective on leading in complex adaptive systems. In J. Hazy, J. Goldstein, & B. B. Lichetenstein (Eds.), *Complex systems leadership theory* (pp. 2–12). Mansfield, MA: ISCE Publishing.

Lieblich, A., Tuval-Mashiach, R., & Zilber, T. (1998). *Narrative research: Reading, analysis, and interpretation.* Thousand Oaks, CA: Sage.

Lindsley, D., Brass, D., & Thomas, J. (1995). Efficacy-performance spirals: A multilevel perspective. *The Academy of Management Review, 20,* 645–678.

Lopez, J. L., & Louis, M. C. (2009). The principles of strengths-based education. *Journal of College & Character, 10*(4), 1–8.

Lord, R. G., Brown, D. J., Harvey, J. L., & Hall, R. J. (2001). Contextual constraints on prototype generation and their multilevel consequences for leadership perceptions. *The Leadership Quarterly, 12,* 311–338.

Lord, R. G., & Hall, R. J. (2005). Identity, deep structure, and the development of leadership skill. *The Leadership Quarterly, 16*, 591–615.

Luthans, F., & Avolio, B. J. (2003). Authentic leadership development. In K. S. Cameron, J. E. Dutton, & R. E. Quinn (Eds.), *Positive organizational scholarship* (pp. 241–258). San Francisco, CA: Berrett-Koehler.

Machiavelli, N. (1997). *The prince.* New Haven, CT: Yale University Press.

Mavroveli, S., Petrides, K. V., Rieffe, C., & Bakker, F. (2007). Trait emotional intelligence, psychological well-being and peer-rated social competence in adolescence. *British Journal of Developmental Psychology, 25,* 263–275.

McCormick, M. (2001). Self-efficacy and leadership effectiveness: Applying social cognitive theory to leadership. *The Journal of Leadership & Organizational Studies, 8*(1), 22–33.

Mezirow, J. (1991). *Transformative dimensions in adult learning.* San Francisco, CA: Jossey-Bass.

Mezirow, J. (2000). *Learning as transformation: Critical perspectives on a theory in progress.* San Francisco, CA: Jossey-Bass.

Nealon, J., & Giroux, S. S. (2012). *The theory toolbox: Critical concepts for the humanities, arts, and social sciences* (2nd ed.). Lanham, MD: Rowman & Littlefield.

Northouse, P. G. (2013, 2016). *Leadership: Theory and practice.* Thousand Oaks, CA: Sage.

Ospina, S., & Foldy, E. (2009). A critical review of race and ethnicity in the leadership literature: Surfacing context, power and the collective dimensions of leadership. *The Leadership Quarterly, 20,* 876–896.

Ospina, S., Foldy, E. G., El Hadidy, W., Dodge, J., Hofmann-Pinilla, A., & Su, C. (2012). Social change leadership as relational leadership. In M. Uhl-Bien & S. Ospina (Eds.), *Advancing relational leadership research: A dialogue among perspectives* (pp. 255–302). Greenwich, CT: Information Age Publishing.

Palmer, P. J. (2000). *Let your life speak: Listening for the voice of vocation.* San Francisco, CA: Jossey-Bass.

Pearce, C. L., & Conger, J. A. (Eds.). (2002). *Shared leadership: Reframing the hows and whys of leadership.* Thousand Oaks, CA: Sage.

Perruci, G. (2011). Millennials and globalization: The cross-cultural challenge of intragenerational leadership. *Journal of Leadership Studies, 5*(3), 82–87.

Pizzolato, J., Nguyen, T. K., Johnston, M., & Wang, S. (2012). Understanding context: Cultural, relational, and psychological interactions in self-authorship development. *Journal of College Student Development, 53,* 656–679.

Plowman, D. A., & Duchon, D. (2007). Emergent leadership: Getting beyond heroes and scapegoats. In J. Hazy, J. Goldstein, & B. B. Lichtenstein (Eds.), *Complex systems leadership theory* (pp. 109–128). Mansfield, MA: ISCE.

Posner, B. Z., & Kouzes, J. M. (1988). Development and validation of the leadership practices inventory. *Educational and Psychological Measurement, 48,* 483–496.

Preskill, S., & Brookfield, S. D. (2009). *Learning as a way of leading: Lessons from the struggle for social justice.* San Francisco, CA: Jossey-Bass.

Reason, R. D., & Davis, T. L. (2005). Antecedents, precursors, and concurrent concepts in the development of social justice attitudes and actions. *New Directions for Student Services, 110,* 5–15.

Rhoads, R. A., & Black, M. A. (1995). Student affairs practitioners as transformative educators: Advancing a critical cultural perspective. *Journal of College Student Development, 36,* 413–421.

Roberson, L., & Block, C. J. (2001). Racioethnicity and job performance: A review and critique of theoretical perspectives on the causes of group differences. *Research in Organizational Behavior, 23,* 247–325.

routenberg, r., & Sclafani, T. (2011, Fall/Winter). Facilitating through "perfectly logical explanations (PLEs)" and other challenging participant comments. *Voices: Commission for Social Justice Educators' Quarterly Newsletter, 6.*

Salovey, P., & Mayer, J. D. (1990). Emotional intelligence. *Imagination, Cognition, and Personality, 9*(3), 185–211.

Savignon, S. J., & Sysoyev, P. V. (2002). Sociocultural strategies for a dialogue of cultures. *The Modern Language Journal, 86,* 508–524.

Shamir, B., Dayan-Horesh, H., & Adler, D. (2005). Leading by biography: Toward a life-story approach to the study of leadership. *Leadership, 1,* 13–29.

Shamir, B., & Eilam, G. (2005). "What's your story?" A life-stories approach to authentic leadership development. *The Leadership Quarterly, 16,* 395–417.

Shankman, M., Allen, S., & Haber-Curran, P. (2015). *Emotionally intelligent leadership: A guide for students* (2nd ed.). San Francisco, CA: Jossey-Bass.

Shapiro, A. (1999). *Everybody belongs: Changing negative attitudes toward classmates with disabilities.* New York, NY: Routledge.

Shapiro, M., Ingols, C., & Blake-Beard, S. (2011). Using power to influence outcomes: Does gender matter? *Journal of Management Education, 35,* 713–748.

Simpson, J. S. (2010). Critical race theory and critical communication pedagogy. In D. L. Fassett & J. T. Warren (Eds.), *The SAGE handbook of communication and instruction* (pp. 361–384). Los Angeles, CA: Sage.

Solórzano, D. (1998). Critical race theory, race and gender microaggressions, and the experiences of Chicana and Chicano scholars. *Qualitative Studies in Education, 11,* 121–136.

Solórzano, D., Ceja, M., & Yosso, T. (2000). Critical race theory, racial microaggressions, and campus racial climate: The experiences of African American college students. *Journal of Negro Education, 69,* 60–73.

Spanierman, L. B., Armstrong, P. I., Poteat, V. P., & Beer, A. M. (2006). Psychosocial costs of racism to Whites: Exploring patterns through cluster analysis. *Journal of Counseling Psychology, 53,* 434–441.

Sue, D. W. (2010). *Microaggressions in everyday life: Race, gender, and sexual orientation.* Hoboken, NJ: Wiley.

Sue, D. W., Capodilupo, C. M., Torino, G. C., Bucceri, J. M., Holder, A. M. B., Nadal, K. L., & Esquilin, M. (2007). Racial microaggressions in everyday life: Implications for clinical practice. *American Psychologist, 62,* 271–286.

Sue, D. W., Lin, A. I., Torino, G. C., Capodilupo, C. M., & Rivera, D. P. (2009). Racial microaggressions and difficult dialogues on race in the classroom. *Cultural Diversity and Ethnic Minority Psychology, 15,* 183–190.

Sue, D. W., & Sue, D. (2013). *Counseling the culturally different: Theory and practice* (6th ed.). Hoboken, NJ: Wiley.

Syed, M. (2013). Identity exploration, identity confusion, and openness as predictors of multicultural ideology. *International Journal of Intercultural Relations, 37,* 491–496.

Teaching for Tolerance: A project of the Southern Poverty Law Center (n.d.). Test yourself for hidden bias. Retrieved from http://www.tolerance.org/P-bias.

Terhune, C. P. (2005). "Can we talk?" Using critical self-reflection and dialogue to build diversity and change organizational culture in nursing schools. *Journal of Cultural Diversity, 13*(3), 141–145.

Theidermen, S. (2014, June 4). Managing unconscious bias: Your workplace advantage [Webinar]. In *Workplace Matters Series*. Retrieved from www .workplaceanswers.com/managing-unconscious-bias-webinar-thank-you/.

Truth, S. (1851, May). *Ain't I a Woman?* Speech presented at the Women's Convention, Akron, OH.

Uhl-Bien, M., Marion, R., & McKelvey, B. (2007). Complexity leadership theory: Shifting leadership from the industrial age to the knowledge era. *The Leadership Quarterly, 18,* 298–318.

Underwood, B., & Moore, B. (1982). Perspective-taking and altruism. *Psychological Bulletin, 91,* 143–173.

Vroom, V. H. (1964). *Work and motivation.* New York, NY: Wiley.

Walker, D., & Walker, G. (2004). *The official rock paper scissors strategy guide.* New York, NY: Simon and Schuster.

Wang, Z., Xu, B., & Zhou, H. J. (2014). Social cycling and conditional responses in the Rock-Paper-Scissors game. Retrieved from: http://arxiv .org/pdf/1404.5199.pdf.

Welkener, M., & Baxter Magolda, M. (2014). Better understanding students' self-authorship through self-portraits. *Journal of College Student Development, 55,* 580–585.

Wheatley, M. J. (1992). *Leadership and the new science: Learning about organization from an orderly universe.* San Francisco, CA: Berrett-Koehler.

Yosso, T. J. (2005). Whose culture has capital? A critical race theory discussion of community cultural wealth. *Race, Ethnicity, and Education, 8,* 69–91.

Zimmerman, B. J., Bandura, A., & Martinez-Pons, M. (1992). Self-motivation for academic attainment: The role of self-efficacy beliefs and personal goal setting. *American Educational Research Journal, 29,* 663–676.

AUTHOR INDEX

SUBJECT INDEX